Guidelines for Physical Education Programs, Grades K-12
Standards, Objectives, and Assessments

Edited by

Steveda Chepko
Springfield College

Ree K. Arnold
Montclair State University

Eastern District Association of the American Alliance for Health, Physical Education, Recreation and Dance

An EDA Council for Services Project

Allyn and Bacon
Boston   London   Toronto   Sydney   Tokyo   Singapore

The definition of a physically educated person that appears on page 3 is reprinted from *Moving Into the Future: National Standards for Physical Education* (1995) with permission from the National Association for Sport and Physical Education (NASPE), 1900 Association Drive, Reston, VA 20191-1599.

Copyright © 2000 by Allyn & Bacon
A Pearson Education Company
160 Gould Street
Needham Heights, Massachusetts 02494-2130

Internet: www.abacon.com

ISBN 0-205-28326-8

Printed in the United States of America

10 9 8 7 6 5 4 3   03 02 01 00

**Eastern District Association of
The American Alliance for Health,
Physical Education, Recreation and Dance**

Task Force to Develop Standards for Quality Programs in HPERD

Task Force Co-Chairpersons

Steveda Chepko, Springfield College, MA
Ree K. Arnold, Montclair State University, NJ

Task Force Members

Peggy Hutter, Kearsarge Middle School, New London, NH
Louise McCormack, Plymouth State College, NH
Larry Moore, Central Berkshire School District, MA
Sandy Reynolds, Portsmouth Middle School, Portsmouth, RI
Maureen Shiel, Mexico High School, NY
Lilyan Wright, Trenton State College, NJ

Editorial Assistants

Lynn Couturier, Springfield College, MA
Barbara G. Hemink, Clarkstown Senior High School, NY

Contributors Grades K-8

Irene Cucina, Plymouth State College, Plymouth, NH
Diana L.Demetrius, Mapleshade Elementary School, East Longmeadow, MA
Elizabeth Guiles-Brown, South Bristol School, ME
Deborah A. Sheehy, Springfield College, Springfield, MA
Jackie Haslett, University of Massachusetts-Boston, Boston, MA

Contributors Grades 9-12

See citations for each activity within Guidelines for Grades 9-12.
See citations for assessment examples in Appendix A.

Table of Contents

Acknowledgments

Preparation of the Guidelines for Physical Education Programs, Grades K - 12, would not have been possible without the continued guidance, support, and input of the membership of the Eastern District Association of AAHPERD. Sincere appreciation is extended to the many individuals who served as reviewers for this document at various stages of its development. Information supplied by respondents to the survey regarding appropriate curricular content for grades 9-12 was invaluable as the Task Force formulated guidelines for the secondary level. The continuous support of the Executive Boards of the Eastern District throughout the eight-year period of development, was critical to the completion of the Guidelines document.

The Task Force wishes to recognize the significant and substantive contributions of those professionals who wrote objectives, sample activities, activity modules, and/or sample assessments for inclusion in the Guidelines. Their willingness to share their expertise was crucial to the strength and validity of the Guidelines.

In addition, the Task Force wishes to acknowledge the significant support and assistance provided by the following individuals:

Marian Frank, NASPE Outcomes Committee; Standards and Assessment Task Force.

Past-Presidents of the Eastern District of AAHPERD:

Carol V. Persson	James Agli
Theresa Purcell	Ronald Feingold
Virginia Overdorf	Thomas Jacoby
Markella Pahnos	Stephen Cone
Steveda Chepko	Robert R. Davidson

Reviewers:

Alan D. Blakeley	Robert Hautala	Jim Ross
Deborah M. Clark	Susan Kogut	Kathleen A. Thornton
Deb Coffin	Cindy Lins	Mary Trotto
Jo Dill	Nancy Lombard	Doris Wooledge
Dennis Docheff	Bennett J. Lombardo	Lilyan B. Wright
Bob Emery	Michelle M. Mach	Karen Zingermann
Fred Garman	Elaine McKay	
Mike Gerich	Marvin Minushkin	
Elizabeth Guiles-Brown	Susan Moss	
Cindy Haigh	Cindy Pentsak	
Gale House	Mary L. Putman	

Student Typists:

Jill Yarkey, Heather Somers, and Jennifer Goff

Preface

In 1989 the Eastern District Association of AAHPERD formed the Task Force to Develop Standards for Quality Programs in HPERD. The Task Force decided to initially focus on program standards for Physical Education. The Program Guidelines for grades K-5 were developed during 1989-1990, as Phase I of the Task Force project. Phase II of the project was initiated in Fall 1990, and the Program Guidelines for grades 6-8 were developed during 1990-1992. The third phase of the project was development of Program Guidelines for grades 9-12, conducted during 1992-1994. The format and content of the guidelines for grades K-12 evolved through a substantial process of review and revision. Input, comments, and suggestions were received from more than 200 individuals throughout the Eastern District. The final phase of the project included reorganization of the Program Guidelines in correspondence to the Content Standards in Physical Education, developed by the National Association for Sport and Physical Education (NASPE) in 1995. Sample assessment techniques were also added to the guidelines for each grade level to illustrate the assessment options identified by NASPE as appropriate for physical education programs.

The intent of the Eastern District in appointing the Task Force was to provide leadership as a professional organization in promoting standards for quality education in HPERD. Thus, the intent of this document is to provide information to those states, school districts, and local schools who seek assistance in developing and maintaining quality programs in Physical Education. It is not the intent of the Eastern District, the Task Force, or the document to promote a prescribed, standardized curriculum guide. Rather, the goal is to provide leadership and service in the effort to demonstrate worth and accountability in our profession.

It is the hope of the Task Force that the program guidelines will be used by individual states and school districts as a part of specific, local workshops and in-service programs devoted to review and revision of curricula. Thus, the Task Force views this document as reference information to stimulate discussion and decision-making at local levels. Program design must, of necessity, be guided by the needs, interests, and resources of specific teachers, students, and schools. To the extent that all Physical Education programs are directed toward a common set of resultant outcomes, it is hoped that the information compiled by the Task Force will serve as a useful operating framework for decision-making.

Introduction

The Guidelines for Physical Education are presented in three sections, representing three grade-ranges: Grades K-5, 6-8, and 9-12. The Guidelines for each grade are based on the definition of a Physically Educated Person, developed by the National Association for Sport and Physical Education (NASPE).

A Physically Educated Person:

- Has learned skills necessary to perform a variety of physical activities

- Is physically fit

- Does participate regularly in physical activity

- Knows the implications of and the benefits from involvement in physical activities

- Values physical activity and its contribution to a healthful lifestyle

(NASPE, 1990)

Content Standards. The guidelines for each grade level are organized in correspondence to the Content Standards in Physical Education, developed by the NASPE Standards and Assessment Task Force. The content standards specify "what students should know and be able to do" (NASPE, 1995, p. vi). The content standards are intended to identify essential areas of knowledge and skills that should result from quality physical education programs, grades K-12. It is assumed that these content standards are broadly applicable and appropriate across a wide variety of schools, programs, and geographic locations.

Behavioral Objectives. For each content standard, at each grade level, specific objectives related to psychomotor, cognitive and/or affective behavior have been developed. Across grade levels, these behavioral objectives illustrate a progressive sequence of curricular content leading to achievement of the knowledge and skills identified in the physical education content standards. Within a particular grade level, the objectives are consistent with the performance benchmarks of progress toward attaining the performance standards, developed by NASPE. The objectives are intended as suggestive of general curricular content within a 5-day-per-week program, rather than as prescriptive of a standard curriculum. It is assumed that these objectives will be useful to those individuals, districts, and/or school seeking guidance, examples, or ideas relative to curricular review, planning, or revision. Clearly it will be necessary for such groups to modify objectives based on length and frequency of physical education classes, size of classes, and the like.

Assessment. The behavioral objectives are stated in terms of observable, measurable behavior, implying both a need for and a possible means of assessment of student achievement. Samples of specific assessment techniques are provided within the guidelines for each grade level to illustrate the variety of options available for use in evaluating student behavior. The samples reflect authentic assessment strategies in which performance is evaluated in a real-life setting, rather than in a contrived context.

The nature of authentic assessment varies with the differences in performance context across grade-levels. For example, the context for assessment of the skill of throwing differs substantially between grade levels K-5 in which the instructional emphasis is on development of fundamental movement patterns, and grade levels 9-12 in which the context is application of the skill within specific sport settings. Similarly, assessment of the application of knowledge and behavior to real-life issues and problems must mirror the authentic social, emotional, and cognitive context at the various grade levels.

Assumptions. The program guidelines are based on the assumption of a 5-day-per-week physical education program, grades K-12. The content of the guidelines for a given grade also assumes that the behavioral objectives for the previous grade(s) have been achieved. Obviously, if these assumptions are not met in a particular program, it will be necessary to modify the objectives and/or delay presentation of some areas of content within the program.

No priority is implied in the ordering of the content standards. In addition, the listing of individual content standards, and accompanying objectives, does not imply that they reflect discrete, unrelated areas of knowledge and ability. Clearly, a lesson involving throwing and catching, for example, can involve objectives relating to skill learning, safety, principles of movement, rules and etiquette, cooperation, and interpersonal skills. Identification of the major content of a particular lesson is often merely a matter of emphasis within the instructional activities.

Grade Levels. A brief introduction is provided at the beginning of each of the three sections of the guidelines: grades K-5, 6-8, and 9-12. These introductions include a general description of content, an explanation of unique elements in the particular grade-level guidelines, and a listing of supplementary material included for a particular section of the guidelines.

Content Standards in Physical Education
(NASPE, 1995)

A physically educated person:

1. **Demonstrates competency in many movement forms and proficiency in a few movement forms.**

   Students acquire the basic skills to participate in a wide variety of leisure physical activities, and develop advanced skills in at least two or three activities.

2. **Applies movement concepts and principles to the learning and development of motor skills.**

   Students develop sufficient knowledge and ability to independently acquire new skills, while continuing to refine existing skills.

3. **Exhibits a physically active lifestyle.**

   Students regularly participate in meaningful physical activity, and evidence a comprehensive perspective on the meaning of a healthy lifestyle.

4. **Achieves and maintains a health-enhancing level of physical fitness.**

   Students accept responsibility for enhancing and maintaining a level of personal fitness commensurate with an active, healthy lifestyle.

5. **Demonstrates responsible personal and social behavior in physical activity settings.**

   Students initiate responsible behavior, function independently and responsibly, and exert a positive influence on the behavior of others in physical activity settings.

6. **Demonstrates understanding and respect for differences among people in physical activity settings.**

   Students willingly participate with persons of diverse characteristics and backgrounds, and develop strategies for inclusion of others.

7. **Understands that physical activity provides opportunities for enjoyment, challenge, self-expression, and social interaction.**

   Students exhibit an awareness of the intrinsic values and benefits of participation in physical activity, and actively pursue lifelong physical activities that provide personal meaning.

EDA GUIDELINES
For Physical Education

Program Standards, Objectives, and Assessments

Grades K - 5

Introduction: Grades K - 5

Behavioral Objectives and Sample Activities. For each of the seven Content Standards, specific grade-appropriate objectives related to psychomotor, cognitive and/or affective behavior have been identified. For each behavioral objective, samples are provided of specific activities that could be used in conjunction with a particular behavioral objective at a particular grade level. The sample activities are intended to illustrate or suggest tasks and activities that can serve as behavioral criteria relative to the accomplishment of the objectives for a particular grade level. It is hoped that these sample activities will serve to suggest additional and/or alternate activities appropriate for a particular physical education program relative to facilities, equipment, and regional/geographical activity interests and opportunities.

Assessment. Examples of a variety of assessment techniques are provided for each grade level. The sample assessment techniques are intended to illustrate some of the many valid, authentic, and appropriate ways to evaluate the extent to which the behavioral objectives have been accomplished. It is hoped that the sample assessments will serve to suggest additional and/or alternate assessment techniques appropriate for a particular program.

Definition of Terms. Listed below are definitions of key terms used in this section of the guidelines document to denote a progressive sequence of skill development for a given activity.

Attempt:	Implies that the skill will be taught but the student will not master or show competency in the skill.
Demonstrate:	Implies that the student will demonstrate competency in the skill.
Explore:	Implies that the student has demonstrated competency in the skill and will explore variations of the movement in dimensions such as speed, flow, or direction.
Review:	Implies the continual review of the skill and serves as a developmental checkpoint.

Structuring Activity Lessons. For a given group of students and a specific activity objective, it is likely that student performances will be distributed across the *attempt, demonstrate,* and *review* continuum of skill development. A general rule-of-thumb for designing activity lessons is to select tasks for which 80% of the students are expected to demonstrate competency. Individualized instruction and practice activities should be designed for the remaining students.

KINDERGARTEN

Did You Know?

A child is born with the potential for the development of trillions of neural connections.

- Which connections are made and retained is determined by the experiences of childhood and these early experiences can determine much of a child's later success or failure.

- The development of neural connections is based on the "use it or lose it" principle. Those "used" are integrated into the brain's circuitry and those not "used" are weeded out.

- If a child is not exposed to a variety of experiences during early childhood (birth to 12 yrs.) a "critical period" might be missed and the window of opportunity may be closed on future development.

- Much of learning that occurs in early childhood is through movement experiences involving the use of sensory systems.

- Early experiences in music and movement help form the brain's circuits for future development of math and language skills.

- Young children need to participate in wide variety of movement experiences to insure that these neural connections are made and these movement experiences must be repeated to insure the retention of these connections.

- Physical education should be scheduled daily in order to insure that "critical periods" are not missed and children have the opportunity to reach their full potential in all domains of learning.

From: Begley, S., (February 19, 1996). "Your Child's Brain", Newsweek.

Standard 1:	Demonstrates competency in many movement forms and proficiency in a few movement forms.

Objective 1.1:   **Demonstrates common body positions.**

Sample Activities:

1.1a: Perform the four body positions of tuck, pike, layout, and straddle

1.1b: Assume various shapes

1.1c: Participate in activities such as Human Obstacle course

> **Definition**
> **Cumulative Records**
> Starting in kindergarten, teachers should record each student's development in the motor domain. Cumulative records should include such items as fitness assessments, height and weight, assessments of the fundamental motor skills, and yearly progress reports.

Objective 1.2:   **Demonstrates moving to various rhythms.**

Sample Activities:

1.2a: Move with even/uneven rhythms

1.2b: Perform exercises, songs, and simple dances to the rhythm of music

1.2c: Participate in activities such as Cookie Jar

Objective 1.3:   **Demonstrates forward rotational skills.**

Sample Activities:

1.3a: Perform log, egg, forward, and shoulder rolls

1.3b: Roll using various shapes

> **Definition**
> **Demonstrate**
> Implies that the student will demonstrate competency in the skill.

Objective 1.4:   **Attempts climbing, supporting, and balancing skills on various apparatus.**

Sample Activities:

1.4a: Walk, turn, mount, and dismount apparatus

1.4b: Hang and swing from inverted positions

1.4c: Climb ladders and cargo nets

1.4d: Maintain support positions on apparatus

1.4e: Move up and down inclines utilizing various body positions

1.4f: Participate in activities such as Treasure Hunt

Objective 1.5: **Demonstrates moving at various levels.**

Sample Activities:
- 1.5a: Move at high and low levels
- 1.5b: Participate in chasing and fleeing activities while varying the levels

Objective 1.6: **Demonstrates the non-locomotor skills of stretching, twisting, curling, bending, holding, lifting, and swaying.**

Sample Activities:
- 1.6a: Perform non-locomotor skills in combination
- 1.6b: Lift and hold equipment used in activity
- 1.6c: Perform non-locomotor skills varying speed and level
- 1.6d: Perform non-locomotor skills varying shape
- 1.6e: Participate in parachute activities

> **Teaching Tip**
> **Teacher Observation**
> - View the skill from different angles.
> - Record the students with problems or showing areas of slower development.
> - Determine the method of observation to be used before making the observation.
> - Utilize different forms of observation such as anecdotal records, checklists, rating scales, or scoring rubrics.
> - Make sure the observation method is appropriate for the skill or activity being observed.
> - Develop criteria before beginning the observation.

Objective 1.7: **Integrates turning with locomotor skills.**

Sample Activities:
- 1.7a: Turn while varying speed, level and direction
- 1.7b: Turn using various locomotor patterns
- 1.7c: Turn using various flows/speeds
- 1.7d: Spin on one foot and maintain balance
- 1.7e: Jump using a turn
- 1.7f: Participate in chasing and fleeing activities which require turning

Objective 1.8: **Demonstrates walking, running, jogging, sliding, and jumping.**

Sample Activities:
- 1.8a: Travel by varying direction, pathway, and effort
- 1.8b: Jump from various heights and over various obstacles
- 1.8c: Change speeds to music
- 1.8d: Participate in chasing and fleeing activities

> **Sample Assessment**
> **Checklist: Running**
> Criteria:
>
> | | | |
> |---|---|---|
> | Lands heel to toe | Yes | No |
> | Places support foot under body | Yes | No |
> | Willing to run at full speed | Yes | No |
> | Leans forward | Yes | No |
> | Swings arms to shoulder level and slightly to midline | Yes | No |

Objective 1.9:   **Demonstrates non-locomotor and manipulative skills in combination.**

Sample Activities

1.9a:	Manipulate objects such as balloons, feathers, bean bags, yarn balls, foam paddles/bats, and ribbons
1.9b:	Perform self-tossing and catching activities
1.9c:	Participate in activities such as Ball Passing

> **Definition**
> **Pre-Assessment**
> Pre-assessment is completed at the beginning of a unit of instruction or the school year.
> * Allows teachers to formulate a picture of where students are in the learning sequence.
> * Includes such things as pretests, teacher observations, and checklists.
> * Allows for the planning of developmentally appropriate sequences.

Objective 1.10:   **Demonstrates locomotor and manipulative skills in combination.**

Sample Activities:

1.10a:	Perform various locomotor movements while manipulating ribbons, feathers or ropes
1.10b:	Self-toss and catch in combination with walking and jogging
1.10c:	Perform various locomotor movements while manipulating objects to a variety of musical accompaniments
1.10d:	Participate in activities such as Circle Straddle Ball

Objective 1.11:   **Attempts the locomotor skills of skipping, hopping, leaping, and galloping.**

Sample Activities:

1.11a:	Gallop forward and backward with either foot
1.11b:	Jump, leap, and hop in all directions with varying effort
1.11c:	Travel over lines and ropes using various approaches
1.11d:	Move to a variety of images in poems or stories

> **Sample Assessment**
> **Checklist: Gallop**
> Criteria:
> * Front-facing position   Yes No
> * Forward step   Yes No
> * Leap onto trailing foot   Yes No
> * Same leg always leads   Yes No
> * Gallop forward or backward   Yes No

Objective 1.12:   **Attempts kicking.**

Sample Activities:

1.12a:	Kick a large stationary ball
1.12b:	Kick a large stationary ball while running forward
1.12c:	Kick using strong and light effort
1.12d:	Kick with different parts of the foot
1.12e:	Participate in activities such as Bottle Kick Ball

Objective 1.13:   **Attempts throwing.**

Sample Activities:
- 1.13a: Throw an object with an overhand and underhand motion
- 1.13b: Attempt throwing an object using various speeds, effort, levels, and directions
- 1.13c: Throw to various tempos
- 1.13d: Participate in activities such as Teacher Ball

Objective 1.14:   **Attempts catching.**

Sample Activities:
- 1.14a: Stop a rolling object with various body parts
- 1.14b: Catch a large object with the hands
- 1.14c: Catch a large object from a rebound with hands
- 1.14d: Give with a catch and collapse
- 1.14e: Catch from a self-toss
- 1.14f: Participate in juggling activities with scarves
- 1.14g: Participate in activities such as Stop Ball

> **Definition**
> **Formative Assessment**
> Formative assessments occur throughout the unit and provide feedback to students and teachers. This type of assessment serves as a motivator for students and facilitates student improvement.

Objective 1.15:   **Attempts striking.**

Sample Activities:
- 1.15a: Strike a large stationary object without and with an implement
- 1.15b: Strike a large moving object (balloon/beachball) without and with an implement
- 1.15c: Strike an object varying effort and force
- 1.15d: Strike in time to music
- 1.15e: Explore striking with different body parts and in different directions
- 1.15f: Participate in activities such as Keep It Up

Objective 1.16:   **Attempts swinging, pushing, and pulling.**

Sample Activities:
- 1.16a: Swing from various body parts
- 1.16b: Push and pull equipment used in activity
- 1.16c: Swing, push, and pull with varying effort
- 1.16d: Swing utilizing various shapes
- 1.16e: Participate in scooter activities and obstacle courses

Standard 2:	Applies movement concepts and principles to the learning and development of motor skills.

Objective 2.1:   **Demonstrates an understanding of general and personal space (where the body moves).**

Sample Activities:

2.1a: Adjust personal space while moving and/or manipulating objects

2.1b: Adjust personal space by varying body positions and levels

2.1c: Move from general space back to personal space on command

2.1d: Move by varying the size of the general space from large/small or small/large

2.1e: Participate in chasing and fleeing activities such as Jack Frost and Jane Thaw

Objective 2.2:   **Demonstrates the concepts of directionality and laterality (relationships).**

Sample Activities:

2.2a: Move front/back, side/side and in/out

2.2b: Move up/down and under/over

2.2c: Move left/right

2.2d: Participate in activities such as Simon Says

Objective 2.3:   **Demonstrates an awareness of spatial relationships between self, others, and objects.**

Sample Activities:

2.3a: Move in opposition and alternately

2.3b: Move in synchrony with others

2.3c: Participate in various obstacle courses

2.3d: Participate in chase and flee activities that includes various spatial relationships

Objective 2.4:   **Demonstrates variations in force/effort (how the body moves).**

Sample Activities:

2.4a: Vary the force/effort in walking, running, and jumping

2.4b: Vary the force/effort in twisting, turning, bending, and stretching

Objective 2.5   **Describes a movement in terms of level and tempo (speed/flow).**

Sample Activities

2.5a: Differentiate between high/low levels

2.5b: Differentiate between fast/slow movements

Objective 2.6:   **Locates the major parts of the body.**

Sample Activities:
2.6a: Point to a specified body part on self or a partner
2.6b: Move specified body parts
2.6c: Participate in activities such as Head, Shoulders, Knees, and Toes

Objective 2.7:   **Solves movement-related problems.**

Sample Activities:
2.7a: Solve movement problems such as "How many different body parts can you use to strike?"
2.7b: Explore concepts of force and effort as they relate to throwing and striking

Standard 3:	*Exhibits a physically active lifestyle.*

Objective 3.1:   **Participates fully in all class activities.**

Objective 3.2:   **Participates outside of class in self-selected movement experiences.**

> **Sample Assessment**
> **Self-Assessment**
> Students identify their levels of participation outside of class through a smiley face exit poll or poker chip survey.

Standard 4:	*Achieves and maintains a health-enhancing level of physical fitness.*

Objective 4.1:   **Participates in anaerobic activities.**

Sample Activities:
4.1a: Participate in movement, dance, and/or games without undue fatigue
4.1b: Participate in activities such as Crazy Cones

Objective 4.2:   **Participates in activities requiring appropriate levels of muscular strength/endurance.**

Sample Activities:
4.2a: Hang by the arms and legs from an elevated bar
4.2b: Explore climbing and swinging activities on apparatus
4.2c: Participate in activities such as seal walks, crab walks, and mule kicks

> **Teaching Tip**
> **Fitness Assessment**
> Fitness assessment should be informal and developmentally appropriate. Time and distances should be modified with no formal testing taking place. Measurements of cardiovascular endurance are inappropriate.

Objective 4.3:   **Demonstrates flexibility.**

Sample Activities:
    4.3a: Participate in movement songs and rhymes
    4.3b: Perform a sequence of shapes that require stretching, bending, and twisting
    4.3c: Perform activities such as see-saws, rolls, and animal mimicry

Standard 5:	*Demonstrates responsible personal and social behavior in physical activity settings.*

Objective 5.1:   **Starts and stops on command.**

Sample Activities:
    5.1a: Start and stop on an auditory or visual signal
    5.1b: Participate in activities such as Red Light, Green Light

Objective 5.2:   **Maintains her/his personal space.**

Sample Activities:
    5.2a: Participate in activities without colliding into other students
    5.2b: Participate in activities such as Shrinking Room

Objective 5.3:   **Follows simple directions.**

Sample Activities:
    5.3a: Go over, under, through, and around objects on command
    5.3b: Solve simple movement challenges
    5.3c: Participate in parachute play

Objective 5.4:   **Follows a series of instructions for an activity.**

Sample Activities:
    5.4a: Sequence two or more prescribed locomotor movements
    5.4b: Create a movement sequence following guidelines provided by the teacher

Sample Assessment
Rating Scale
Students follow a series of three instructions through an obstacle course. For example, "Go over an obstacle, around an obstacle, and then go under another obstacle." Use a rating scale to assess the performance.
Criteria:
3 = completes sequence without error
2 = completes sequence with one error
1 = does not complete sequence or has two or more errors

Objective 5.5:   **Participates in activity without arguing.**

Sample Activities:
  5.1a: Ask and answer questions in an appropriate manner
  5.1b: Speak at appropriate times

Objective 5.6:   **Accepts responsibility when asked by the teacher.**

Sample Activities:
  5.6a: Pick up and put away equipment
  5.6b: Use equipment properly

Objective 5.7:   **Demonstrates cooperative skills.**

Sample Activities:
  5.7a: Share equipment with a partner
  5.7b: Solve movement problems with a partner
  5.7c: Create a movement sequence with a partner

> **Sample Assessment**
> **Self-Assessment**
> Students evaluate their feelings about working with a partner in a cooperative activity by circling a shining sun, a dark cloud, or a thunderstorm according to their reaction to the experience.

Standard 6:	*Demonstrates understanding and respect for differences among people in physical activity settings.*

Objective 6.1:   **Demonstrates respect for individuals.**

Sample Activities:
  6.1a: Interact with classmates in an appropriate manner
  6.1b: Play without interfering with others

Standard 7:	*Understands that physical activity provides opportunities for enjoyment, challenge, self-expression, and social interaction.*

Objective 7.1:   **Creates a sequence of non-locomotor movements.**

Sample Activities:
  7.1a: Develop an original sequence within given parameters

Objective 7.2:   **Develops self-confidence in a physical activity setting.**

> **Sample Assessment:**
> **Event Task**
> Students draw a picture of a movement sequence and then perform the sequence.

Sample Activities:
  7.2a: Participate in activities that are developmentally appropriate

Objective 7.3:   **Explores her/his physical capabilities.**

Sample Activities:
  7.3a: Participate in personal movement challenges such as "How high can you jump?" or
              "How far can you throw?"
  7.3b: Participate in informal fitness assessment

> Teaching Tip
> **Developmental Assessment**
> All students in kindergarten should participate in a
> developmental assessment of the fundamental motor
> skills (running, jumping, kicking, throwing, catching,
> and striking) in order to begin tracking their progress
> in the motor domain. Testing in developmental skills
> should occur in grades K, 3, and 5. A test with
> established norms or criteria such as "The Test for
> Gross Motor Development" or a locally developed
> test could be used.

FIRST GRADE

Did You Know?

- Research has shown that exercise increases nerve connections and provides nutrients in the form of glucose to the brain. This makes it easier for students of all ages, sizes, and shapes to learn.

- William Greenough from the University of Illinois at Urbana-Champaign has stated that numerous research studies have found that children who exercise regularly do better in school.

- The implications for schools are clear. Children need to be more physically active during the school day and in the classroom, not sitting at desks completing worksheets.

- Children retain knowledge longer if they connect emotionally and physically to the material.

- By using more then one sensory modality, children form a multidimensional mental model from the learning experience allowing for easier retrieval.

- It is clear from the current research that physical educators and classroom teachers must integrate movement into the daily instruction of children in order to maximize learning in all domains.

From: Hancock, L. (February 19, 1998). "Why Do Schools Flunk Biology?", Newsweek.

Standard 1:	Demonstrates competency in many movement forms and proficiency in a few movement forms.

Objective 1.1: **Explores different body positions while jumping.**

Sample Activities:
- 1.1a: Explore different body positions when jumping from an elevation
- 1.1b: Mimic different sport jumping skills

Objective 1.2: **Explores moving to various rhythms.**

Sample Activities:
- 1.2a: Demonstrate even/uneven rhythms
- 1.2b: Explore rhythmical movements using small musical aids
- 1.2c: Explore moving to a range of musical rhythms and styles
- 1.2d: Perform a singing dance in a group

> **Definition**
> **Explore**
> Implies that the student has demonstrated competency in the skill and will try variations in movement dimensions such as speed, flow, or direction.

Objective 1.3: **Explores rotational skills.**

Sample Activities:
- 1.3a: Explore backward rolling movements
- 1.3b: Explore rolling movements in combinations
- 1.3c: Participate in activities such as Pivot Tag

Objective 1.4: **Explores balancing skills.**

Sample Activities:
- 1.4a: Balance at different levels on different body parts
- 1.4b: Explore static and dynamic balance
- 1.4c: Participate in activities such as Palm Push

Objective 1.5: **Demonstrates climbing, supporting, and balancing skills on various apparatus.**

Sample Activities:
- 1.5a: Balance on one body part
- 1.5b: Support weight alternately on one body part and then another
- 1.5c: Climb a rope no higher than 7 feet

Objective 1.6: **Reviews walking, running, jogging, and sliding.**

> **Definition**
> **Demonstrating Competency**
> The term "demonstrate" implies that the student will demonstrate competency in the skill. An objective that includes the term "Demonstrate" implies that 80% of the students will consistently perform the skill at a developmental level associated with their age.

Objective 1.7: **Demonstrates hopping, jumping, and galloping.**

Sample Activities:
- 1.7a: Hop on one foot
- 1.7b: Jump backward
- 1.7c: Jump up onto a piece of apparatus
- 1.7d: Gallop forward and backward with either foot leading
- 1.7e: Participate in activities such as High Water/Low Water

```
                        Sample Assessment
                      Checklist: Jumping
Criteria:

•  Preparatory crouch         Yes   No
•  Forward trunk lean         Yes   No
•  Feet spaced 5 to 10
      inches apart            Yes   No
•  Hips extend at take-off    Yes   No
•  Arms extended overhead     Yes   No
•  Knees flex on landing      Yes   No
```

Objective 1.8: **Attempts leaping, turning, and skipping.**

Sample Activities:
- 1.8a: Participate in activities that involve leaping over objects on the floor
- 1.8b: Participate in activities that involve combining leaping and running
- 1.8c: Participate in activities that involve skipping and turning

Objective 1.9: **Attempts kicking.**

Sample Activities:
- 1.9a: Kick a large moving ball
- 1.9b: Attempt running and kicking a moving ball
- 1.9c: Attempt kicking a ball toward various targets at different levels
- 1.9d: Participate in activities such as Frantic Ball

```
              Definition
              Attempt
Implies the skill will be taught,
but the student will not master
or show competency in the
skill.
```

Objective 1.10: **Attempts throwing.**

Sample Activities:
- 1.10a: Throw a small object toward a large target
- 1.10b: Throw a small object using various speeds and levels
- 1.10c: Throw a small object for distance using the entire arm in an overhand motion
- 1.10d: Participate in activities such as Snow Man

Objective 1.11: **Attempts catching.**

Sample Activities:
- 1.11a: Catch a small object from a rebound
- 1.11b: Participate in activities such as Hot Potato

```
              Teaching Tip
       Performance Assessment
Make sure that the assessment
task or condition is appropriate to
assess the skill. For example,
having students throw at small
targets from short distances is
inappropriate because the task
does not require a full throwing
motion. A more appropriate task
would be to have students throw
for distance. This task requires a
full throwing motion and allows
for a more appropriate evaluation
of the throwing pattern.
```

Objective 1.12: **Attempts striking with and without a short handled implement.**

Sample Activities:

1.12a: Strike a large stationary ball (beach or nerf) without and with an implement

1.12b: Strike a large moving ball (beach or nerf) without and with an implement

1.12c: Participate in such activities as Hit and Run

Objective 1.13: **Reviews the non-locomotor skills of stretching, twisting, curling, bending, holding, lifting, and swaying.**

Sample Activities:

1.13a: Demonstrate various shapes as a response to imagery, such as trees in the wind

> **Teaching Tip**
> **Developmental Levels**
> All children go through stages of development which are age-related but not age-dependent. Each child's development is unique, but certain development checkpoints or benchmarks occur for most children within a specific time frame. These windows of opportunity are crucial for the mastery of the fundamental motor skills. By 5th grade, most students should demonstrate mature forms of the six fundamental motor skills. Any skill that does not meet the mature standard is considered developmental. Many adults continue to exhibit developmental throwing patterns. This is why these patterns are considered age-related and not age-dependent.

Objective 1.14: **Demonstrates swinging, pushing, and pulling.**

> **Sample Assessment**
> **Role Playing**
> Students act out an imagined movement pattern. The teacher should accept responses in a nonjudgmental way.

Sample Activities:

1.14a: Swing from rung to rung on a ladder

1.14b: Move across an apparatus with a hand-to-hand motion

1.14c: Participate in obstacle course activities

1.14d: Push and pull equipment greater than her/his body weight

Objective 1.15: **Demonstrates non-locomotor and manipulative skills in combination.**

Sample Activities:

1.15a: Move implements such as wands or hula hoops

1.15b: Juggle scarves

Objective 1.16: **Demonstrates locomotor and manipulative skills in combination.**

Sample Activities:

1.16a: Catch and throw on the run

1.16b: Participate in jump-rope activities

1.16c: Strike while running or jumping

Standard 2:	*Applies movement concepts and principles to the learning and development of motor skills.*

Objective 2.1:   **Explores general and personal space.**

Sample Activities:
- 2.1a: Explore general space by varying speed and direction
- 2.1b: Explore personal space using elastic bands or movement sacks
- 2.1c: Participate in activities such as Bumper Cars

Objective 2.2:   **Explores the concepts of directionality and laterality.**

Sample Activities:
- 2.2a: Move left/right
- 2.2b: Move in opposition and in alternation
- 2.2c: Participate in activities such as the Hokey Pokey

Objective 2.3:   **Demonstrates locomotor skills in various pathways.**

Sample Activities:
- 2.3a: Move in curved, zig-zag, and straight pathways using skipping, galloping, and sliding movements
- 2.3b: Design various pathways with a jump rope and move across the rope

> **Sample Assessment**
> **Event Task**
> The teacher uses a series of flash cards to illustrate movement pathways. Students duplicate the pathway with a jump rope. The teacher identifies a locomotor skill that the students use to travel a particular pathway.

Objective 2.4:   **Explores variations in force/effort.**

Sample Activities:
- 2.4a: Vary force and effort while running, jumping, and throwing
- 2.4b: Mimic various animal movements while changing the purpose of the movements

Objective 2.5:   **Explores throwing and striking activities by varying force/effort.**

Sample Activities:
- 2.5a: Strike objects of various sizes and weights such as balloons, yarn balls, and nerf balls
- 2.5b: Throw objects of various shapes, sizes, and weights
- 2.5c: Throw objects from various levels and positions such as kneeling and lying

Objective 2.6:   **Compares movements in terms of level and tempo (speed/flow).**

Sample Activities:
- 2.6a: Contrast high/low levels
- 2.6b: Contrast slow/fast tempos

Objective 2.7:   **Identifies the major parts of the body.**

Sample Activities:
2.7a:	Move various body parts
2.7b:	Catch a scarf on a designated body part

Objective 2.8:   **Identifies the heart, lungs, and parts of the skeleton.**

Sample Activities:
2.8a:	Locate parts on an anatomical model
2.8b:	Place labels on an anatomical model

> **Sample Assessment**
> **Group Project**
> Students work in small groups to label various body parts on a skeleton. Labels should include the name of the body part and a picture of the part to be labeled. Labels can be fixed using velcro. This project can be used as a theme lesson during the month of October.

Standard 3:   *Exhibits a physically active lifestyle.*

Objective 3.1:   **Participates fully in all class activities.**

Objective 3.2:   **Participates outside of class in self-selected movement experiences.**

Standard 4:   *Achieves and maintains a health-enhancing level of physical fitness.*

Objective 4.1:   **Participates in anaerobic activities.**

Sample Activities:
4.1a:	Participate in movement, dance, and/or games without undue fatigue

Objective 4.2:   **Participates in activities requiring appropriate levels of muscular strength/endurance.**

> **Definition**
> **Anaerobic Activity**
> Anaerobic activity is defined as high intensity movement that can not be sustained for long periods of time.

Sample Activities:
4.2a:	Support her/his body weight for a minimum of 10 seconds
4.2b:	Hang by the arms or legs from an elevated bar
4.2c:	Support a portion of a partner's body weight
4.2d:	Participate in activities such as fitness challenges

Objective 4.3:   **Demonstrates flexibility.**

> **Teaching Tip**
> **Anaerobic Activity**
> The most appropriate activities for young children are those that require them to participate fully for short periods of time. The focus of lessons should be anaerobic activities.

Sample Activities:
4.3a:	Perform locomotor and non-locomotor skills at full extension and full flexion

Objective 4.4:   **Identifies types of activities that increase muscular strength/endurance and flexibility.**

> **Sample Assessment**
> **Group Project**
> Students bring in pictures of activities that requires muscular strength/endurance and flexibility (photographs, magazines, drawings, etc.). Pictures are displayed on a bulletin board near the gymnasium.

Standard 5:	*Demonstrates responsible personal and social behavior in physical activity settings.*

Objective 5.1:   **Utilizes personal and general space appropriately.**

Sample Activities:

5.1a:	Stop and start on command
5.1b:	Participate in games and activities without bumping into others
5.1c:	Maintain proper spacing when utilizing apparatus or equipment

Objective 5.2:   **Identifies safety rules for the activity and area being used.**

Objective 5.3:   **Listens and follows instructions.**

Sample Activities:

5.3a:	Combine prescribed movement sequences
5.3b:	Participate in activities such as Simon Says

> **Sample Assessment**
> **Checklist: Listening Skills**
>
> Criteria:
>
> | | | |
> |---|---|---|
> | • Follows a single, simple direction | Yes | No |
> | • Listens without interrupting | Yes | No |
> | • Asks questions for clarification | Yes | No |
> | • Focuses eyes on the speaker | Yes | No |
> | • Follows three directions given in sequence. | Yes | No |

Objective 5.4:   **Follows the rules of the activity.**

Sample Activities:

5.4a:	Perform a sequence of movements within given parameters
5.4b:	Perform a short dance sequence within given parameters
5.4c:	Develop three rules for an activity and participate in the activity while following the rules
5.4d:	Follow the rules for simple games

Objective 5.5:   **Sets realistic, short-term movement goals with the help of the teacher.**

Sample Activities:
    5.5a: Set a movement goal such as stepping in opposition while throwing
    5.5b: Set a goal for participating in physical activity beyond the class

Objective 5.6:   **Accepts responsibility when asked by the teacher.**

Sample Activities:
    5.6a: Help put away and take out equipment
    5.6b: Help another student

Objective 5.7:   **Accepts corrective feedback when delivered by the instructor.**

Objective 5.8:   **Demonstrates cooperative skills.**

Sample Activities:
    5.8a: Share equipment
    5.8b: Participate with a partner in cooperative problem solving activities
    5.8c: Share space effectively

Sample Assessment
Scoring Rubric: Cooperation

Each student moves about general space inside a hula hoop. On command, students find a partner. One student is to drop her/his hoop and join the partner in her/his hula hoop. The partners move around general space sharing the hula hoop. The teacher varies the type of locomotor skills to be used. If students effectively share a hoop, the partners join another group of two and form a group of four. Cooperative skills are assessed by using a scoring rubric.

Criteria:
Level 3:   willing to relinquish her/his hula hoop and cooperate with partner, alternating the leader of the movement.

Level 2:   willing to share her/his hula hoop, but often forces the direction of the movement.

Level 1:   not willing to share her/his hula hoop or join a partner.

Standard 6:	Demonstrates understanding and respect for differences among people in physical activity settings.

Objective 6.1: **Demonstrates acceptance of individual differences.**

Sample Activities:
    6.1a: Work with partners of various abilities in throwing activities

Standard 7:	Understands that physical activity provides opportunities for enjoyment, challenge, self-expression, and social interaction.

Objective 7.1: **Creates a sequence of locomotor movements.**

Sample Activities:
    7.1a: Develop an original sequence within given parameters

Objective 7.2: **Develops self-confidence in a physical activity setting.**

Objective 7.3: **Selects appropriate levels of challenges.**

Sample Activities:
    7.3a: Participate in various self-testing activities
    7.3b: Participate in creative play
    7.3c: Participate in activities that provide for different levels of challenge

> **Sample Assessment**
> **Group Project**
> The teacher places symbols for various directions and movements on a series of index cards. Students create and perform a movement sentence using the sequence on the cards. The teacher assesses the accuracy of the sentence content.

> Teaching Tip
> **Individualized Challenges**
> Activities should provide students with choices of individual challenges. For example, in jumping activities students should choose the height over which to attempt the jump. Ashworth and Mosston (1994) advocate the use of a rope placed on a slant for jumping challenges. By slanting the rope, students can choose the level they will attempt to clear on the jump. The teacher assesses if students are choosing appropriate levels of challenge.

GRADE TWO

Did You Know?

- Repeated and persistent exposure to movement activities for children between the ages of three and ten is necessary to keep neural circuits alive and functioning at optimal levels. Not only must the neural connections be established through participation in a wide variety of activities, but repetition is necessary to maintain these connections for a lifetime.

- The cerebellum is the area of the brain most commonly linked to movement. It takes up 1/10th of the brain volume and contains over half of the neurons.

- The part of the brain that processes movement also processes learning.

- Researchers Dr. James Pollatschek and Dr. Frank Hagen have found that children who engage in daily physical education have improved motor performance, like school better, and demonstrate superior academic performance.

- The Vanves and Blanchard project from Canada revealed that when physical education time was increased at the elementary level to 1/3 of the school day, academic scores improved.

- Sensory-motor activities feed directly into the pleasure centers of the brain. Some researchers have identified a direct link between the cerebellum and the pleasure centers in the emotional system.

From: Jabs, C., (November, 1996). "Your Baby's Brain", WorkingMother.

Jensen, E. (1997). "Movement & Learning", Turning Point.

Standard 1:	*Demonstrates competency in many movement forms and proficiency in a few movement forms.*

Objective 1.1: **Demonstrates rotational skills.**

Sample Activities:

1.1a: Roll forward and backward
1.1b: Perform combinations of rolling skills
1.1c: Roll down an inclined plane
1.1d: Perform a log roll

Objective 1.2: **Demonstrates balancing skills.**

Sample Activities:

1.2a: Stand on one foot for 7 seconds
1.2b: Balance objects on various body parts while in various positions
1.2c: Balance on lines or low beams/benches

> **Teaching Tip**
> **Developmental Assessment**
> At the 2nd or 3rd grade level a reassessment of students' fundamental motor skills should occur. The same assessment tool used at the kindergarten level should be repeated in order to document progress or to identify specific areas of concern. Scores on the assessment should be recorded in the student's cumulative file. Teachers should chart the progress of the group and of individual students.

Objective 1.3: **Demonstrates different body shapes/positions including round, narrow, twisted, symmetrical and asymmetrical, while jumping and landing.**

Sample Activities:

1.3a: Jump off an object using different body positions
1.3b: Balance using various body shapes
1.3c: Jump with a half turn and a full turn

Objective 1.4: **Demonstrates moving to various rhythms using time, force, and flow.**

Sample Activities:

1.4a: Travel to a variety of rhythms changing time and force
1.4b: Travel to a rhythm varying the flow of the movement
1.4c: Clap to rhythms led by the teacher
1.4d: Participate in a variety of dance activities

Objective 1.5: **Reviews walking, running, jogging, sliding, galloping, jumping/landing, and hopping.**

> **Definition**
> **Review**
> Implies the continual review of the skill and serves as a developmental checkpoint. Students reviewing a skill have already demonstrated competency in the skill.

Objective 1.6:   **Demonstrates leaping, turning, and skipping.**

Sample Activities:
1.6a: Leap over objects on the floor
1.6b: Turn while jumping
1.6c: Skip backwards

Objective 1.7:   **Demonstrates kicking with dominant and non-dominant foot.**

Sample Activities:
1.7a: Dribble a ball continuously with dominant and non-dominant foot
1.7b: Approach and kick a moving ball with dominant and non-dominant foot
1.7c: Kick a ball toward various targets at different levels with dominant and non-dominant foot

Sample Assessment **Checklist: Kicking**		
Criteria:		
• Non-kicking foot is placed beside object	Yes	No
• Kicking leg is flexed during backswing	Yes	No
• Kicking leg is extended at contact	Yes	No
• Arms swing in opposition to legs	Yes	No
• Follow through is upward and high	Yes	No
• Balance is maintained while kicking	Yes	No

Objective 1.8:   **Attempts overhand throw.**

Sample Activities:
1.8a: Throw a small object overhand using various speeds and levels
1.8b: Throw a small object with an overhand motion attempting weight transfer, stepping in opposition, and use of the entire arm
1.8c: Throw a small object overhand toward a target with each hand
1.8d: Participate in simple throwing activities with a partner

Objective 1.9:   **Attempts catching**

Sample Activities:
1.9a: Catch an object from a rebound
1.9b: Catch various shaped objects such as balloons, bean bags, nerf footballs, and rubber rings
1.9c: Catch an object with a scoop

Sample Assessment **Scoring Rubric: Catching**	
Level 3:	Arms slightly ahead of body, elbows flexed. Ball is contacted with hands and grasped with fingers. Palms are adjusted to size and flight of object.
Level 2:	Arms in front of body, elbows slightly flexed. Arms encircle ball against the chest. Hands and arms hold ball to chest.
Level 1:	Arms are outstretched, elbows extended, palms upward. Ball is contacted with arms and elbows flexed. Object is trapped against body.

Objective 1.10:   **Attempts striking a ball with short and long-handled implements.**

Sample Activities:
1.10a:	Strike a ball held in hand
1.10b:	Strike a moving ball with an implement
1.10c:	Strike a moving ball from a rebound with an implement
1.10d:	Attempt to strike (volley, dribble) a moving ball with an implement while traveling
1.10e:	Strike balloons/nerf balls using small paddles

Objective 1.11:   **Attempts dribbling using her/his hand(s).**

```
┌─────────────────────────────────────┐
│         Sample Assessment            │
│      Rating Scale: Dribbling         │
│  Students contact ball with fingers, │
│  keeping head up.                    │
│  Criteria:                           │
│  4 = evident  90% of time            │
│  3 = evident 75% of time             │
│  2 = evident 50% of time             │
│  1 = evident less than 25% of the time│
└─────────────────────────────────────┘
```

Sample Activities:
1.11a:	Dribble a ball using one hand
1.11b:	Dribble a ball alternating hands

Objective 1.12:   **Reviews the non-manipulative skills of stretching, twisting, and curling.**

Sample Activities:
1.12a:	Combine several of non-manipulative skills into a pattern
1.12b:	Contrast movements such as curling, twisting, and stretching

Objective 1.13:   **Demonstrates locomotor and manipulative skills in combination.**

```
┌─────────────────────────────────────┐
│            Definition                │
│          Rating Scale                │
│  Rating scales are used to specify the│
│  degree to which criteria for        │
│  successful performance have been    │
│  met. In contrast to a "Yes or No"   │
│  checklist, a rating scale is used to │
│  assess how well or how often the    │
│  performance criteria are being met. │
└─────────────────────────────────────┘
```

Sample Activities:
1.13a:	Dribble a ball with hands while traveling
1.13b:	Toss ball, turn, and catch
1.13c:	Tap a ball along the ground and move with it

Objective 1.14:   **Demonstrates locomotor and balancing skills in combination.**

Sample Activities:
1.14a:	Travel and stop in various balanced positions
1.14b:	Jump and land, balancing on various body parts

28

Standard 2:	Applies movement concepts and principles to the learning and development of motor skills.

Objective 2.1: **Reviews combinations of directions, levels, and pathways.**

Sample Activities:
- 2.1a: Move forward and backward using walk, run, skip, hop, and gallop
- 2.1b: Move forward/backward, up/down, and right/left in response to a signal
- 2.1c: Travel straight, curved, and zigzag pathways while changing directions and levels
- 2.1d: Gallop using various pathways, alternating the lead foot

> **Sample Assessment**
> **Written Test**
> Students are given a worksheet on which several pathways are drawn. The teacher names a pathway and students circle the corresponding pathway on the sheet or trace the pathway named by the teacher using a specific color (a curved pathway is yellow, straight pathway is red, etc).

Objective 2.2: **Demonstrates the concepts of weight transfer in non-locomotor and locomotor skills.**

Sample Activities:
- 2.2a: Transfer weight to various body parts while traveling across a mat
- 2.2b: Throw overhand for distance

Objective 2.3: **Develops concepts of effort (how the body moves), space awareness (where the body moves), and relationships (with whom or what the body moves).**

Objective 2.4: **Identifies the structure and function of the heart and lungs.**

Sample Activities:
- 2.4a: Draw the heart and the lung
- 2.4b: Identify how the heart and lungs function in activities such as skipping or running

Objective 2.5: **Identifies good health habits.**

Sample Activities:
- 2.5a: Identify methods to keep the body healthy and clean
- 2.5b: Identify foods from the food pyramid

Standard 3:	Exhibits a physically active lifestyle.

Objective 3.1: **Participates fully in all class activities.**

Objective 3.2: **Participates outside of class in self-selected physical activities.**

Sample Activities:
3.2a: Identify and pursue opportunities in the areas of dance, in-line skating, gymnastics, cycling, swimming, and/or martial arts

> **Sample Assessment**
> **Written Assignment**
> Students write a three sentence paragraph about any physical activity in which they have participated outside of class. This assignment could be completed in conjunction with the classroom teacher.

Objective 3.3: **Applies knowledge in the areas of health and physical activity outside of the classroom setting.**

Objective 3.4: **Participates in activity outside of class to meet her/his short-term, self-selected fitness goal.**

Standard 4:	Achieves and maintains a health-enhancing level of physical fitness.

Objective 4.1: **Identifies the components of health-related fitness (cardiovascular endurance, muscular strength/endurance, and flexibility.)**

Sample Activities:
4.1a: Identify and demonstrate an activity for each component of health-related fitness

Objective 4.2: **Demonstrates cardiovascular endurance.**

Sample Activities:
4.2a: Participate in 30 minutes of continuous movement, dance, or rhythmic gymnastics without undue cardiovascular fatigue

Objective 4.3: **Demonstrates muscular strength/endurance.**

Sample Activities:
4.3a: Hold head and shoulders off mat in a curl for 10 seconds
4.3b: Participate in activities involving scooters
4.3c: Jump a turned rope for 3 minutes

Objective 4.4:   **Demonstrates flexibility.**

Sample Activities:
    4.4a: Participate in activities requiring stretching, twisting, and curling
    4.4b: Participate in such activities as Thread the Needle

Objective 4.5:   **Sets a short-term fitness goal for one component of health-related fitness with the help of the teacher.**

Sample Assessment
Student Project
Students use the results of their fitness assessment to set a goal in an appropriate area of health-related fitness. Students will need the help of the teacher to set realistic goals. Teachers should emphasize the need for each goal to be specific and individualized. The achievement of a health-related fitness goal will require students to participate in activities beyond class time. This assignment will cross over to Standard 3 of exhibiting a physically active lifestyle. Most activities will involve more than one standard.

Standard 5:	*Demonstrates responsible personal and social behavior in physical activity settings.*

Objective 5.1:   **Maintains personal space while using an implement.**

Sample Activities:
    5.1a: Participate in activities involving use of an implement without contacting another individual

Sample Assessment
Rating Scale: Use of Personal Space
Criteria:
Students use an implement in an appropriate manner.
  3 = Appropriate use observed most of the time
  2 = Appropriate use observed some of the time
  1 = Appropriate use observed occasionally

Objective 5.2:   **Identifies safety rules for the activity and the area he/she is using.**

Objective 5.3:   **Listens and follows directions.**

Sample Activities:
    5.3a: Start and stop on command
    5.3b: Get and return equipment appropriately
    5.3c: Move within designated boundaries

Objective 5.4:   **Identifies the purpose of rules for an activity.**

Objective 5.5:   **Follows the rules of an activity.**

Sample Activities:
    5.5a: Participate in a variety of age-appropriate movement experiences

Objective 5.6:   **Demonstrates cooperative skills.**

Sample Activities:
    5.6a: Share equipment with more than one person
    5.6b: Participate with partners in cooperative problem-solving activities
    5.6c: Work with a partner to spot a third person

Standard 6:	*Demonstrates understanding and respect for differences among people in physical activity settings.*

Objective 6.1:   **Demonstrates proper etiquette and regard for others.**

Sample Assessment		
Checklist: Etiquette and Regard for Others		
Criteria:		
•Shows concern for others in activities.	Yes	No
•Shows willingness to work with anyone in the class.	Yes	No
•Is willing to work with anyone in the class.	Yes	No
•Is courteous to classmates and teachers	Yes	No

Standard 7:	*Understands that physical activity provides opportunities for enjoyment, challenge, self-expression, and social interaction.*

Objective 7.1   **Creates a sequence utilizing locomotor and manipulative movements.**

Sample Activities:
    7.1a: Develop an original movement sequence within given parameters

Objective 7.2:   **Describes and demonstrates the shape and flow of a movement.**

Sample Activities:
    7.2a: Create various shapes through movement and dance
    7.2b: Identify things in nature which have flowing movements
    7.2c: Perform flowing movements using imagery such as "blowing trees" or "flowing water"

Objective 7.3:   **Develops self-confidence in a physical activity setting.**

Sample Assessment		
Checklist: Self-confidence		
Criteria:		
• Volunteers to go first	Yes	No
• Asks questions during class	Yes	No
• Accepts skill challenges	Yes	No
• Extends skill challenges	Yes	No
• Volunteers to demonstrate a skill	Yes	No
• Volunteers to work with less skilled students	Yes	No

33

GRADE THREE

Did You Know?

- The American Academy of Pediatrics has found that fewer than half of school-aged children get enough exercise to develop healthy hearts and lungs.

- Dr. Dan Landers of Arizona State University has found that exercise promotes growth in developing brains and slows deterioration in older adults.

- The brain weighs just 3.3 pounds and contains between 50 billion to 100 billion cells. Up until 2 years of age, brain cells (neurons) can regenerate themselves, but after the age of 2 they are meant to last a lifetime.

- A child's brain is the hardware s/he is born with and experience (via stimulation) is the software that determines how much of the hardware gets used.

- The more senses involved in the process of learning the faster the acquisition and an increase in retention occurs.

From: Nichols, M. & Hawaleshka, D. , (January 22, 1996). "Secrets of the Brain". Maclean's.

Olsen, E. (1994). Fit Kids, Smart Kids: New Research Confirms that Exercise Boosts brainpower. Parents Magazine, 69(10), 33.

Standard 1:	Demonstrate competency in many movement forms and proficiency in a few movement forms.

Objective 1.1: **Demonstrates moving to various rhythms.**

Sample Activities:

1.1a: Jump rope to various tempos (speed/flow)

1.1b: Toss and catch a ball with a partner to music

1.1c: Combine bouncing, tossing, and catching to music

1.1d: Participate in a dramatic play venture such as a Trip to Mt. Everest

1.1e: Participate in activities such as Moon Ball

Teaching Tip
Checks for Understanding
Students identify key concepts in the lesson by answering a series of questions at the end of the class.

Sample Questions:
1. Identify the five ways of getting off of the floor (elevating).
2. How can each kind of jump be applied to dance, gymnastics, and game activities?

Objective 1.2: **Explores ways of elevating.**

Sample Activities:

1.2a: Use three ways of elevating from the floor in activities such as Lummi Sticks, Tininkling, and other dances

1.2b: Explore variations in jumping, hopping, and leaping

Objective 1.3: **Demonstrates rotational skills.**

Sample Activities:

1.3a: Perform forward and backward, log, and shoulder rolls with variations

1.3b: Combine two or more rotational skills.

1.3c: Participate in activities such as Human Wheel

Objective 1.4: **Demonstrates inverted skills.**

Sample Activities:

1.4a: Perform tripod and headstand

1.4b: Perform mule kicks, headstands, and cartwheels

1.4c: Perform inverted Follow Me skills

Sample Assessment
Rating Scale: Elevating
Students demonstrate three (3) of five (5) ways of elevating from the floor:
a. jumping (2 feet to 2 feet)
b. jumping (1 foot to 2 feet)
c. jumping (2 feet to 1 foot)
d. hopping (1 foot to 1 foot)
e. leaping (1 foot to the other foot)

A rating scale is used to assess performance.
Criteria:
4 = correctly demonstrates 3 techniques
3 = correctly demonstrates 2 techniques
2 = correctly demonstrates 1 technique
1 = fails to demonstrate elevating

Objective 1.5: **Demonstrates climbing, supporting, and balancing skills on various apparatus.**

Sample Activities:
1.5a: Use various combinations of body parts to perform climbing, supporting, and balancing skills
1.5b: Participate in Circus Day using scooters, ropes, climbing apparatus, and adventure activities

Objective 1.6: **Attempts dribbling a ball using her/his feet.**

Sample Activities:
1.6a: Dribble a ball using the inside and outside of the foot
1.6b: Dribble at different speeds and identify the effort used to change speeds

Objective 1.7: **Attempts trapping.**

Sample Activities:
1.7a: Participate in partner activities such as Throw, Bounce, and Trap
1.7b: Trap a ball from a roll, a kick, and a rebound

Objective 1.8: **Demonstrates a mature overhand throwing pattern.**

Objective 1.9: **Demonstrates throwing with two hands.**

Sample Assessment		
Checklist: Throwing		
Criteria:		
• Side to target	Yes	No
• Elbow up and back	Yes	No
• Hip rotation initiates forward motion	Yes	No
• Elbow leads forearm	Yes	No
• Steps with opposite foot	Yes	No
• Stride towards target	Yes	No
• Follow-through across body	Yes	No

Sample Activities:
1.9a: Self-toss to music using a two-handed underhand motion
1.9b: Throw a ball to a spot on the wall with a two-handed overhand motion
1.9c: Pass a ball at different levels to a partner using a two-handed overhand motion

Objective 1.10 **Attempts shooting a ball from a stationary position.**

Sample Activities:
1.10a: Throw a ball with two hands at targets at various heights (overhand, underhand)
1.10b: Throw a ball with one hand at targets at various heights (overhand, underhand)
1.10c: Participate in activities such as Beat Ball

Objective 1.11   **Attempts catching.**

Sample Activities:
    1.11a: Catch balls of various shapes and sizes
    1.11b: Catch a ball in a stationary position and while moving
    1.11c: Participate in rhythmic gymnastic ball skills
    1.11d: Participate in activities such as Beat Ball

Objective 1.12:   **Attempts striking a ball with short and long-handled implements.**

Sample Activities:
    1.12a: Bat/strike a ball from a stationary position
    1.12b: Bat/strike a ball that is suspended from a string
    1.12c: Bat/strike a ball that is thrown by a partner
    1.12d: Bat a ball with a modified implement
    1.12e: Participate in activities such as Paddle Ball

Objective 1.13:   **Demonstrates dribbling using her/his hand(s).**

Sample Activities:
    1.13a: Dribble a ball using dominant and non-dominant hands
    1.13b: Dribble a ball using one hand
    1.13c: Dribble a ball using alternate hands

> **Teaching Tip**
> **Authentic Assessment**
> One method of assessing dribbling skills is to have students participate in such activities as Dribbling Knockout. This activity requires students to keep their heads up while dribbling and requires the use of both hands. The activity is game-like and requires the application of the skill in a realistic setting.

Standard 2:	*Applies movement concepts and principles to the learning and development of motor skills.*

Objective 2.1:   **Identifies activities that necessitate crossing the midline of the body.**

Sample Activities:
    2.1a: Describe movements that require crossing the midline, such as batting and writing on a blackboard

Objective 2.2:   **Explores locomotor skills by varying force/effort.**

Sample Activities:
    2.2a: Participate in movement challenges by varying weight factors (firmness and fine touch) while walking/running/jumping
    2.2b: Attempt to control various weighted balls in a keep-away situation
    2.2c: Participate in movement challenges by varying time factors (suddenness and sustained) while walking/running/jumping

Objective 2.3:   **Explores non-locomotor skills by varying the location of the center of gravity.**

Sample Activities:
   2.3a: Participate in movement challenges by varying levels and bases of support
   2.3b: Perform a two, three, and four point balance

Sample Assessment
Event Task

Students work with a partner to explore the relative stability of various body positions. One member of the pair assumes various bases of support by changing foot positions (staggered, narrow, or wide). In each position, the partner attempts to push the student off balance from the rear. The partners change roles to explore the effect of changes in the location of the center of gravity by kneeling and standing on tip toes. Students answer the following questions:
   1. Which positions are most stable? Why?
   2. How did standing on tip toes affect your center of gravity?
   3. How did kneeling effect your center of gravity?

Objective 2.4:   **Describes and demonstrates concepts related to stability.**

Sample Activities:
   2.4a: Identify the most stable and the most unstable positions from two, three, and four point balances
   2.4b: Identify stable and unstable body positions through symmetric and asymmetric shapes
   2.4c: Participate in activities such as Sailors and Sharks

Objective 2.5:   **Explores kicking a ball by varying weight and time factors.**

Sample Activities:
   2.5a: Pass a ball to a partner with the inside/outside of the foot using combinations among firmness and fine touch, and suddenness and sustained movement
   2.5b: Pass a ball to a partner with the instep of the foot, varying speed and distance

---

Standard 3:	*Exhibits a physically active lifestyle.*

Objective 3.1:   **Participates fully in all class activities.**

Objective 3.2:   **Participates outside of class in self-selected physical activities.**

Definition
Student Log

Logs allow students to document or record specific behaviors over a period of time. Logs can be kept by individual students, groups, or classes, and are useful in recording such things as regularity of participation, feelings or reflections, and progress. Usually the teacher provides a format for recording the specific information in the log.

Standard 4:	*Achieves and maintains a health-enhancing level of physical fitness.*

Objective 4.1:   **Describes and demonstrates cardiovascular endurance.**

Sample Activities:
4.1a:	Participate in various kinds of aerobic activities and workouts
4.1b:	Participate in activities such as Amoeba Tag

Objective 4.2:   **Describes and demonstrates muscular/strength endurance.**

Sample Activities:
4.2a:	Participate on apparatus such as monkey bars, climbing ropes, horses, and Swedish boxes
4.2b:	Participate in a fitness circuit

Objective 4.3:   **Demonstrates flexibility.**

Sample Activities:
4.3a:	Stretch specific muscle groups
4.3b:	Participate in individual tumbling activities
4.3c:	Participate in partner stunts, such as Chinese Get-up

> **Sample Assessment**
> **Student Log**
> Students keep a log of their out-of-class participation in physical activity. Activities such as soccer, skating, walking, or intramural participation should be included. Log format should contain date, time, who participated, how long participation lasted, the level of activity, and any other important information. Assessment of the log should take into consideration the frequency, intensity, and duration of each activity.

Objective 4.4:   **Defines cardiovascular endurance, muscular strength/endurance, and flexibility.**

Objective 4.5:   **Participates in formal physical fitness assessment.**

Sample Activities:
4.5a:	Participate in formal fitness tests such as Physical Best

> **Teaching Tip**
> **Fitness Assessment**
> Assessment of health-related fitness components should be appropriate for the developmental level of the students. Test items should be modified as necessary. All assessment results should be private and the emphasis should be placed on using the information to better understand the relationship between fitness and wellness. The focus should be on improvement of individual scores and not on setting records or competition. Fitness assessment can be formative and/or summative.

Standard 5:	Demonstrates responsible personal and social behavior in physical activity settings.

Objective 5.1: **Identifies appropriate footwear/clothing for safe participation in various activities.**

Sample Activities:

5.1a: Collect advertisements for appropriate footwear/clothing

Objective 5.2: **Identifies unsafe behaviors on the playground.**

> **Sample Assessment**
> **Group Project**
> Students develop safety rules for the playground. Rules should focus on both personal and group behaviors. Classroom teachers could have students illustrate and post the rules in the classroom and/or gymnasium.

Objective 5.3: **Develops safety rules for physical education with the help of the teacher.**

Sample Activities:

5.3a: Produce a safety list for each major activity/game
5.3b: Design safety posters for each major activity/game

Objective 5.4: **Demonstrates positive behavior and language in a winning or losing situation.**

Sample Activities:

5.4a: Identify the positive happenings during an activity
5.4b: Congratulate partner, opponent, or team upon conclusion of the game or activity

Standard 6:	Demonstrates understanding and respect for differences among people in physical activity settings.

Objective 6.1: **Accepts and gives constructive feedback.**

Sample Activities:

6.1a: Participate in simple reciprocal teaching activities
6.1b: Attempt to identify correct technique or sequencing with a peer

Objective 6.2: **Encourages and supports peers.**

Sample Activities:

6.2a: Praise peers for effort and accomplishments during movement, dance, or games

> **Sample Assessment**
> **Checklist: Feedback**
> Criteria:
> * Uses criteria provided by the teacher — Yes   No
> * Accepts feedback from peer without complaint — Yes   No
> * Provides verbal encouragement during the activity — Yes   No
> * Correctly identifies performance error — Yes   No

Objective 6.3: **Participates in a cooperative problem-solving activity.**

Sample Activities:
6.3a: Complete an obstacle course with a partner
6.3b: Participate in New Games activities such as Poison River

Standard 7:	*Understands that physical activity provides opportunities for enjoyment, challenge, self-expression, and social interaction.*

Objective 7.1: **Evaluates level, tempo (speed/flow), and shape of movement.**

Sample Activities:
7.1a: Describe level (high, medium, low), speed, shape (pin-like, wall-like, ball-like, screw-like), and flow (successive flow/simultaneous flow, or continuous flow) of a partner's movement
7.1b: Develop a script of movements
7.1c: Mirror a partner in a variety of activities

Objective 7.2: **Demonstrates leadership skills.**

Sample Activities:
7.2a: Lead a warm-up or cool-down activity

Objective 7.3: **Demonstrates the aesthetic and creative qualities of movement by completing an original routine using nonlocomotor, locomotor, and manipulative movements.**

Sample Activities:
7.3a: Complete an original routine using all three subcategories of movement (listed in obj. 7.3)
7.3b: Complete a creative, dramatic problem such as Volcano

Sample Assessment
Checklist: Routine
Criteria:
- All three components included   Yes   No
- One movement flows to the next   Yes   No
- Variation in speed and flow demonstrated   Yes   No
- Routine is memorized   Yes   No

Definition
Summative Assessment

Summative assessment occurs at the end of a unit of instruction or grading period. This type of assessment determines the student's level of achievement at the end of a teaching unit and is a summation of the student's progress. Summative assessments include such things as report cards, fitness test scores, skill checklists, or tests of motor skill development.

GRADE FOUR

Did You Know?

- Children are born with 100 billion neurons.

- Child's formative years (birth through age 11 or 12) trillions of connections (synapses) are wired.

- These synapses act as bridges and establish the brain's circuitry.

- A brain with higher quality synapses can process information more quickly, with less energy.

- Critical periods exist in which the brain must be used in order for certain kinds of development to take place.

- Critical Periods have been identified for:

  Sight
  Language
  Emotion
  Movement

- Interaction and stimulation are physical determinants of how intricately the neuro-circuity of the brain is wired.

Standard 1:	Demonstrates competency in many movement forms and proficiency in a few movement forms.

Objective 1.1:   **Demonstrates rotational skills.**

Sample Activities:
1.1a: Perform the backward roll in the tuck, pike and straddle positions
1.1b: Perform the forward roll in the tuck and pike position

Objective 1.2:   **Demonstrates inverted skills.**

Sample Activities:
1.2a: Perform inverted skills such as tripod, mule kick, headstand, and cartwheel

Objective 1.3 :   **Explores moving to various rhythms.**

Sample Activities:
1.3a: Dribble, pass, and throw to various rhythms
1.3b: Perform traditional dances such as the Virginia Reel

Objective 1.4:   **Demonstrates efficient running techniques.**

Sample Activities:
1.4a: Run at different paces
1.4b: Run with various stride lengths
1.4c: Jog a set distance
1.4d: Participate in fleeing activities, relays, and dashes

Definition
Authentic Assessment
Authentic assessments are designed to take place in real-life settings rather than in an artificial or contrived setting. They determine if the student can use/apply skill, knowledge, or behavior in a "real" environment. Authentic assessments answer such questions as, "Does the student's throwing pattern remain the same as s/he participates in a game?" and include such things as applying strategies during game play, using fitness components to plan a personal program, problem solving, etc.

Objective 1.5: **Demonstrates throwing and catching in combination with locomotor skills.**

Sample Activities:
- 1.5a: Toss a ball overhead, move to another spot, and catch it
- 1.5b: Toss a ball against a wall and catch the ball on the rebound
- 1.5c: Toss a small ball against a wall and slide right or left to retrieve it
- 1.5d: Participate in team juggling activities

Sample Assessment
Checklist: Catching
Criteria:

- Elbows flexed in preparation   Yes   No
- Uses hands exclusively   Yes   No
- "Gives" with the catch at elbows and shoulders   Yes   No
- Shows no evidence of a fear reaction   Yes   No
- Visually tracks ball throughout flight   Yes   No

Objective 1.6: **Demonstrates catching and kicking skills in combination.**

Sample Activities:
- 1.6a: Catch a bean bag tossed from the right or left foot
- 1.6b: Toss a bean bag from the right foot and catch the bean bag with the left foot
- 1.6c: Punt a yarn ball and catch it
- 1.6d: Participate in activities such as Punt and Catch

Objective 1.7: **Demonstrates dribbling and passing with the feet.**

Sample Activities:
- 1.7a: Dribble and pass to a partner
- 1.7b: Participate in activities such as Soccer Touch Ball

Objective 1.8: **Explores dribbling with the hands.**

Teaching Tip
Grid Activities
Students entering fourth grade begin to participate in activities that require them to use fundamental motor skills with various game strategies. One method of practicing game concepts in conjunction with motor skills is to use various size grids. A grid is a space of a specific dimension which defines the boundaries for the participants in the activity. Students practice specific skills within the grid. For example, students may dribble and pass a soccer ball to a partner while remaining within their grid. The type of pass can be specified or a single defender can be added. A variety of concepts or skills can be practiced effectively within a grid. Grid activities lend themselves to authentic assessments of motor skills.

Sample Activities:
- 1.8a: Dribble a ball with the non-dominant hand
- 1.8b: Dribble a ball while moving in different directions using various locomotor movements
- 1.8c: Participate in activities such as Basketball Tag

Objective 1.9:   **Demonstrates striking with a short-handled implement.**

Sample Activities:
1.9a:	Bounce a ball in the air using a paddle
1.9b:	Dribble a ball with a paddle
1.9c:	Bounce a ball alternately in the air and on the floor with a paddle
1.9d:	Scoop a ball from the floor with a paddle
1.9e:	Roll a ball and scoop it from the floor with a paddle
1.9f:	Bounce a ball back and forth with a partner using a paddle
1.9g:	Participate in activities such as Tennis Volleyball

Objective 1.10:   **Participates in small group activities requiring knowledge and application of fundamental game concepts.**

Sample Activities:
1.10a:	Participate in grid activities with various numbers of participants and types of implements/equipment
1.10b:	Participate in grid activities using simple offensive and defensive strategies
1.10c:	Play Dribble Take Away, Captain Ball, Basketball Tag, Circle Guard, or Pass Around the Key
1.10d:	Play Beachball, Four-square, Mini-Volleyball, Keep It Up, Or Three-and-Over
1.10e:	Play Easy Football, Everyone's Eligible, or Fun Football

---

Sample Assessment
Event Task

Students use specific offensive and defensive strategies in a grid activity. Students work in groups of four (4) within a 15x15 yard grid. Two students serve as neutral posts between cones, while the other two students play 1-on-1 inside the grid. The offensive player can pass to the posts on both sides. A player scores by successfully receiving a ball beyond the end line. A player continues on offense until there is a turnover; then the player is immediately on defense. This activity is tiring, and the offensive/defensive players should switch positions with the post players after one (1) minute. Award points for the skill being emphasized in the lesson, such as the give-and-go or closing pathways. The assessment of the activity can be either qualitative (were pathways closed) or quantitative (how many points were scored). A rating scale or scoring rubric could be created for the activity.

Standard 2:	Applies movement concepts and principles to the learning and development of motor skills.

Objective 2.1: **Moves in clockwise and counterclockwise directions.**

Sample Activities:
2.1a: Form a human clock
2.1b: Participate in circle activities that involve passing and catching in clockwise and counterclockwise directions

Objective 2.2: **Locates objects in space from a personal frame of reference.**

Sample Activities:
2.2a: Follow footsteps through an obstacle course
2.2b: Walk through a maze
2.2c: Follow a map through an obstacle course
2.2d: Estimate the number of steps between herself/himself and a stationary object

Objective 2.3: **Demonstrates non-locomotor and locomotor skills with various combinations of shape, level, and effort.**

Sample Activities:
2.3a: Form the shape of an inanimate object using various body parts
2.3b: Play tug of war with a partner at various levels

Objective 2.4: **Describes and demonstrates concepts related to the Laws of Motion.**

Sample Activities:
2.4a: Create, with a partner, an activity that demonstrates one of the Laws of Motion
2.4b: Participate in relay races which demonstrate each of the Laws of Motion
2.4c: Complete stations which illustrate each law of motion

Sample Assessment
Group Project
Students participate in small groups to work through a maze. The maze is a series of boxes which must be stepped on in the correct sequence. One student, the "Maze Master", consults a map which has the correct sequence and guides the group through the maze. A scoring rubric can be used to assess performance.

Scoring Rubric
Level 3: All students successfully complete the sequence and work together cooperatively.
Level 2: Students complete the sequence, but take undue time interacting.
Level 1: Students fail to complete the maze.

Sample Assessment
Written Worksheet
Students lie on a scooter and propel themselves forward and backward.
Students answer the following questions:
1. In which direction do you predict you will have to apply force in order to move forward?
2. On what law of motion did you base your prediction?
3. Was your prediction accurate? Why or why not?
4. In what direction do you predict you will need to apply force in order to move backward?
5. Can you move with equal forcefulness forward and backward?

Standard 3:	*Exhibits a physically active lifestyle.*

Objective 3.1:   **Participates fully in all class activities.**

Objective 3.2:   **Participates outside of class in self-selected activities.**

Objective 3.3:   **Participates in activity outside of class to meet her/his personal fitness goals.**

> **Sample Assessment**
> **Parental Report**
> Parents can participate in the assessment of their children's goals by recording out-of-class participation. Parental documentation can take the form of an anecdotal record, signing off on activity logs, or recording activities in which they participate with their children.

Standard 4:	*Achieves and maintains a health-enhancing level of physical fitness.*

Objective 4.1:   **Demonstrates cardiovascular endurance.**

Sample Activities:
 4.1a: Participate in activities requiring cardiovascular endurance such as in-line skating, cycling, or swimming
 4.1b: Participate in activities such as Astronaut Drills and challenge courses

Objective 4.2:   **Demonstrates muscular strength/endurance.**

Sample Activities:
 4.3a: Participate in circuit training
 4.3b: Participate in activities such as Crab Soccer

Objective 4.4:   **Demonstrates flexibility.**

Sample Activities:
 4.4a: Explore all the ways the body can bend
 4.4b: Participate in activities such as Nose-and-Toe Tag

> **Sample Assessment**
> **Event Task**
> Students rotate through a series of activity stations, each of which focuses on one component of health-related fitness. Task cards at each station specify the activity to be performed. A checklist or scoring rubric can be used to assess performance.

Objective 4.5:   **Participates in formal physical fitness assessment.**

Sample Activities:
 4.5a: Participate in organized fitness testing such as Physical Best

Objective 4.6   **Differentiates between strength and endurance and describes how each is developed through exercise.**

Sample Activities:
 4.6a: Demonstrate an activity that develops strength
 4.6b: Demonstrate an activity that develops endurance

Objective 4.7:   Defines "overload" as it applies to strength and endurance.

Sample Activities:
4.7a: Plan an activity that will increase strength or endurance

Objective 4.8:   Describes how to maintain and improve flexibility at a joint.

Objective 4.9:   Sets personal fitness goals for each health-related fitness component.

Standard 5:	*Demonstrates responsible personal and social behavior in physical activity settings.*

Objective 5.1:   Identifies proper safety equipment for participation in dance, games, and sports.

Sample Activities:
5.1a: List proper footwear for various activities

Objective 5.2:   Works with a partner in the development of an activity, dance, or game to be played by the class.

Objective 5.3:   Demonstrates appropriate etiquette for movement, dance, and games.

> **Sample Assessment**
> **Group Project**
> Students work in small groups to design bulletin boards that illustrate items such as helmets, pads, or mouth guards. Students should indicate how these safety items provide protection for athletes.

Sample Activities:
5.3a: Ask a partner to dance
5.3b: Congratulate classmates for a well-excuted movement

Objective 5.4:   Participates in peer observations.

> **Definition**
> **Peer Observation**
> Students participate in peer observations of other students in order to provide feedback on the performance of specific skills. These observations are based on criteria identified by the teacher. Various forms of feedback can be used such as hand signals, discussions, or written checklists.

> **Sample Assessment**
> **Peer Observation**
> Students work with a partner and use a checklist to assess each other's throwing pattern. Criteria are provided by the teacher, including diagrams and/or pictures of the correct technique for throwing. Students limit their feedback to the criteria identified on the checklist.

Standard 6:	*Demonstrates understanding and respect for differences among people in physical activity settings.*

Objective 6.1: **Explores the ethnic background of activities, dances and games.**

Sample Activities:
6.1a: Prepare an oral report, bulletin board, or book report on the ethnic background of a chosen activity

Objective 6.2: **Serves as a group leader.**

> Sample Assessment
> **Oral Report**
> Students prepare and deliver an oral report on the ethnic background of the assigned sport, dance, or activity. Assignments can be made in conjunction with the classroom teacher as different cultures are studied.

Standard 7:	*Understands that physical activity provides opportunities for enjoyment, challenge, self-expression, and social interaction.*

Objective 7.1: **Creates a routine to music.**

Sample Activities:
7.1a: Place movements in a sequence to music
7.1b: Create a square dance

Objective 7.2: **Teaches an activity, dance or game to classmates that he/she has created.**

Sample Activities:
7.2a: Produce a book of games as created by the class

Objective 7.3: **Defines the aesthetic qualities of movement.**

Objective 7.4: **Develops self-confidence in a physical activity setting.**

> Sample Assessment
> **Peer Observation**
> Students work in groups of two (2) to describe the qualities of a movement prescribed by the teacher. Each student observes the performance of her/his partner and describes the qualities of the movement by circling the appropriate descriptor of flow, tempo, effort, shape, and level.
>
> | Flow: | Even | Uneven |
> | --- | --- | --- |
> | Tempo: | Fast | Slow |
> | Effort: | Hard | Small |
> | Shape: | Large | Small |
> | Level: | High | Low |

GRADE FIVE

Did You Know?

- The brain changes physiologically as a result of experience over time with the environment determining to some degree the functioning ability of the brain.

- The brain exhibits "neural plasticity" or the ability of the brain to change in response to outside stimuli.

- The brain is curious and needs stimulation to survive. Learning environments must give children the opportunity to relate what they are learning to what they already know.

- The brain is social and collaborative which mandates a learning environment that provides opportunities for children to cooperate and solve problems in small groups or with a partner.

- Enriched learning environments include:

  * Activities that stimulate all the senses
  * Opportunities for children to make choices
  * Activities that promote the fun of learning

From: Wolfe, P. (Nov., 1998). "What Do We Know from Brain Research?" Educational Leadership, 56, (3).

Standard 1:	Demonstrates competency in many movement forms and proficiency in a few movement forms.

Objective 1.1:   **Demonstrates various body positions while elevated.**

Sample Activities:
- 1.1a: Jump from a Reuther board in tuck, pike, and straddle positions
- 1.1b: Participate in activities such as Follow the Leader

Definition
Portfolio

Portfolios are an excellent method of documenting student achievement over time. Generally portfolios are maintained by students, and students have the freedom to choose what to include in their portfolios. Portfolios allow students to document their progress in achieving a specific goal using a variety of resources. The teacher decides which goals can be documented by using the portfolio, and students then begin gathering evidence. The teacher must be willing to accept a wide variety of documentation. Certificates for participation outside of class in recreational activities, achievement of a fitness badge in Boys or Girls Scouts, or pictures, themes or other written materials can all be included to document achievement of a specific goal. Portfolios are assessed relative to the extent to which the materials indicate that the class goal has been met.

Objective 1.2:   **Demonstrates rotational and inverted skills.**

Sample Activities:
- 1.2a: Perform skills such as cartwheel, roundoff, handstand forward roll, or front limber
- 1.2b: Rebound and outlet a basketball

Objective 1.3:   **Demonstrates mechanically efficient patterns of kicking.**

Sample Activities:
- 1.3a: Participate in a formal assessment of her/his pattern of kicking
- 1.3b: Evaluate a partner's pattern of kicking

Objective 1.4:   **Demonstrates mechanically efficient patterns of throwing.**

Sample Activities:
- 1.4a: Participate in a formal assessment of her/his pattern of throwing
- 1.4b: Evaluate a partner's pattern of throwing

Teaching Tip
Developmental Assessment

The same assessment given at K and 2nd grade should be repeated in the 5th grade. This should be the final check on the achievement of fundamental motor skills. Research findings indicate that if children leave 5th grade without competency in fundamental motor skills they will probably never reach their full movement potential.

Objective 1.5:   **Demonstrates mechanically efficient patterns of catching.**

Sample Activities:
  1.5a: Participate in a formal assessment of her/his pattern of catching
  1.5b: Evaluate a partner's pattern of catching

Objective 1.6:   **Demonstrates mechanically efficient patterns of striking without and with an implement.**

Sample Assessment Checklist: Striking		
Criteria:		
• Step, turn, and swing in sequence	Yes	No
• Hip rotation/de-rotation	Yes	No
• Weight transfer to forward foot	Yes	No
• Correct timing on contact	Yes	No
• Full extension of the arm on contact	Yes	No
• Follow through	Yes	No

Sample Activities:
  1.6a: Participate in a formal assessment of her/his pattern of striking
  1.6b: Evaluate a partner's pattern of striking

Objective 1.7:   **Demonstrates basic competence in dance.**

Sample Activities:
  1.7a: Perform square/folk/contemporary dances
  1.7b: Perform a jump routine to music

Definition
Scoring Rubric

A scoring rubric is similar to a rating scale but with multiple criteria used simultaneously. The teacher identifies criteria that describe different levels of performance of a task. The levels of the rubric represent gradations in achievement of the objective. Scoring rubrics are typically used for more complex assessments.

Standard 2:	*Applies movement concepts and principles to the learning and development of motor skills.*

Objective 2.1:   **Demonstrates basic competence in game strategies and concepts.**

Objective 2.2:   **Demonstrates third-party perspective in team activities.**

Sample Activities:
   2.2a: Participate in activities such as Zone Soccer

Sample Assessment		
Scoring Rubric: Concept of Open Space/Player		
Level 3:	Level 2:	Level 1:
Moves to open space with ball	Sometimes moves to open space with ball	Seldom moves to open space with ball
Moves to open space without ball	Sometimes moves to open space without ball	Seldom moves to space without ball
Always passes to open teammates	Sometimes passes to open teammates	Seldom passes to open teammates

Objective 2.3:   **Describes and demonstrates concepts related to the effective use of levers.**

Objective 2.4:   **Identifies major muscles in the body.**

Sample Activities:
   2.4a: Label major muscles on an outline of her/his body

Objective 2.5:   **Describes concepts related to cardiovascular fitness.**

Sample Activities:
   2.5a: Monitor heart rate at rest and following activity
   2.5b: Compare the effects of various exercises on heart rate

> Sample Assessment
> **Written Worksheet**
> Students work in partners to identify concepts related to levers. One student is in the wheelbarrow position with the other partner providing the force. Partners move forward 10 feet and switch roles. Students answer the following questions:
> 1. What type of lever are you using to propel your partner in the wheelbarrow position?
> 2. Where is the fulcrum, the resistance, and the point of force application?

Sample Assessment
Student Log
Students record in a log resting heart rates, exercise heart rates during various activities, and recovery heart rates following activity. To ensure more accuracy, heart rate monitors could be used.

Standard 3: **Exhibits a physically active lifestyle.**

Objective 3.1:   **Participates fully in all class activities.**

Objective 3.2:   **Participates outside of class in self-selected activities.**

> Definition
> **Student Journal**
> A student journal is used to record perceptions, reflections, or feelings about participation in physical activity. Journals are kept for specific amounts of time and students record in their journals at regular intervals. Journals often provide teachers with important information about how students are feeling which may not be evident through observation. Assessment of the journal by the teacher is not based on right or wrong answers, but on rating scales involving the depth of self-reflection.

Objective 3.3:   **Participates in activities designed to improve self-diagnosed weaknesses in health-related fitness components.**

> Sample Assessment
> **Student Journal**
> Students record progress in improving health-related fitness including goals, activity, and reflections on feelings before, during, and after activity.

Standard 4:	*Achieves and maintains a health-enhancing level of physical fitness.*

Objective 4.1:   **Demonstrates cardiovascular endurance.**

Sample Activities:
- 4.1a: Follow a videotaped aerobic workout
- 4.1b: Follow instructor's aerobic workout to music for 20 minutes
- 4.1c: Participate in Jump Rope for Heart

Objective 4.2:   **Demonstrates muscular strength/endurance.**

Sample Activities:
- 4.2a: Participate in a strength-training circuit
- 4.2b: Participate in gymnastics apparatus activities

Objective 4.3:   **Demonstrates flexibility.**

Sample Activities:
- 4.3a: Participate in aerobic and dance work-outs that emphasize range of motion
- 4.3b: Describe the benefits of adequate flexibility

Objective 4.4:   **Participates in formal physical fitness assessment.**

Objective 4.5:	**Designs a personal fitness program.**

Sample Assessment
Scoring Rubric: Fitness Program Design

Level 3:
 Sets realistic goals
 Participates 3x per week
 Includes all 4 fitness components
Level 2:
 Goals too easy/hard
 Participates 2x per week
 Includes 3 of 4 fitness components
Level 1:
 Sets no goal/s
 Participates 1x per week
 Includes 2 of 4 fitness components

Objective 4.6: **Identifies beverages which are effective in fluid replacement.**

Sample Activities:
 4.6a: Rank-order beverages as to their effectiveness in fluid replacement.

Objective 4.7: **Sets a long term goal for improvement in an area of a self-diagnosed weakness.**

Standard 5:	*Demonstrates responsible personal and social behavior in physical activity settings.*

Objective 5.1: **Identifies safety factors related to bicycling, skate boarding, and skating.**

Sample Activities:
 5.1a: Prepare an oral report, bulletin board, or poster on safety factors for a chosen activity

Objective 5.2: **Describes and demonstrates responsible behavior while participating in physical activity.**

Sample Assessment
Scoring Rubric: Responsible Behavior
Level 3:
 Completes task without supervision
 Helps settle disagreements among classmates
 Returns equipment without being asked
Level 2:
 Needs some supervision to complete tasks
 Does not argue with classmates
 Returns equipment when asked
Level 1:
 Needs constant supervision to complete tasks
 Argues with classmates
 Does not return equipment when asked

Objective 5.3: **Officiates an activity, game, or sport.**

Sample Activities:
 5.3a: Make line calls while participating in games

Objective 5.4: **Displays respect for the person who is officiating.**

Objective 5.5: **Participates with a group in cooperative problem-solving activities.**

Sample Activities:
 5.5a: Develop a group dance using assigned movement elements
 5.5b: Develop a team strategy for a game/sport
 5.5c: Participate in Project Adventure activities

Standard 6:	Demonstrates an understanding and respect for differences among people in physical activity settings.

Objective 6.1: **Participates in reciprocal evaluations of movement patterns.**

Objective 6.2: **Demonstrates acceptance of teammates' skill levels.**

Sample Activities:
    6.2a: Participate with assigned partner(s) or teammates without complaint

Standard 7:	Understands that physical activity provides opportunities for enjoyment, challenge, self-expression, and social interaction.

Objective 7.1: **Evaluates movement for aesthetic qualities.**

Sample Activities:
    7.1a: Depict the effort, shape, and flow of a movement through drawing

Objective 7.2: **Participates with a group in creating a movement activity, dance, or game.**

Objective 7.3: **Develops self-confidence in physical activity settings.**

Objective 7.4: **Chooses appropriate skill challenges based on proficiency.**

> **Sample Assessment**
> **Rating Scale: Self-confidence**
> Criteria:
>
> 5 = Extends movement challenges when appropriate.
> 4 = Extends movement challenges upon request of the teacher.
> 3 = Meets movement challenges without extending the skill.
> 2 = Modifies movement challenges to ensure success.
> 1 = Does not meet movement challenges.

EDA GUIDELINES
For Physical Education

Program Standards, Objectives, and Assessments

Grades 6 - 8

Introduction: Grades 6-8

Characteristics of Middle School Children. A discussion of the unique characteristics and needs of middle school children is presented, and implications are drawn for the content and structure of the physical education program.

Objectives for the Middle School Teacher. Objectives for the middle school teacher in designing instructional activities are also presented in this section. The teacher objectives are based on the characteristics and needs of middle school children, and are intended to suggest strategies for designing effective activities to achieve the various behavioral objectives.

Behavioral Objectives and Sample Activities. For each of the seven Content Standards, specific, grade-appropriate objectives related to psychomotor, cognitive and/or affective behavior have been identified. For each behavioral objective, samples are provided of specific activities that could be used in conjunction with a particular behavioral objective at a particular grade level. The sample activities are intended to illustrate or suggest tasks and activities that can serve as behavioral criteria relative to the accomplishment of the objectives for a particular grade level. It is hoped that these sample activities will serve to suggest additional and/or alternate activities appropriate for a particular physical education program relative to facilities, equipment, and regional/geographic activity interests and opportunities.

Assessment. Examples of a variety of assessment techniques are provided for each grade level. The sample assessment techniques are intended to illustrate some of the many valid, authentic, and appropriate ways to evaluate the extent to which the behavioral objectives have been accomplished. It is hoped that the sample assessments will serve to suggest additional and/or alternate assessment techniques appropriate for a particular program.

Activity Matrices. For Standard 1, which relates to skill acquisition, activity matrices are provided for each grade level to illustrate the content suggested in the behavioral objectives. A complete activity x grade level matrix is included at the end of the section to illustrate the content progression for the skill acquisition standard across the three grades, 6-8.

Principles for Designing Practice. Principles for designing appropriate practice activities for the acquisition of specific motor skills in grades 6-12 are presented at the beginning of the grades 9-12 section. Included in this information is a task analysis used to examine the complexity of the performance environment and the movement pattern associated with a particular skill, and examples to simplify the practice environment.

Definition of Terms. Listed below are definitions of key terms used in this section of the guidelines document to denote a progressive sequence of skill development for a given activity.

Attempt   Implies that the skill will be taught but the student will not master or show competency in the skill.

Demonstrate: Implies that the student will demonstrate competency in the skill.

Explore: Implies that the student has demonstrated competency in the skill and will explore
                    variations of the movement in dimensions such as speed, flow, or direction.

Review: Implies the continual review of the skill and serves as a developmental checkpoint.

Structuring Activity Lessons. For a given group of students and a specific activity objective, it is likely that
student performances will be distributed across the *attempt, demonstrate,* and *review* continuum of skill
development. A general rule-of-thumb for designing activity lessons is to select tasks for which 80% of the
students are expected to demonstrate competency. Individualized instruction and practice activities should be
designed for the remaining students.

GRADE SIX

Did You Know?

- Physical activity programs for young people are most likely to be effective when they:

  *emphasize enjoyable participation in physical activities that are easily done throughout life

  *offer a diverse range of noncompetitive and competitive activities appropriate for different ages and abilities

  *give young people the skills and confidence they need to be physically active

  *promote physical activity through all components of a coordinated school health program and develop links between school and community programs

- Inactivity and poor diet cause at least 300,000 deaths a year in the United States. Only tobacco use causes more preventable deaths.

From: U.S. Department of Health and Human Services (March 1997). CDC's Guidelines for School and Community Programs Promoting Lifelong Physical Activity. (brochure). Available on the Internet at http://www.edc.gov/nccdphp/dash.

Standard 1:	*Demonstrates competency in many movement forms and proficiency in a few movement forms.*

Objective 1.1:   **Demonstrates body, spatial, and temporal awareness.**

Objective 1.2:   **Demonstrates rotational skills.**

Sample Activities:
  1.2a: Forward or backward rolls in different body shapes
  1.2b: Cartwheels

Objective 1.3:   **Demonstrates static balancing skills.**

Sample Activities:
  1.3a: Front or side scale
  1.3b: Headstand or handstand

Objective 1.4:   **Demonstrates dynamic balancing skills.**

Sample Activities:
  1.4a: Various leaps
  1.4b: Turns and pivots at different levels

Objective 1.5:   **Demonstrates vaulting skills.**

Sample Activities:
  1.5a: Travel over objects of varying heights and distances
  1.5b: Flank vault

Objective 1.6:   **Demonstrates supporting skills.**

Sample Activities:
  1.6a: Skin-the-cat or inverted hang
  1.6b: Front support

> Sample Assessment
> **Checklist: Flank Vault**
> Students observe a partner and provide feedback on performance of the flank vault. Criteria for observations are identified by the teacher. Feedback is provided through verbal discussion.
> Criteria:
> * Running approach   Yes   No
> * Two-foot takeoff   Yes   No
> * Arms extended on contact with apparatus   Yes   No
> * Legs extended to side   Yes   No
> * Hips elevated   Yes   No

Objective 1.7:   **Demonstrates beginning square and/or line dance skills.**

Sample Activities:
  1.7a: Grapevine
  1.7b: Allemande right and left

Objective 1.8:   **Demonstrates body control while performing movement activities, dances, games, and sports.**

Sample Activities:
    1.8a: Run within her/his lane on the track
    1.8b: Perform a cartwheel and land within a designated area

Objective 1.9:   **Demonstrates receiving and projecting objects without and with an implement while stationary and moving.**

Sample Activities:
    1.9a: Move into open spaces while passing an object back and forth with a partner, using various pathways
    1.9b: Juggle with a small group, keeping the members of the group moving

Objective 1.10:   **Participates in swimming and water survival skills commensurate with her/his ability.**

Sample Activities:
    1.10a: Enter the water fully clothed and demonstrate the ability to use clothing as a flotation device

---

Teaching Tip
Teacher Observation
- View the skill from different angles.
- Record the students with problems or showing areas of slower development.
- Determine the method of observation to be used before making the observation.
- Utilize different forms of observation such as anecdotal record, checklist, rating scales, or scoring rubrics.
- Make sure the observation method is appropriate for the skill or activity being observed.
- Develop criteria before beginning the observation.

1.10b?

Objective 1.11:   **Demonstrates or attempts the following basketball skills:**

REVIEW	DEMONSTRATE	ATTEMPT
	Dominant hand dribble	Non-dominant hand dribble
	Pivot	Speed dribble
	Defensive slides	Change-of- pace dribble
		Crossover dribble
		Spin dribble
		Chest pass
		Bounce pass
		Two-hand overhead pass
		Flip pass
		Outlet pass
		Baseball pass
		Set shot
		Dominant hand lay-up
		Foul shot
		Jump shot
		Turn on rebound

Definition
Demonstrate
Implies that the student will perform the skill competently, at the age-appropriate developmental level.

Definition
Attempt
Implies the skill will be taught, but the student will not master or show competency in the skill.

Objective 1.12:   **Demonstrates or attempts the following field hockey skills:**

REVIEW	DEMONSTRATE	ATTEMPT
	Grip	Drive pass
		Flick pass
		Flat pass
		Through pass
		Push pass
		Drive shot
		Flick shot
		Scoop shot
		Ground trap
		Air trap
		Hand trap
		Forward tackle
		Side tackle
		Dribble

Objective 1.13: **Demonstrates or attempts the following football skills:**

REVIEW	DEMONSTRATE	ATTEMPT
	Giving and receiving handoff	Long hike
	Carrying the ball	Forward pass
	Kickoff	Lateral pass
	Blocking	Punting
		Over the shoulder catch
		Above the shoulder catch
		Below the knees catch

> **Teaching Tip**
> **Assessing Achievement**
> The teacher can use checklists, scoring rubrics, rating scales, skill tests, verbal quizzes, and/or written tests to evaluate student progress in mastery of grade - appropriate skills. Samples of the various types of assessments are provided in the appendix at the end of this document.

Objective 1.14: **Demonstrates or attempts the following racket sport skills:**

REVIEW	DEMONSTRATE	ATTEMPT
	Forehand grip	Forehand swing
	Backhand grip	Backhand swing
		Volley
		Drop serve

Objective 1.15: **Demonstrates or attempts the following soccer skills:**

REVIEW	DEMONSTRATE	ATTEMPT
	Instep kick	Outside kick
	Dribble	Heel kick
	Foot trap	Square pass
		Through pass
		Aerial pass
		Throw-in
		Drive shot
		Chip shot
		Body trap
		Leg trap
		Thigh juggle
		Foot juggle

Objective 1.16:   **Demonstrates or attempts the following softball skills:**

REVIEW	DEMONSTRATE	ATTEMPT
	Underhand throw	Overhand throw from outfield
	Base running	Fielding ground balls
	Overhand throw from infield	Fielding line drives
	Catching with glove	Fielding fly balls
		Hitting
		Pitching

> **Teaching Tip**
> **Assessing Improvement**
> Many teachers base part of a student's evaluation on improvement. In order to measure improvement, students must participate in some type of pre-instructional assessment, and the same assessment must be conducted at the end of the instructional unit (summative assessment). The improvement is measured in terms of the difference between the pre- and post-assessments. Many teachers use rating scales or skill tests to assess improvement.

Objective 1.17:   **Attempts the following track and field skills:**

REVIEW	DEMONSTRATE	ATTEMPT
		Sprint
		High jump
		Relays

Objective 1.18:   **Attempts the following volleyball skills:**

REVIEW	DEMONSTRATE	ATTEMPT
		Underhand serve
		Set
		Forearm pass
		Dominant hand hit

> **Sample Assessment**
> **Skill Test: Volleyball**
> Although skill tests do not assess performance in a game setting, some skill tests correlate with individual skills used in game play. The Volleyball Wall Volley Test (Latcxhaw, 1954) has appropriate criterion validity and is designed for use with 6th grade students.

Objective 1.19:   **Attempts the skills of compass and map reading necessary to complete a beginning orienteering course.**

Objective 1.20:   **Attempts the offensive skills of pick, give-and-go, pick and roll, fake, and screen for a variety of team sports.**

Sample Activities:

1.20a: Participate in 2 on 2 and/or 3 on 3 games

1.20b: Keep away

Objective 1.21:   **Attempts player-to-player defense in a variety of team sports.**

Sample Activities:

1.21a: Participate in 2 on 2 and/or 3 on 3 games

1.21b: Keep away

> Sample Assessment
> **Grid Activity**
> Students participate in 3 on 3 play in a grid, attempting to pass a ball to a teammate over the end line. In addition students attempt to use a pick, give-and-go, pick-and-roll, fake, and/or screen. A team scores a point for a pass beyond the end line, and additional points for using one of the offensive skills.

Standard 2:	**Applies movement concepts and principles to the learning and development of motor skills.**

Objective 2.1:   **Explores the application of force.**

Sample Activities:

2.1a: Throw, kick, and strike objects of different sizes and shapes

2.1b: Pull and push objects of different weights

Objective 2.2:   **Explores various trajectories through throwing and catching.**

Sample Activities:

2.2a: Throw and catch a ball on the rebound

Objective 2.3:   **Identifies the mechanical advantage of movement in opposition.**

Objective 2.4:   **Identifies the purpose of the follow-through phase of movement.**

Objective 2.5:   **Identifies gross errors in personal movements.**

Objective 2.6:   **Participates in activities that enhance awareness of spatial relationships between and among the ball, the goal, the opponent, and her/himself (third party perspective).**

Sample Activities:
     2.6a: 2 on 1 game
     2.6b: 3 on 2 game

Sample Assessment
Student Project
Students solve movement problems designed by the teacher. The problems are designed to provide students an opportunity to demonstrate knowledge of various movement concepts. Sample Problem: When Janey plays 3 on 3 basketball with her friends she does very well handling the ball and shooting. When she doesn't have the ball she is never quite sure what she should do. Identify two (2) options Janey has when she does not have the ball. Be sure to be very clear with your suggestions and use complete sentences.

Standard 3:	*Exhibits a physically active lifestyle.*

Objective 3.1:   **Participates in self-selected aerobic activities outside of class.**

Sample Activities:
     3.1a: Rope jumping
     3.1b: Jogging
     3.1c: Step Aerobics

Objective 3.2:   **Participates in self-selected activities outside of class that require muscular strength/endurance.**

Sample Activities:
     3.2a: Tumbling/gymnastics activities
     3.2b: Climbing activities

Objective 3.3:   **Attempts beginning activities in a variety of geographically-appropriate outdoor pursuits.**

Sample Activities:
     3.3a: Snow shoeing
     3.3b: Bicycling

Sample Assessment
Student Log
Students keep a daily log of their physical activities. Logs can be part of the morning routine, and recording can be done during attendance or lunch count. Logs are collected at the end of each month and comments are made by the physical education teacher. Teachers should provide a weekly focus for the log, such as activities requiring muscular strength/ endurance, aerobic endurance, or flexibility.

Standard 3 + 4 combine w/ EPEC

Standard 4:	*Achieves and maintains a health-enhancing level of physical fitness.*

Objective 4.1:   **Calculates maximum and target heart rates.**

Objective 4.2:   **Identifies appropriate activities to enhance each component of health-related fitness.**

Objective 4.3:   **Identifies the three factors manipulated to achieve overload.**

Objective 4.4:   **Identifies appropriate methods of increasing flexibility.**

> Sample Assessment
> **Group Project**
> Students work in small groups to design a fitness routine that includes activities that will enhance each of the components of fitness assigned by the teacher.

> Sample Assessment
> **Student Project**
> Students design a personal flexibility routine based on the results of their fitness assessment. Music is chosen by the classroom community. During class time devoted to flexibility, students perform their routines.

Objective 4.5:   **Identifies appropriate methods of increasing strength.**

Objective 4.6:   **Differentiates between muscular strength and muscular endurance.**

Objective 4.7:   **Differentiates between aerobic and anaerobic capacity.**

> Sample Assessment
> **Group Project**
> Students work with a partner to design a series of activities to increase upper body strength. During class time devoted to developing upper body strength, students perform their activity routine with their partner.

Objective 4.8:   **Participates in activities that will sustain a target heart rate of 60% to 85% of maximum heart rate for a minimum of 20 minutes.**

Objective 4.9:   **Participates in activities that will increase range of motion.**

> Sample Assessment
> **Worksheet**
> Students complete a worksheet involving calculation of maximum and target heart rates. These worksheets are available from the American Heart Association.

Sample Activities:
    4.9a: Sport-specific stretching exercises
    4.9b: Systematic stretching exercises

Objective 4.10:   **Participates in health-related fitness assessment.**

Teaching Tip
Fitness Assessment
Middle school is a very difficult time period for most students. Their physical characteristics are changing rapidly, and they can be extremely uncomfortable with their bodies. Therefore, assessment activities should be carefully planned to avoid any student embarrassment. Results of the assessment should be kept confidential between the individual student and the teacher.

Sample Activities:

4.10a: Physical Best
4.10b: Fitness Gram
4.10c: Set personal goals for fitness based on health-related standards and previous fitness scores

Objective 4.11:   **Identifies possible injuries that may result from improper warm-up, conditioning, or cool-down.**

Standard 5:	*Demonstrates responsible personal and social behavior in physical activity settings.*

Objective 5.1:   **Identifies safety factors in the utilization of space without and with an implement.**

Sample Activities:
5.1a: Maintain a safe distance from others when using a jump rope

Objective 5.2:   **Identifies safety factors associated with the utilization of athletic equipment/apparatus.**

Sample Activities:
5.2a: Demonstrate safe use of sticks, rackets, and bats in a crowded area

Sample Assessment
Group Project
Students design a pamphlet on physical education safety. Illustrations and information are included to educate the reader regarding the safety considerations for physical activity.

Objective 5.3:   **Differentiates between safe and unsafe participation/environment.**

Sample Activities:
5.3a: Attempt transverse rock climb or peg board climb only if a safety mat is in place

Objective 5.4:   **Identifies the function of rules.**

Sample Activities:
5.4a: Create a game
5.4b: Modify a game

Objective 5.5:   **Follows all game rules to maintain safe playing conditions.**

Sample Activities:
  5.5a: Participate in a floor hockey game without body-checking opponents.

Objective 5.6:   **Applies the rules and regulations for the activity.**

Sample Activities:
  5.6a: Self-officiate an activity
  5.6b: Teach rules to peers

Objective 5.7:   **Demonstrates an understanding of the relative importance of winning and losing.**

Sample Activities:
  5.7a: Participate in team activities with individuals of various skill levels

> **Sample Assessment**
> **Checklist: Winning/Losing**
>
> Criteria:
> - Avoids trash talking   Yes No
> - Avoids excessive celebrating
>   upon victory   Yes No
> - Accepts decision of officials   Yes No
> - Congratulates opponents
>   after the game   Yes No
> - Recognizes and acknowledges
>   outstanding play by opponents   Yes No

Standard 6:	*Demonstrates understanding and respect for differences among people in physical activity settings.*

Objective 6.1:   **Identifies the historical and cultural origins of a variety of dances.**

Objective 6.2:   **Participates in folk and line dances from different cultures.**

Sample Activities:
  6.2a: Schottiche
  6.2b: Tucker
  6.2c: Troika
  6.2d: Hora

Objective 6.3:   **Demonstrates an acceptance of differences among classmates in physical development.**

Objective 6.4:   **Demonstrates the ability to resolve conflict with peers.**

> **Sample Assessment**
> **Rating Scale: Conflict Resolution**
>
> Criteria:
> 3 = Self mediation
> 2 = Peer mediation
> 1 = Teacher mediation

Objective 6.5:   **Teaches a movement activity identified with the student's culture.**

Sample Activities:
    6.5a: Curling

Objective 6.6:   **Participates in activities with modified rules, structure, and/or equipment to increase the parity of the movement, dance, game, or sport.**

Sample Activities:
    6.6a: Scooter basketball
    6.6b: Half-court tennis

> **Sample Assessment**
> **Group Project**
> Students are given a written description of a game of elimination. Students work in small groups to modify the rules so that players are included, not excluded, from the game. Each group then teaches the game to classmates.

Standard 7:	*Understands that physical activity provides opportunities for enjoyment, challenge, self-expression, and social interaction.*

Objective 7.1:   **Observes creative movement phrases or sentences performed by a more experienced model and discuss her/his movement.**

Objective 7.2:   **Develops, in cooperation with a group, creative movement phrases or sentences based on a theme.**

Objective 7.3:   **Creates movement sentences in response to music, props, literature, or other appropriate stimuli.**

Sample Activities:
    7.3a: Create a dance in a square formation
    7.3b: Interpret a poem through dance

> **Sample Assessment**
> **Self-Assessment**
> Students evaluate their performance or progress in selected skills or behaviors. Self-assessment can include the use of checklists, journals, or rating scales.

Objective 7.4:   **Chooses a motivator (for example: music, teacher involvement, student selection of activity) that will enhance fun and enjoyment in the class.**

Sample Activities:
    7.4a: Participate in warm-ups to music of her/his choice

Objective 7.5:   **Participates in initiative and cooperative learning activities.**

Sample Activities:
    7.5a: Project Adventure
    7.5b: Rock Climbing

Objective 7.6:   **Participates in activities which will allow her/him to set and achieve dual and team goals.**

Sample Activities:
    7.6a: Everyone up
    7.6b: Cooperation tag

Objective 7.7:   **Participates in a variety of non-competitive games.**

Characteristics of Middle School Students, Implications for Physical Education Programs, and Objectives for the Middle School Teacher

The content of the middle school program in physical education should be based on the needs and interests of the middle school child. Unfortunately, many middle school physical education curricula are simply adaptations of either elementary or secondary programs. To more effectively meet the needs of young adolescents, it is essential to understand the developmental changes - physical, intellectual, emotional, and social - that occur during the middle school years. Curricular decisions within the physical education program should be based on an understanding of the unique characteristics of the middle school child.

Physical Growth and Development

Physically, adolescents are trying to master a new body. Secondary sexual characteristics are now more apparent. Girls experience breast development, growth of pubic hair, widening of the hips, and accumulation of body fat. Boys encounter growth of facial and pubic hair, development of genitalia, deepening of the voice, and an increase in muscle mass. Given these changes, gender role identification becomes a significant issues for students.

A rapid and uneven growth pattern occurs. The growth spurt for females occurs 1.5 years earlier than for males. Girls are taller and more physically mature than boys. However, once boys enter puberty, they will surpass girls in height, weight, strength, and endurance. Girls continue to demonstrate superiority in balance and flexibility. Boys who have not entered puberty will not be as strong or quick, and, therefore, some may be uneasy about physical contact activities.

The range of motor abilities among students broadens due to differences in growth velocity within and between genders. Both awkward and highly coordinated individuals can be found in the same class. Mastery of new skills can be difficult for some students, resulting in feelings of physical inadequacy for both girls and boys. Consequently, some students may avoid learning new skills to assure they will not be embarrassed in front of peers and teachers.

The range of activities within the physical education program must correspond to the range of individual differences among students. Programs should include activities related to physical fitness, individual and dual sports, team sports, gymnastics, rhythm and dance, aquatics, and outdoor pursuits that provide opportunities for students to enjoy physical education and to experience success with respect to their individual interests and ability levels. The degree of difficulty of activities should be adapted to the physical and emotional development of individual students through modifications in equipment, rules, space, and the like. In this way, young adolescents will be able to acquire skill within a productive learning environment, despite the diversity found in body size and ability level.

Intellectual Development

Middle school students are faced with increased demands to process information and make informed choices. Therefore, it is important to incorporate decision-making and problem-solving tasks in physical education. Students need to develop and apply critical thinking skills in a structured, supportive environment that minimizes the potential stress of decision-making.

Adolescents are capable of handling abstract concepts. Conceptual thinking allows students to generalize information and project hypothetical conclusions, as well as to assign conceptual values from one realm of behavior to another. The physical education program should include concepts from biomechanics, motor learning and development, and exercise physiology. These concepts should be discussed relative to the developmental changes that are taking place among the students. Understanding the changes that are taking place within their bodies is a first step toward development of identity for adolescents.

Emotional Development

Emotional changes among adolescents parallel their rapid physical changes. These emotional changes impact behavior, which, at times, can be unpredictable. Moods appear to fluctuate quickly. Therefore, physical education programs should incorporate strategies for stress reduction and emotional control to meet the emotional needs of students.

A positive self-concept is critical to the emotional development of an individual. Programs should provide opportunities for students to develop, change, and test perceptions of themselves, and to develop a sense of self-worth. Activities and teaching styles should be carefully selected to enable students to achieve a level of success. Success in physical activity provides reinforcement and recognition, which are essential to the development of self-esteem.

Social Development

Adolescents are striving for greater independence from parents, and intimacy among peers becomes a primary social characteristic. It is essential to recognize the need for peer acceptance and approval among middle school students. However, middle school students are often torn between adult and peer values. Therefore, the middle school program must provide opportunities for adolescents to receive approval from both peers and adults. Educators may facilitate the growth of independence by providing activities that require responsibility, leadership, and decision-making skills. However, guidance in decision-making is still necessary. Students seek well-defined parameters for their learning experiences, and clear limits and goals are essential for successful teaching.

Middle school students are interested in and self-conscious about their bodies, appearance, and abilities. Most adolescents link their social acceptance to their physical appearance. Explanation of the physiological changes that are characteristic of adolescence helps students to become more accepting of individual differences among peers.

Competition is viewed by the adolescent as a means of attaining social prominence. This belief places an undue emphasis on winning. Highly competitive games often lead to feelings of inadequacy and failure for a large number of students. Often the losers in competition are the individuals who are most in need of peer acceptance due to real or perceived deficiencies in physical abilities. Small group activities should be emphasized with the focus on developing competency in a nurturing environment. Practice activities must be well-designed, allowing sufficient time for skill development without the fear of public humiliation. Because of the diversity of skill found among students in the same grade, programs must be carefully designed to achieve a balance between competitive and cooperative activities. Cooperative experiences can assist in promoting both leadership and group membership skills that are needed at this level.

Summary

The middle school years are a period of transition. Students in this age group are experiencing a myriad of physical, emotional, intellectual, and social changes. They are attempting to establish identity, develop peer relationships, assert independence, and cope with emerging sexuality. As students struggle with these issues, physical education has a unique opportunity to "ease the way". The nature of the physical education program lends itself to numerous teachable moments that can help students make informed decisions and clarify values. To effectively facilitate physical, intellectual, emotional, and social growth for middle school students, the physical education curriculum must be based on the unique characteristics and special needs of the middle-school age group.

Teacher Objectives

The following objectives for designing appropriate instructional activities in physical education are based on the unique characteristics and needs of middle school children. The objectives provide suggestions relative to effective methodology for achieving curricular objectives, and are expressed in terms of desired teacher behaviors.

The teacher should provide opportunities for students to experience:
   *Self-growth, self-exploration, and self-expression
   *Success, achievement, and mastery
   *Acceptance and approval by peers
   *Leadership
   *Feelings of competence
   *Self- and peer-assessment
   *Responsibility
   *Creativity
   *Goal-setting

The teacher should provide activities that include:
   *Cooperative and initiative learning
   *Clear objectives and competency goals
   *Clear guidelines for acceptable behavior
   *Small group participation focused on the development of competency
   *Sufficient practice for mastery to occur
   *Specific feedback
   *Non-competitive participation with numerous individuals and rotating groups
   *Modification of regulation games

Submitted by: Dr. Louise McCormack, Plymouth State College
                Dr. Ree K. Arnold, Montclair State University

GRADE SEVEN

Did You Know?

- Nearly half of young people ages 12-21 are not vigorously active on a regular basis.

- Physical activity declines dramatically with age during adolescence.

- Female adolescents are much less physically active than male adolescents.

- People who are usually inactive can improve their health and well-being by becoming moderately active on a regular basis.

- A moderate amount of physical activity is roughly equivalent to physical activity that uses approximately 150 Calories of energy per day, or 1,000 Calories per week.

- Examples of moderate amounts of activity include:
  *washing and waxing a car for 45-60 minutes
  *playing touch football for 30-45 minutes
  *wheeling self in wheelchair for 30-40 minutes
  *bicycling 5 miles in 30 minutes
  *bicycling 4 miles in 15 minutes
  *raking leaves for 30 minutes
  *shoveling snow for 15 minutes

From: U.S. Department of Health and Human Services (March 1997). CDC's Guidelines for School and Community Programs Promoting Lifelong Physical Activity. (brochure). Available on the Internet at http://www.edc.gov/nccdphp/dash.

Standard 1:	*Demonstrates competency in many movement forms and proficiency in a few movement forms.*

Objective 1.1:   **Reviews rotational skills.**

Objective 1.2:   **Demonstrates rotational skills on apparatus.**

Sample Activities:
 1.2a: Pull-over or sole circle
 1.2b: Forward or backward rolls

Objective 1.3:   **Reviews static balancing skills.**

Objective 1.4:   **Demonstrates static balancing skills on apparatus.**

Sample Assessment Checklist: Static Balance		
Criteria:		
• Hold balance for 3 seconds	Yes	No
• Full extension of extremities	Yes	No
• Proper alignment	Yes	No
• Head up and eyes forward	Yes	No
• Stillness achieved	Yes	No

Sample Activities:
 1.4a: Knee scale or V-seat
 1.4b: Shoulder stand

Objective 1.5:   **Reviews dynamic balancing skills.**

Objective 1.6:   **Demonstrates dynamic balancing skills on apparatus.**

Sample Activities:
 1.6a: Forward or backward walking
 1.6b: Leaps or jumps

Objective 1.7:   **Reviews vaulting skills.**

Objective 1.8:   **Demonstrates vaulting skills using a springboard or reuther board.**

Sample Assessment Checklist:Support Hierarchy for Parallel Bars		
Level 1 Criteria:		
• Front support	Yes	No
• Front support to straddle seat	Yes	No
• Flank dismount	Yes	No
Level 2 Criteria:		
• Walk forward in front support	Yes	No
• Shoulder swing to front support	Yes	No
• ½ turn to front support	Yes	No
Level 3 Criteria:		
• Shoulder stand	Yes	No
• Forward roll to straddle seat	Yes	No
• Flank dismount	Yes	No

Sample Activities:
 1.8a: Landing on top
 1.8b: Flank or squat

Objective 1.9:   **Demonstrates supporting skills.**

Sample Activities:
 1.9a: L-seat or double leg stem rise
 1.9b: Swings or hangs

Objective 1.10:   **Performs rotational and balancing skills to music.**

Objective 1.11:   **Demonstrates beginning folk dance skills.**

Sample Activities:
     1.11a: Polka step
     1.11b: Schottiche step

> **Sample Assessment Activity**
> **Group Project**
> Students are divided into small groups. Each group randomly selects a folk dance from those taught in class. After a short practice period, the group performs the dance for the class.

Objective 1.12:   **Reviews, demonstrates, or attempts the following basketball skills:**

REVIEW	DEMONSTRATE	ATTEMPT
Dominant hand dribble	Non-dominant hand dribble	Crossover dribble
Pivot	Speed dribble	Spin dribble
Defensive slides	Change-of-pace dribble	Dominant hand lay-up
	Chest pass	Turn on rebound
	Bounce pass	Drop step
	Two-hand overhead pass	Baseball pass
	Flip pass	
	Outlet pass	
	Set shot	
	Foul shot	
	Jump stop	

Objective 1.13:   **Demonstrates the offensive skills of pick, give-and-go, pick-and-roll, fake, and screen for a variety of team sports.**

> **Sample Assessment**
> **Scoring Rubric: Basketball Game Play**
>
> Level 1:
> Moves to open space without ball
> Passes ball to open players
> Uses a variety of passes
> Executes dominant side lay-up
> Executes set shot
> Dribbles with dominant hand
> Executes jump stop
> Uses pivot to create open space
>
> Level 2:
> Executes give-and-go
> Executes jump shot
> Sets picks
> Sets screens
> Uses a variety of fakes
> Dribbles with dominant and non-dominant hand
> Executes non-dominant side lay-up

Objective 1.14:   Demonstrates or attempts the following field hockey skills:

REVIEW	DEMONSTRATE	ATTEMPT
Grip	Drive pass	Flick shot
	Flick pass	Scoop shot
	Flat pass	Side tackle
	Through pass	Come-from-behind tackle
	Push pass	Scoop pass
	Drive shot	
	Ground trap	
	Air trap	
	Hand trap	
	Dribble	
	Forward tackle	

> **Sample Assessment Activity**
> **Checklist : Field Hockey Drive Shot**
> Students execute 10 drive shots from various angles, while the ball is stationary, and after receiving the ball from a pass. A tally is kept of how many shots were successful out of 10 attempts, and a checklist is used to assess technique.

Objective 1.15:   Reviews, demonstrates or attempts the following football skills:

REVIEW	DEMONSTRATE	ATTEMPT
Giving and receiving handoff	Long hike	Punting
Carrying the ball	Forward pass	Over the shoulder catch
Kickoff	Lateral pass	
Blocking	Above the shoulder catch	
	Below the knees catch	

Objective 1.16:   Attempts the following lacrosse skills:

REVIEW	DEMONSTRATE	ATTEMPT
		Cradle
		Catch
		Underhand throw
		Overhand throw
		Scoop

> **Sample Assessment**
> **Checklist: Lacrosse Throwing**
> * Full extension of dominant arm   Yes No
> * Pull on bottom of stick   Yes No
> * Step in opposition   Yes No
> * Follow through in direction of pass Yes No

> **Sample Assessment**
> **Checklist: Lacrosse Catching**
> * Give at elbow and shoulder   Yes No
> * Recoil of dominant arm on contact Yes No
> * Begin cradle immediately   Yes No
> * Keep cross vertical   Yes No

Objective 1.17: **Participates in lead-up activities for racket sports.**

Objective 1.18: **Reviews, demonstrates, or attempts the following racket sport skills:**

REVIEW	DEMONSTRATE	ATTEMPT
Forehand grip	Forehand swing	Backhand swing
Backhand grip	Drop serve	Serve
	Volley	Lob
		Smash

Objective 1.19: **Reviews, demonstrates or attempts the following soccer skills:**

REVIEW	DEMONSTRATE	ATTEMPT
Instep kick	Outside kick	Aerial pass
Dribble	Heel kick	Chip shot
Foot trap	Flat pass	Thigh juggle
	Through pass	Foot juggle
	Throw in	Punting
	Drive shot	Side tackle
	Body trap	Come-from-behind tackle
	Leg trap	

Sample Assessment
Soccer Skill Test
A soccer test battery is available from AAHPERD that can be used for pre- and post-assessment to evaluate improvement.

Objective 1.20: **Reviews, demonstrates, or attempts the following softball skills:**

REVIEW	DEMONSTRATE	ATTEMPT
Underhand throw	Overhand throw from outfield	Pitching
Base running	Fielding ground balls	
Overhand throw from infield	Fielding line drives	
Catching with glove	Fielding fly balls	
	Hitting	

Objective 1.21:   Demonstrates the following track and field skills:

REVIEW	DEMONSTRATE	ATTEMPT
	Sprint	Running long jump
	High jump	Triple jump
	Relays	Hurdling
		Middle distance running

Sample Assessment
Student Project
Following instruction and trials in all of the events of the track and field unit, students choose their top three events. For each of the three events, students must describe the event, state the proper technique for executing the skills, and list their three best scores in each of the three events.

Objective 1.22:   Reviews, demonstrates or attempts the following volleyball skills:

REVIEW	DEMONSTRATE	ATTEMPT
	Underhand serve	Set
	Forearm pass	Dominant hand hit
		Overhand serve
		Block

Sample Assessment
Rating Scale: Forearm Pass Volleyball
Students' use of the forearm pass is assessed during several games of 3 on 3 volleyball.

4 = Consistently controls and effectively redirects serve reception with forearm pass
3 = Sometimes controls and effectively redirects with forearm pass on serve reception
2 = Controls serve reception, but does not redirect with forearm pass
1 = Does not control forearm pass on serve reception

Objective 1.23:   Demonstrates the skills of compass and map reading necessary to complete a beginning level orienteering course.

Objective 1.24:   Attempts an intermediate level orienteering course.

Standard 2:	Applies movement concepts and principles to the learning and development of motor skills.

Objective 2.1: Explores trajectory of moving objects.

Sample Activity:
  2.1a: Toss and catch a ball on the rebound

Objective 2.2: Identifies the mechanical advantage of a third class lever.

Sample Activities:
  2.2a: Toss a ball for distance with a lacrosse stick

Objective 2.3: Maintains proper positioning and spacing for a variety of games and sports while playing player-to-player defense.

> **Sample Assessment**
> **Group Project**
> Students, working in partners or small groups, attempt to predict where a thrown or hit ball will rebound from a wall. Groups locate around the gym allowing each group enough wall, gym, and floor space to participate in the game. Students mark a spot on the wall to which the ball will be thrown/hit. Before the throw/hit, each group member predicts where the ball will hit after the wall rebound. Students should use a series of impact targets, and the type of balls and implements should be varied. Students could develop a game from the activity, based on their ability to predict the location of the ball.

Objective 2.4: Identifies the open player in a variety of games and sports.

Objective 2.5: Participates in activities that enhance third party perspective.

> **Sample Assessment**
> **Grid Activity**
> Students play a game of "Keep Away" (in appropriate sport) in which players are paired with an opponent inside a small grid. One partner plays offense while the other partner uses player-to- player defense. The passer is a neutral post who is outside of the grid. Upon an interception, all players rotate to a new position.

Standard 3:	Exhibits a physically active lifestyle.

Objective 3.1: Participates in self-selected activities outside of class that enhance cardiovascular fitness.

> **Sample Assessment**
> **Portfolio**
> Students keep a log in their portfolio in which they record their weekly participation in activities to enhance cardiovascular fitness, flexibility, and muscular strength/endurance.

Sample Activities:
  3.1a: Group walking
  3.1b: Step aerobics

Objective 3.2:   Participates in self-selected activities that will increase muscular strength/endurance outside of class.

Sample Activities:
   3.2a: Dynabands
   3.2b: Hand weights

Objective 3:3:   Demonstrates beginning activities in a variety of geographically-appropriate outdoor pursuits.

> **Sample Assessment**
> **Group Project**
> Students work in small groups to prepare a "Guide Book" for an outdoor pursuit of their choice. Each "Guide Book" must include equipment information, safety information, basic skills needed for this activity, and suggested locations to pursue the activity.

Sample Activities:
   3.3a: Ice skating
   3.3b: Rock climbing
   3.3c: Bowling

Objective 3.4:   Attempts more challenging activities in a variety of geographically-appropriate outdoor pursuits.

Standard 4:	*Achieves and maintains a health-enhancing level of physical fitness.*

Objective 4.1:   Identifies the components of physical fitness that s/he would like to improve upon, and designs a program to meet those needs.

Objective 4.2:   Participates in warm-up activities to increase range of motion (flexibility).

Sample Activities:
   4.2a: Quadriceps stretch
   4.2b: Butterflies (sitting/soles of the feet together)

Objective 4.3:   Identifies the relationship among physical activity, weight, and body type.

Objective 4.4:   Participates in a variety of relaxation exercises.

Sample Exercises:
   4.4a: Progressive relaxation
   4.4b: Visualization

Objective 4.5:   Participates in fitness assessment.

Sample Activities:
   4.5a: Physical Best
   4.5b: Fitness Gram

> **Sample Assessment**
> **Peer Assessment**
> Students participate in a "Partner Fit-Check" in which each student administers a set of fitness tests to a partner to assess cardiovascular fitness, muscular strength and endurance, and flexibility.

Objective 4.6: **Differentiates between components of health-related and performance-related fitness.**

Sample Activities:
4.6a: Compare the fitness components required by a shuttle run, a sprint, and a mile run
4.6b: Identify fitness components utilized in an obstacle course

Objective 4.7: **Reviews the calculation of maximum and target heart rates.**

Objective 4.8: **Selects and participates in warm-ups for each component of health-related fitness.**

Objective 4.9: **Demonstrates appropriate pace when participating in aerobic activities.**

> Sample Assessment
> **Written Report**
> Students submit a written summary of the results of their "Partner Fit-Check". Students identify their areas of greatest strength and weakness. In addition, students identify the activities in which they currently participate to enhance their documented strengths, and suggest additional activities to improve their documented weaknesses.

Objective 4.10: **Describes principles of training and conditioning for a chosen activity.**

Sample Activities:
4.10a: Creative dance
4.10b: Team sport

Objective 4.11: **Describes the role of exercise and nutrition in weight management.**

> Sample Assessment
> **Fitness Test**
> Students participate in one of the National Youth Fitness assessments. Upon completion of the assessment, students prepare a written report to be sent home to their parents.

Standard 5:	*Demonstrates responsible personal and social behavior in physical activity settings.*

Objective 5.1: **Reviews safety factors in the utilization of space, athletic equipment/apparatus.**

Sample Activities:
5.1a: Perform warm-up stretches with appropriate spacing
5.1b: Kick a soccer ball only in uncongested areas during warm-ups

> Sample Assessment
> **Group Project**
> Students identify rules and procedures for maintaining safety in the gym. After each class has had an opportunity for input, the consolidated list is displayed in the gym as a safety poster.

Objective 5.2: **Reviews the components of safe participation and what constitutes a safe environment.**

Sample Activities:
5.2a: Refrain from bringing liquids or food into playing area
5.2b: Put equipment and apparatus away appropriately

Objective 5.3: **Follows the rules of the activities to maintain safe playing conditions.**

Sample Activities:
5.3a: Keep hockey sticks below waist level

Objective 5.4: **Identifies the difference between ethical and unethical behavior of participants during play.**

Objective 5.5: **Strives to contribute to the achievement of a team goal.**

Objective 5.6: **Participates in group cooperation games and adventure activities to encourage team building and fun.**

> **Sample Assessment**
> **Role Playing**
> Students are given a series of ethical dilemmas that might occur in sport. Working in groups of three or four, students identify what they would do if confronted with the dilemma. Students must justify their decisions.

> **Sample Activity**
> **Group Project**
> Students work with a partner to create, teach to the class, and conduct a drill for a specific sport. Students submit a copy of their drill, including an explanation and diagrams, for inclusion in a handbook of original skill drills to be compiled by the teacher.

Standard 6:	*Demonstrates understanding and respect for differences among people in physical activity settings.*

Objective 6.1: **Identifies the cultural and historical origins of a variety of games, sports, and dances.**

Objective 6.2: **Participates in culturally diverse games and sports.**

> **Sample Assessment**
> **Group Project**
> Students choose a culture that they have studied in another subject area during the school year. Students work in small groups to create a dance, game, or sport that they believe could have been played in that culture. A history of the culture, a list of equipment, and a set of rules or steps of the dance must be included. Students will present their project to the class.

Sample Activities:
6.2a: Bocci
6.2b: Rugby
6.2c: Cricket

Objective 6.3:   Teaches a game or sport identified with the student's heritage.

Objective 6.4:   Demonstrates an understanding that proficiency is dependent upon practice rather than upon gender, race, or ethnicity

Objective 6.5:   Participates in individual activities with modified rules, structure, and/or equipment to increase the parity of the movement, dance, game or sport.

> **Teaching Tip**
> **Activity Modification**
> - Reduce the number of participants
> - Reduce the amount of space
> - Reduce the number of decisions to be made
> - Reduce the speed of objects or implements
> - Modify equipment
> - Create rules that ensure that all participants are involved in the play

Standard 7:	*Understands that physical activity provides opportunities for enjoyment, challenge, self-expression, and social interaction.*

Objective 7.1:   Observes the aesthetic qualities of an exemplary choreographed work through live demonstration or film.

Sample Activities:
   7.1a: Attend a dance concert

Objective 7.2:   Compares and contrast various movement phrases.

Objective 7.3:   Cooperates with another student to create, develop and refine movement phrases based on a theme.

Objective 7.4:   Demonstrates the ability to succeed at assigned roles within a team activity.

> **Sample Assessment**
> **Checklist: Dance**
> Criteria:
> - Transitions are smooth   Yes No
> - Contrast exists between even and uneven rhythms   Yes No
> - Dance flows from element to element   Yes No
> - Superior extension is exhibited   Yes No
> - Elements are executed with appropriate technique   Yes No

Sample Activities:
   7.4a: Leader or captain
   7.4b: Player
   7.4c: Coach
   7.4d: Official

Objective 7.5:   Creates a game, movement, dance or sport with a group.

Objective 7.6:   **Participates in games in which the opponent is a standard of performance.**

Sample Activities:
  7.6a: Frisbee-golf
  7.6b: Archery

Objective 7.7:   **Participates in modified team or individual sports without keeping score.**

Objective 7.8:   **Chooses motivators (for example: music, teacher involvement, student selection of activity) that will enhance fun and enjoyment in the class.**

Sample Activities:
  7.8a: Participate in "open gym" where the students may select the activity of the day from a number of options

> **Sample Assessment Event Task**
> Students play a variety of "New Games" which discourage scoring and elimination from the game. Teachers "debrief" the activity to encourage students to express what they like and dislike about the activity.

Principles for Designing Appropriate Practice Activities
for the Acquisition of Specific Motor Skills

Activities related to the grade-level objectives for content standard 1 of the program guidelines typically take the form of what are commonly called practice drills for a specific skill such as passing, dribbling, or shooting. The design of these practice activities should be based on a consideration of both the theory and research findings regarding factors affecting the learning of motor skills. The following material describes several principles, drawn from the motor learning literature, that should be considered in designing practice activities for the acquisition of specific motor skills.

Task Analysis

Prior to deciding on a practice activity or drill for a specific skill, it is imperative to identify and analyze the essential performance characteristics and requirements of the skill in its "real-world" or "game-related" form. This process is referred to as a task analysis. The elements of the task analysis correspond to components of practice about which decisions must be made in structuring the practice situation. That is, for practice activities to be effective, the characteristics of the practice drill must correspond to the essential characteristics of the skill, as identified in the task analysis.

Performance Environment. The first element of a task analysis is identification of the performance environment of the skill. How variable is the real-world performance of the specific skill? That is, is the task a closed or an open skill? In some cases, the performance context may not vary at all during execution of the skill. Such activities are called closed skills; examples include skills related to tumbling and gymnastics. For other activities, the performance environment may be quite variable over time; such activities are called open skills. Examples of open skills are the component skills of basketball and soccer.

Attentional Demands. The second element of the task analysis requires identification of the attentional demands of the skill. The complexity of the demands on the learner's attention is related to the first element of the analysis, the environmental context of performance. How many objects and/or people are included in the performance environment? Are the objects and/or people moving or stationary? These factors determine the extent and complexity of the demands on the learner's attention. Motor skills vary considerably in the nature of their attentional demands. For example, an activity may involve no other players and a stationary target (archery), one other player and a moving object (tennis), or many moving players and a moving object (team sports).

Decision-Making Requirements. The third element of the task analysis is identification of the requirements for decision-making by the performer. Motor skills vary in the number of viable response options available to the performer at a given point in performance. The number of response options to be considered dictates the type and complexity of the decisions the learner must make. Some skills may require a single decision between two response options (e.g., swing or don't swing). Other skills may involve multiple response options and concomitant decisions. For example, the learner may be required to decide which of several types of passes to execute and where to direct the pass (left, right, front, back, etc.).

Pattern of Movement. The first three elements of the task analysis are related to the complexity of the performance environment relative to variability, predictability, and demands on attention and decision-making abilities. The final two elements of the task analysis are related to the complexity of the movement required by the specific skill. The required movement must be analyzed relative to the length of the movement sequence and the interdependence of the parts of the sequence. How many body segments are involved in the "finished form" of the movement? Is the performer moving or stationary? Is the skill performed with or without an implement? Is a transition in the type of movement required (e.g., from horizontal to vertical movement in a jump or spike)? Are components of movement performed simultaneously (step and throw) or sequentially (run, stop, and throw)? Does the skill require a continuous sequence of movement to develop maximum force or velocity (discus throw), or several discrete phases of movement with a change of direction between phases (golf swing)? Results of the analysis of the nature and complexity of the required movement, dictate whether the skill can or should be practiced as a whole or as component parts.

Simplified, But Realistic Practice

The purpose of the initial task analysis is to identify the complexity of both the performance environment and the movement associated with a specific skill. Based on the analysis, the teacher must decide how to reduce the complexity of some or all of the elements of performance during practice, without changing or eliminating the essential nature of the skill. It is inappropriate, for example, to simplify the practice situation by changing an open, or moving environment, to a closed (non-moving) performance environment. Instead of eliminating the essential movement in the performance environment, the practice activity should be designed to reduce the complexity of the open environment. For example, the speed of moving objects or people can be reduced or made more predictable. Balls can be rolled or tossed (rather than hit), to only the dominant side of the performer, within a designated area of the court or field. A pitch, for example, can be delivered underhand, at a moderate speed, rather then eliminating the moving ball and using a batting tee; striking a stationary ball is appropriate in practicing the golf swing, but not in practicing batting.

A similar strategy should be used in planning practice activities relative to the attentional and decision-making requirements of performance. Rather than eliminating these elements from practice, they should be simplified in the practice setting. For example, the number of response options and concomitant decisions to be made in a given situation can be reduced (either pass left or dribble straight ahead). The number of opponents can be reduced and/or their movement can be slowed or restricted, rather than totally eliminating the presence and movement of opposing players.

Consideration must also be given to the most appropriate way to simplify the required movement involved in the skill. Sometimes it is possible to reduce the length of the movement sequence without losing the essential continuity of the pattern ("back-scratch" tennis serve). In other cases, components of the movement sequence can be initially practiced in isolation (jump and strike in volleyball spike), before being combined with an approach.

For the student to acquire skill in a motor task, the practice situation must include all the essential elements required in skilled performance. Clearly, the performance requirements must be simplified in accord with the level of development and skill of the student. However, it is critical that the learner understand and practice all the components of motor skill performance. Practice activities must be designed to provide opportunities to develop all the requisite abilities including analysis and prediction of moving/stationary objects and people, identification of response options and consequences, making appropriate decisions, and planning and controlling the pattern of movement.

Progressive Increases in Complexity of Practice

The results of the task analysis and the subsequent decisions regarding which elements of performance to simplify, and how, are used to plan the progression of practice activities for the specific skill. As practice continues, plans must be made to systematically increase the complexity of the practice activities. That is, practice must be designed to provide sequential progression toward real-world, "finished form", performance characteristics of the specific skill. Practice activities should include progressive increases in the variability of the performance environment. Similarly, progressive increases should be made in the attentional demands of the performance environment. The number of response options and concomitant decisions should be systematically increased. The required pattern of movement should be progressively increased in length and continuity requirements. That is, elements of performance that were simplified during initial practice of the specific skill, must be systematically and progressively increased in complexity during subsequent practice situations.

Increased Variety of Movement Tasks

In addition to adding complexity to the practice activities for a specific skill, progressive practice should also include variations in the setting in which the skill is performed. Systematic alterations should be made in characteristics of performance such as the distance, direction and angle of performers or objects, or the location, speed, height, and spin of a moving object. Providing for variations in performance settings during practice is essential for the development of a general movement schema, or flexible formula for performance. The ability to adapt performance to changing environmental/game requirements cannot be developed if practice activities are limited to repeated practice of one movement pattern, from one distance, in one direction, etc.

Provide Specific Corrective Feedback

Throughout the practice period, the learner should receive specific, corrective feedback regarding the quality and effectiveness of performance. In order to improve future performance of a specific skill, the learner must first evaluate current performance based on information regarding the movement that was executed and its effect in the performance environment. Based on the analysis and evaluation of performance, the learner decides whether to repeat or alter the pattern of movement on subsequent performance attempts. The ability of the teacher to describe performance and identify needed changes is an essential element in skill development. Practice activities should include time for performance evaluation by the teacher and peers, as well as for self-evaluation by the student. Feedback to the student should include information regarding both the technique of the movement and the results of the movement in the performance environment. Feedback concerning the result of the performance should reinforce or clarify "what happened" as a result of the executed movement (where the pass went, what happened next). In open skills, this type of feedback should precede correction of movement technique. That is, corrective feedback regarding movement execution should be based on an assessment of the effectiveness of the attempt relative to the desired results of performance. In closed skills, feedback regarding performance should emphasize style and consistency of the pattern of movement.

Summary

To be effective in developing motor skill, practice activities must be both realistic and progressive. Practice activities must provide an opportunity for development of all the component abilities required in skilled performance: perceptual analysis, decision-making, and planning/control of movement. A task analysis is useful in identifying the essential characteristics and degree of complexity of performance in its skilled form. Results of the analysis are used to plan realistic practice activities for a specific skill. To be effective, practice activities should involve a systematic progression in complexity of requirements for performance, within a realistic environmental context.

Submitted by: Dr. Ree K. Arnold
              Montclair State University

GRADE EIGHT

Did You Know?

- The percentage of children and adolescents who are overweight has more than doubled in the past 30 years; most of this increase has occurred since the late 1970's.

- Of U.S. children and adolescents ages 6-17 years, about 4.7 million, or 11% are seriously overweight.

- Obese children and adolescents are more likely to become obese adults; overweight adults are at increased risk for heart disease, high blood pressure, stroke, diabetes, some types of cancer, and gallbladder disease.

- More than 60% of adults do not achieve the recommended amount of regular physical activity. In fact, 25% of all adults are not active at all.

- Inactivity is more common among women than men, and among those with lower income and less education than among those with higher income or education.

- In 1991, 19% of students enrolled in a physical education class reported that they did not exercise for 20 or more minutes in an average physical education class; this figure rose to 30% in 1995

From: U.S. Department of Health and Human Services (July 1996). Physical Activity and Health: A Report of the Surgeon General. Available on the Internet at http//www.cdc.gov/nccdphp/ sgr/ataglan.htm (March 1997), Physical Activity and the Health of Young People. Available on the Internet at hhtp//www.cdc.gov/nccdphp/dash/phactfac.htm

Standard 1:	Demonstrates competency in many movement forms and proficiency in a few movement forms.

Objective 1.1: Demonstrates combinations of rotational, balancing, and supporting skills.

Sample Activities:
  1.1a: Handstand forward roll
  1.1b: Backward extension

Objective 1.2: Demonstrates combinations of rotational, balancing, and supporting skills on apparatus.

Sample Activities:
  1.2a: Front support, ¼ turn, straddle back on beam
  1.2b: Squat, ½ turn dismount

Objective 1.3: Creates and performs a timed routine using rotational, balancing, and supporting skills.

Objective 1.4: Creates and performs an apparatus routine composed of a mount, rotational, balancing, supporting skills, and a dismount.

Objective 1.5: Demonstrates vaulting skills using a springboard or reuther board.

> **Sample Assessment**
> **Checklist: Gymnastics Routine**
> Criteria:
> • At least 5 elements included in routine   Yes   No
> • Elements performed from all skill categories   Yes   No
> • Completed within time limit   Yes   No
> • Acceptable level of technique used throughout routine   Yes   No
> • Smooth transitions from one element to the next   Yes   No
> • All levels of difficulty displayed in routine   Yes   No

Sample Activities:
  1.5a: Bent hip squat vault
  1.5b: Horizontal squat vault
  1.5c: Straddle vault

Objective 1.6: Demonstrates beginning social dance skills.

Sample Activities:
  1.6a: Promenade
  1.6b: Waltz step

> **Sample Assessment**
> **Peer Observation**
> Students perform one social dance of their choice with a partner. Students use a checklist to complete peer evaluations on the dances presented. The checklist should be developed by students early in the unit.

Objective 1.7:   **Attempts beginning social dances.**

Sample Activities:
  1.7a: Waltz
  1.7b: Fox trot

Objective 1.8:   **Reviews, demonstrates, or attempts the following basketball skills:**

REVIEW	DEMONSTRATE	ATTEMPT
Dominant hand dribble	Crossover dribble	Non-dominant hand lay-up
Non-dominant hand dribble	Spin dribble	Boxing out
Speed dribble	Baseball pass	Drop step
Change-of-pace dribble	Dominant hand lay-up	
Chest pass	Turn on rebound	
Bounce pass	Jump shot	
Two-hand overhead pass		
Flip pass		
Outlet pass		
Set shot		
Foul shot		
Jump stop		

Objective 1.9:   **Participates in a regulation basketball game.**

Objective 1.10:   **Reviews, demonstrates, or attempts the following field hockey skills:**

REVIEW	DEMONSTRATE	ATTEMPT
Drive pass	Scoop shot	Flick shot
Flick pass	Air trap	Come-from-behind tackle
Flat pass	Side tackle	Reverse stick tackle
Through pass	Scoop pass	Goalie clear
Push pass		
Drive shot		
Ground trap		
Hand trap		
Forward tackle		
Dribble		

Objective 1.11:   **Participates in a regulation field hockey game.**

Sample Assessment
Rating Scale: Field Hockey Ball Control
Criteria:
4 = controls ball upon reception and while passing 90% of the time
3 = controls ball upon reception and while passing 75% of the time
2 = controls ball upon reception and while passing 50% of the time
1 = controls ball upon reception and while passing less than 25% of the time

Objective 1.12:   **Reviews, demonstrates, or attempts the following football skills:**

REVIEW	DEMONSTRATE	ATTEMPT
Giving and receiving handoff	Over the shoulder catch	Punting
Carrying the ball		
Kickoff		
Long hike		
Forward pass		
Lateral pass		
Blocking		
Above the shoulder catch		
Below the knees catch		

Objective 1.13:   **Participates in a regulation flag football game.**

Sample Assessment
Scoring Rubric: Football Game Play

Level 2:
Executes over the shoulder catch
Uses fakes to allude tackles
Consistently handles lateral passes
Consistently catches ball while moving
Executes forward pass with accuracy to a stationary target

Level 1:
Consistently catches ball above shoulder
Changes directions while carrying the ball
Consistently executes hand-offs
Consistently catches ball while stationary
Executes forward pass with accuracy to a moving target

Objective 1.14:   **Demonstrates the following lacrosse skills:**

REVIEW	DEMONSTRATE	ATTEMPT
	Cradle	
	Catch	
	Underhand throw	
	Overhand throw	
	Scoop	

Objective 1.15:   **Participates in a modified game of lacrosse.**

> **Sample Assessment**
> **Group Project**
> Students design a game of lacrosse for a small group, ensuring maximum participation and enjoyment for all skill levels represented. Number of participants, rules and regulations, and equipment may be altered.

Objective 1.16:   **Reviews , demonstrates, or attempts the following racket sport skills:**

REVIEW	DEMONSTRATE	ATTEMPT
Forehand grip	Backhand swing	Serve
Backhand grip		Lob
Forehand swing		Smash
Volley		Drop shot
Drop serve		

Objective 1.17:   **Participates in a regulation game in a chosen racket sport.**

Objective 1.18:   **Reviews, demonstrates, or attempts the following soccer skills:**

REVIEW	DEMONSTRATE	ATTEMPT
Instep kick	Punting	Thigh juggle
Outside kick	Aerial pass	Foot juggle
Heel kick	Chip shot	Come-from-behind tackle
Flat pass	Side tackle	Goalie throw
Through pass		Goalie hand trap
Throw-in		
Drive shot		
Foot trap		
Body trap		
Leg trap		
Dribble		

Objective 1.19:   **Participates in a regulation game of soccer.**

> **Sample Assessment**
> **Student Observation: Videotape**
> Students watch a soccer game on videotape. Using an evaluation form provided by the teacher, students will identify both offensive and defensive strategies employed by the teams.

Objective 1.20:   Reviews, demonstrates, or attempts the following softball skills:

REVIEW	DEMONSTRATE	ATTEMPT
Overhand throw from outfield Fielding ground balls Fielding line drives Fielding fly balls Base running Hitting	Pitching	Hitting a pitched ball to a predetermined location

Objective 1.21:   Participates in a regulation softball game.

Objective 1.22:   Reviews, demonstrates, or attempts the following track and field skills:

REVIEW	DEMONSTRATE	ATTEMPT
Sprint High jump Relays	Running long jump Hurdling Middle distance running	Triple jump

Objective 1.23:   Selects two events in which to participate during an intraclass track and field meet.

Objective 1.24:   Reviews, demonstrates, or attempts the following volleyball skills:

REVIEW	DEMONSTRATE	ATTEMPT
Underhand serve Forearm pass	Dominant hand hit	Set Non-dominant hand hit Overhand serve Block

Objective 1.25:   Participates in a regulation volleyball game.

Objective 1.26:   Reviews the skills of compass and map reading necessary to complete an intermediate level orienteering course.

Objective 1.27:   Attempts to use the concept of "cunning running" in an intermediate level orienteering course.

Standard 2:	Applies movement concepts and principles to the learning and development of motor skills.

Objective 2.1: **Explores the effect of changing the length of the lever on striking skills.**

Sample Activities:
2.1a: Utilize and compare junior and regulation tennis rackets

Objective 2.2: **Demonstrates effective timing and sequencing for throwing and striking.**

Objective 2.3: **Identifies and utilizes open space or player while participating in a variety of games and sport.**

Objective 2.4: **Attempts to create an open space by causing an opponent to move in a variety of games and sports.**

Sample Activities:
2.4a: Utilize head fake in basketball
2.4b: Utilize same preparatory movements for drop shot and clear in badminton

Objective 2.5: **Attempts basic player-to-player defense.**

> Sample Assessment
> **Student Observation**
> Students practice a series of striking skills using different length levers, and observe the effects of changing the length of the lever on the speed of the swing, control of the swing, and distance traveled by the struck object. Students discuss results of the observations.

Standard 3:	Exhibits a physically active lifestyle

Objective 3.1: **Maintains a log of her/his physical activity both in and out of school.**

Objective 3.2: **Plans and implements a personal fitness program including all the components of health-related fitness.**

Objective 3.3: **Designs and participates outside of class in activities that will enhance cardiovascular fitness.**

Sample Activities:
3.3a: Individual walking program

Objective 3.4: **Participates outside of class in activities that will increase muscular strength and endurance.**

> Sample Assessment
> **Student Project**
> Students complete a personal fitness profile which includes a physical activity log and fitness assessment scores for the last three years. Based on this profile, students plan a six-week program for increasing their health-related fitness levels. Students complete the planned program outside of class and keep a log of their activities over a six-week period.

Objective 3.5: Participates in a variety of recreational activities appropriate to the geographical area.

Sample Activities:
  3.5a: Downhill skiing
  3.5b: Fishing

> **Sample Assessment**
> **Student Project**
> Students identify two recreational activities available in the community in which they have not participated, but think they might enjoy. Students visit the activity site and prepare a written or oral report describing the activity, required equipment, cost of participation, location, and whether instruction is available.

Standard 4: *Achieves and maintains a health-enhancing level of physical fitness.*

Objective 4.1: Participates in health-related fitness assessment.

Sample Activities:
  4.1a: Physical Best

Objective 4.2: Identifies the effects of activity on stress levels.

Objective 4.3: Leads peers in a relaxation exercise.

Objective 4.4: Describes the relationship between body composition amd health-related fitness.

Objective 4.5: Demonstrates techniques of weight training.

Objective 4.6: Demonstrates techniques for warming up, stretching, and cooling down prior to and following physical activity.

Objective 4.7: Identifies symptoms of and dangers in the use of performance-enhancing drugs.

> **Sample Assessments**
> **Written Report**
> Students write a paper summarizing the research findings relative to the dangers involved in the use of performance-enhancing drugs. The teacher develops a scoring rubric to assess content and organization of the report.

> **Definition**
> **Journal**
> Journals kept by students are self-reflections on assigned topics. Journals should not be assessed on how well they are written, but should be assessed on how well students reflect on the assigned topic. The purpose of a journal is to encourage students to analyze and express their feelings about physical activity without fear of being judged right or wrong.

Standard 5:	Demonstrates responsible personal and social behavior in physical activity settings.

Objective 5.1: **Modifies participation based on risk factors.**

Sample Activities:
5.1a: Pass only when the receiver is ready
5.1b: Change pace of pass based on distance from receiver

Objective 5.2: **Decides to participate or not participate, based on the safety of the environment.**

Objective 5.3: **Follows the rules of activities to maintain safe playing conditions.**

Sample Activities:
5.3a: Play McWhipit lacrosse with no stick checking

Objective 5.4: **Strives to contribute to the achievement of a class goal.**

> Sample Assessment
> **Student Journal**
> Students reflect on risk-taking in physical education class and the extent to which they are influenced by peers to take or not take risks. The assignment should include both physical and psychological risks associated with participation. Students may elect to share their journal entries with peers in small group discussions.

> Sample Assessment
> **Student Observation**
> Students identify, during debriefing, the goals that were accomplished through a class activity, what was learned, what experiences were stressful, and the importance of the group support system.

Standard 6:	Demonstrates understanding and respect for differences among people in physical activity settings.

Objective 6.1: **Demonstrates acceptance of differences among classmates based on gender.**

Objective 6.2: **Identifies the historical and cultural origin of a selected dance, game or sport.**

> Sample Assessment
> **Written Report/Project**
> Students research and submit a paper on similarities and differences among various cultures regarding game, sport, activity, or dance. Students instruct peers in one game, sport, activity, or dance of a self-selected culture.

> Sample Assessment
> **Role Playing**
> Students participate in a small group activity/game requiring them to act as if they are the opposite gender. Girls will take the role of boys and boys will take the role of girls in the activity/game. After participating in the activity/game, students discuss how they felt as the opposite gender, and identify any observed negative stereotyping.

101

Standard 7:	Understands that physical activity provides the opportunity for enjoyment, challenge, self-expression, and social interaction.

Objective 7.1: **Creates, develops, and refines movement phrases based on self-generated themes.**

Sample Activities:
    7.1a: Run like lightning
    7.1b: Land softly like a feather

Objective 7.2: **Integrates information from other subject matter into creative movement works.**

Sample Activities:
    7.2a: Create a dance illustrating environmental issues
    7.2b: Create a game based on mathematical concepts

> **Sample Assessment**
> **Group Project**
> Students work in small groups to create a dance related to a school-wide theme or required book for their age group. Students self-select their music from choices provided by the teacher. Dance creations should integrate the assigned topic area with the music and the movements. Students present their dance to their classmates and parents.

Objective 7.3: **Combines movement phrases and sentences into more extensive choreographed pieces.**

Objective 7.4: **Participates in individual and team sports with modified rules, structure, and/or equipment to increase the opportunities for participation and enjoyment.**

> **Sample Assessment**
> **Student Log**
> Students record negative and positive incidents that occurred during a unit of instruction. Students tabulate and discuss why the incidents may have occurred.

Objective 7.5:   **Leads initiative or cooperative activities.**

Sample Assessment
Group Project
Students, in small groups, share or create an initiative or cooperative activity. After the class participates in the activity, students are in charge of debriefing the group about the activity. A scoring rubric may be used to evaluate student participation in the project.

Level 4:
Interacts openly during debriefing
Participates fully in activity
Works well with others in group
Creates own initiative activity

Level 3:
Interacts during debriefing
Participates well in activity
Leads an activity

Level 2:
Does not interact often during debriefing
Moderate involvement in activity
Follows others, but does not participate fully

Level 1:
Unwilling to interact in debriefing
Uninvolved in group activity or remains "outside" activity
Uncooperative or unsupportive

Objective 7.6:   **Participates in activities in which the opponent is the environment.**

Sample Activities:
  7.6a: Sailing
  7.6b: Rock climbing
  7.6c: Skiing

Objective 7.7:   **Identifies elements that contribute to her/his enjoyment for several self-selected activities.**

Sample Assessment
Student Journal

Students record feelings about participation in activity, and reflect on characteristics of activities that are personally enjoyable. Students are given a choice of who may read the journal.

Activity x Grade Matrix

Attempt: Implies that the skill will be taught but the student will not master or show competency in the skill. This is a first level progression.

Demonstrate: Implies that the student will demonstrate competency in the skill. This is a second level progression.

Review: Implies the continual review of the skill and serves as a developmental checkpoint.

ACTIVITY	6th Grade			7th Grade			8th Grade		
	REV	DEM	ATT	REV	DEM	ATT	REV	DEM	ATT
BASKETBALL									
Dominant hand dribble		D		R			R		
Pivot		D		R					
Defensive slides		D		R					
Non-dominant hand dribble			A		D		R		
Speed dribble			A		D		R		
Change-of-pace dribble			A		D		R		
Crossover dribble			A			A		D	
Spin dribble			A			A		D	
Chest pass			A		D		R		
Bounce pass			A		D		R		
Two-hand overhead pass			A		D		R		
Flip pass			A		D		R		
Outlet pass			A		D		R		
Baseball pass			A			A		D	
Set shot			A		D		R		
Dominant hand lay-up			A			A		D	
Jump shot			A			A		D	
Foul shot			A		D		R		
Jump stop			A		D		R		
Turn on rebound			A			A		D	
Drop step						A			A
Non-dominant hand lay-up									A
Boxing out									A

Activity x Grade Matrix

ACTIVITY	6th Grade			7th Grade			8th Grade		
	REV	DEM	ATT	REV	DEM	ATT	REV	DEM	ATT
FIELD HOCKEY									
Grip		D		R					
Drive pass			A		D		R		
Flick pass					D		R		
Flat pass			A		D		R		
Through pass			A		D		R		
Push pass			A		D		R		
Drive shot			A		D		R		
Flick shot			A			A			A
Scoop shot			A			A		D	
Ground trap			A		D		R		
Air trap			A			A		D	
Hand trap			A		D		R		
Forward tackle			A		D		R		
Side tackle			A			A		D	
Dribble			A		D		R		
Scoop pass						A		D	
Come-from-behind tackle						A			A
Reverse stick tackle									A
Goalie clear									A
FOOTBALL									
Giving & receiving handoff		D		R			R		
Carrying the ball		D		R			R		
Kickoff		D		R			R		
Blocking		D		R			R		
Long hike			A		D		R		
Forward pass			A		D		R		
Lateral pass			A		D		R		
Punting			A			A			A
Over shoulder catch			A			A		D	
Above shoulder catch			A		D		R		
Below knees catch			A		D		R		
LACROSSE									
Cradle						A		D	
Catch						A		D	
Underhand throw						A		D	
Overhand throw						A		D	
Scoop						A		D	

Activity x Grade Matrix

ACTIVITY	6th Grade			7th Grade			8th Grade		
	REV	DEM	ATT	REV	DEM	ATT	REV	DEM	ATT
RACKET SPORT									
Forehand grip		D		R			R		
Backhand grip		D		R			R		
Forehand swing			A		D		R		
Volley			A		D		R		
Drop serve			A		D		R		
Backhand swing			A			A		D	
Serve						A			A
Lob						A			A
Smash						A			A
Drop shot									A
SOCCER									
Outside kick			A		D		R		
Heel kick			A		D		R		
Flat pass			A		D		R		
Through pass			A		D		R		
Aerial pass			A			A		D	
Throw-in			A		D		R		
Drive shot			A		D		R		
Chip shot			A			A		D	
Body trap			A		D		R		
Leg trap			A		D		R		
Thigh juggle			A			A			A
Foot juggle			A			A			A
Instep kick		D		R			R		
Dribble		D		R			R		
Foot trap		D		R	-		R		
Punting						A		D	
Side tackle						A		D	
Come-from-behind tackle						A			A
Goalie throw									A
Goalie hand trap									A

Activity x Grade Matrix

ACTIVITY	6th Grade			7th Grade			8th Grade		
	REV	DEM	ATT	REV	DEM	ATT	REV	DEM	ATT
SOFTBALL									
Underhand throw		D		R					
Base running		D		R			R		
Overhand throw from infield		D		R					
Catching with glove		D		R					
Overhand throw from outfield			A		D		R		
Fielding ground balls			A		D		R		
Fielding line drives			A		D		R		
Fielding fly balls			A		D		R		
Hitting			A		D		R		
Pitching			A			A		D	
Hitting a pitched ball to a predetermined location									A
TRACK AND FIELD									
Sprint			A		D		R		
High jump			A		D		R		
Relays			A		D		R		
Running long jump						A		D	
Triple jump						A			A
Hurdling						A		D	
Middle distance running						A		D	
VOLLEYBALL									
Underhand serve			A		D		R		
Set			A			A			A
Forearm pass			A		D		R		
Dominant hand hit			A			A		D	
Overhand serve						A			A
Block						A			A
Non-dominant hand hit									A

EDA GUIDELINES
For Physical Education

Program Standards, Objectives, and Assessments

Grades 9 - 12

Introduction: Grades 9-12

The emphasis within the guidelines for grades 9-12 is preparation for a lifetime of wellness-related activity. Collectively, the guidelines focus on self-evaluation, lifetime values, and carry-over activities. The intent of the guidelines is to suggest means by which individual students can evidence characteristics of a Physically Educated Person.

Format of the Guidelines. The format for the program guidelines, grades 9-12, is substantially different from the K-8 guidelines. *First,* the secondary school guidelines are not grade specific. Rather, the guidelines reflect a collective approach to the physical education program for grades 9-12. *Second,* recommendations are made concerning the percentage of the 9-12 physical education program which should focus on fitness/wellness, dance, sport, and recreational activities. These content recommendations are based on the results of a survey of 70 individuals from the Eastern District.

Third, the guidelines include student selection of specific activities in grade 11 and 12. As part of the survey of physical educators, respondents were asked to indicate in which grades activities should be prescribed (teacher-selected), and in which grades activities should be elective (student-selected). Based on the responses to the survey, the program guidelines recommend a prescribed curricular content for all students for grades 9 and 10, and student election of specific activities within required activity categories for grades 11 and 12. *Fourth,* the emphasis in the program guidelines is sequential, progressive instruction enabling students to master curricular objectives related to acquisition of skill in movement activities. This emphasis is consistent with Content Standard 1, which specifies achieving competency in a variety of activities and proficiency in selected activities.

Behavioral Objectives. For each of the seven Content Standards, specific objectives related to psychomotor, cognitive and/or affective behavior have been identified for grades 9-12, collectively. These behavioral objectives reflect possible areas of curricular content that relate directly to the achievement of the physical education content standards. Within the program guidelines, behavioral objectives are presented in the form of activity modules.

Activity Modules. A module is a self-contained unit of curricular content, based on 15 days of class participation. The content within a module should be sequential and progressive. Program content for grades 9-12 consists of 9 different modules per year. Specific modules are not to be repeated by an individual student. The 4-year curriculum in physical education for grades 9-12 includes a total of 36 activity modules.

A list of suggested activity modules for each of six categories of curricular content is presented in **Table 1**. The suggested activities are based on the responses to the survey mentioned above. Activities indicated as appropriate for grades 9-12 by at least 35% of the survey respondents are included in Table 1.

```
┌─────────────────────────────────────────────────────────────────────────────┐
│                                                                               │
│  Table 1                                                                      │
│  Suggested Activity Modules for Physical Education, Grades 9-12               │
│                                                                               │
│  Fitness Activities    Team Sports    Individual/      Recreational    Dance  │
│                                       Dual Sports      Activities             │
│                                                                               │
└─────────────────────────────────────────────────────────────────────────────┘
```

Fitness Activities	Team Sports	Individual/ Dual Sports	Recreational Activities	Dance
Aerobic Dance	*Basketball	*Archery	Backpacking	Ballroom
Cross-Country Skiing	Field Hockey	*Badminton	Camping	*Creative
Cycling	Flag Football	*Bowling	Canoeing	Folk
Gymnastics	*Lacrosse	*Golf	Cross-Country Skiiing	Line
Jogging	*Soccer	*Gymnastics		Modern
Step Aerobics	*Softball	Paddleball	*Floor Hockey	Square
Strength Training	Team Handball	*Racquetball	*Mountain Biking	
Swimming	*Volleyball	Swimming	Ice Skating	
Walking		Table Tennis	*New Games	
Weight-Training		*Tennis	*Orienteering	
		*Track & Field	Project Adventure	
			Recreational Leadership	
			Rock Climbing	
			Roller Blading	
			Self-Defense	
			Ultimate Frisbee	
			Water Safety	

Note: Activities listed were identified as appropriate for
      grades 9-12 by at least 35% of survey respondents.

      *Sample Module(s) included in guidelines

Table 2 presents the recommended number of modules to be included in the curriculum for each activity category (e.g., individual sports, dance, etc.). The number of modules per category corresponds to the percentage of the curriculum that should focus on each of the six activity categories, as indicated by the results of the survey. For example, the recommendation that 22% of the physical education curriculum for grades 9-12 consist of individual sport activities, translates to 8 individual sport modules across the 4-year program.

Table 2 also differentiates among **levels** of activity modules for four of the activity categories. Activity modules designed to develop **competency** in a variety of dance forms, activities, and sports, are labeled **Level A** modules. Activity modules designed to develop **proficiency** in selected dance forms, activities, and sports, are labeled **Level B** modules. The content between modular levels for a given activity is progressive and sequential. That is, a Level B module represents a higher level of skill/knowledge than does Level A.

Table 2
Number and Level of Curricular Modules by Activity Category for
Physical Education, Grades 9-12

Category	# modules	% Program	# Level A Modules	# Level B Modules
Fitness/Wellness	8	22%		
Fitness Activities	4	11%		
Team Sports	6	17%	4	2
Individual Sports	8	22%	6	2
Recreational Activities	8	22%	(any combination of levels A and B)	
Dance	2	6%	2	
	36	100%		

Sample Activity Modules. The program guidelines include 28 sample activity modules for sports, recreational activities, and dance; 18 Level A and 10 Level B modules. The guidelines also include 12 sample modules in Fitness/Wellness across grades 9-12. Six of the modules are labeled according to the specific element of fitness/wellness addressed in the module (e.g., muscular strength, cardiovascular risk factors, etc.). Four of the modules represent fitness activities. Modules 11 and 12 involve application of fitness/wellness principles as a culminating activity.

The sample modules for the curricular categories of team and individual sports, recreational activities, and dance primarily include behavioral objectives related to Content Standards 1-2 and 4-7. Behavioral objectives related to Content Standard 3 are included in the sample modules within the category of Fitness/Wellness. The sample modules are intended to illustrate the sequence and progression of skills, knowledge, and tasks that could be included within various types and level of modules. Additional and/or alternative modules could and should be developed at the local level.

Development of a Curricular Plan. Development of a specific curriculum plan for a specific school or district involves two steps. First, the number and level of modules to be offered within each category at each of the four grade levels must be determined. **Table 2** presents guidelines for the total number of modules to be included within each of the categories of curricular content. It is recommended that each grade level include 9 modules, 3 of which focus on fitness/wellness content. The remaining 6 modules per grade level should be distributed across activity categories in a manner deemed appropriate by the physical education staff.

Second, the specific activity modules to be offered must be selected. For example, if two Level A individual sport modules are to be required in grade 9, the specific activities are selected from the list in **Table 1** (badminton, tennis, etc.). No student should repeat either a Level A or a Level B module.

Sample Modular Curriculum. An example of a modular curriculum plan for grades 9-12 is presented in **Table 3**. Selection of the specific modules to be included within a particular activity category should be based on the characteristics of a specific school, including facilities, equipment, geographic location, expertise of the staff, and interests of the students.

The sample modular curriculum is based on the assumption of a 5-day-per-week physical education program, grades 9-12. For those 9-12 programs which do not include four years of daily physical education, it will be necessary to reduce the number of activity modules offered within each content category. However, the recommended percentage of the curriculum which focuses on each of the content areas should be maintained.

Table 3
Sample Modular Curriculum Plan for Physical Education, Grades 9-12

Activity Categories	Grade	Fitness/ Wellness	Fitness Activities	Team Sports		Individual Sports		Recreational Activities		Dance	Total
Level of Modules			A	A	B	A	B	A	B	A	
			Number of Modules								
(Prescribed)	9	2	1	2		2		2			9
(Prescribed)	10	2	1	2		2		1		1	9
(Elective)	11	2	1		1	2		3			9
(Elective)	12	2	1		1		2	2		1	9
Total # of Modules		8	4	6		8		8		2	36

Assessment. Examples of a variety of assessment techniques are provided for each activity module. The sample assessment techniques are intended to illustrate some of the many valid, authentic, and appropriate ways to evaluate the extent to which the behavioral objectives have been accomplished. It is hoped that the sample assessments will serve to suggest additional and/or alternate assessment techniques appropriate for a particular program. In grades 9-12, assessment should focus on evaluation of the extent to which students evidence characteristics of a physically-educated person. The context of the assessment should require students to apply skills and knowledge in real-life settings that are likely to be encountered outside the school environment.

Definition of Terms. Listed below are definitions of key terms specific to this section of the guidelines document. The first three terms denote a progressive sequence of skill development for a given activity. The next three terms are used to denote a progressive sequence of skill development both within a specific module and across levels of modules for a given activity.

Attempt	Implies that the skill will be taught but the student will not master or show competency in the skill.
Demonstrate:	Implies that the student will demonstrate competency in the skill.
Review:	Implies the continual review of the skill and serves as a mastery checkpoint.
Module:	A self-contained unit of content, based on 15 days of class participation.
Level A Module:	An activity module designed to develop competency in a variety of dance forms, activities, and sports.
Level B Module:	An activity module designed to develop proficiency in selected dance forms, activities, and sports.
Competency:	Implies that the learner has mastered the fundamental skills of the activity and can apply these skills in game situations or performances. Demonstrating competency includes using fundamental game strategies or applying skills to solve advanced movement problems.
Proficiency:	Implies that the learner has mastered advanced skills of the activity and can adapt these skills in game situations or performances. Demonstrating proficiency includes using advanced game strategies, creating movement patterns, or creating unique combinations of movements.

DANCE MODULES

Recommended Percentage of Program: 6%

Recommended Number of Modules: 2 Level A

Note: **It is recommended that:**

    a.   **modules in grades 9 and 10 be prescribed (teacher-selected) for all students**

    b.   **modules in grades 11 and 12 be elective (student-selected) within required activity categories**

    c.   **modules not be repeated by an individial student**

Dance

Standard 1:	*Demonstrates competency in many movement forms and proficiency in a few movement forms.*

Objective 1.1:   **Reviews the following movement skills:**

Locomotor movements:

walk	leap
run	gallop
hop	slide
jump	skip

Non-locomotor/axial movements:

bend	stretch
twist	swing

Objective 1.2:   **Reviews the following movement elements:**

Shape:

curved	straight
twisted	symmetrical
angular	asymmetrical

Space:
pathways (curved/straight)
levels (high/medium/low)
focus (up/down/right/left)
direction (forward/backward/side/diagonal/turn)
range (big/little)

Time:
rhythm (beat)
tempo (changes)

Force:
energy (sustained/swing/percussive/collapse/vibratory/
strong/light)

Objective 1.3:   **Attempts the following steps/movements in modern/jazz dance and demonstrates competency in four (4) self-selected steps/movements:**

> Contraction
> Triplet
> Three-step turn
> Pivot turn
> Seat turn
> Knee fall
> Isolation

Objective 1.4:   **Attempts the following steps/movements in ballet and demonstrates competency in five (5) self-selected steps/movements:**

> Plie
> Releve
> Five basic arm/feet positions
> Chasse
> Battement
> Arabesque
> Tour
> Saute
> Sissone
> Jete

Objective 1.5:   **Demonstrates the ability to combine, memorize, and perform a sequence of steps/movements from modern/jazz or ballet.**

> Sample Assessment
> **Student Log**
> Students should practice the skills learned in class until they feel proficient. Practice sessions should be documented in the log and validated with a parent signature.

Objective 1.6:   **Demonstrates competency in modern/jazz or ballet by performing with technical skill, artistic expression, clarity, musicality, and stylistic nuance.**

> Sample Assessment
> **Group Project**
> Individual skills are placed on index cards. Small groups of students randomly select five cards and create a combination/dance using all five skills. Students then set the dance to music and perform the dance emphasizing performance qualities (artistic expressions musicality, technical skill, etc.) and give the piece a finished performance quality.

Standard 2:	Applies movement concepts and principles to the learning and development of motor skills.

Objective 2.1: Defines and explains the following movement principles:

Alignment
Balance
Initiation of movement
Articulation of isolated body parts
Weight shifts
Elevation and landing
Fall and recovery

> Sample Assessment
> **GroupProject**
> Students work in small groups to create a lecture-demonstration which provides an understanding of the following movement principles: alignment, balance, articulation of isolated body parts, weight shifts, elevation and landing, fall and recovery. Students present a lecture-demonstration to an audience which is unfamiliar with the subject matter.

Objective 2.2: Observes and discusses how dance is different from other forms of human movement.

> Sample Assessment
> **Student Debate**
> Students plan and carry out a debate addressing the question: Is dance different from other forms of movement?

Objective 2.3: Refines techniques through self-evaluation and correction.

> Sample Assessment
> **Student Project**
> Students establish a set of aesthetic criteria and apply the criteria in evaluating their work and that of others.

Objective 2.5: Uses improvisation to generate movements for choreography.

Objective 2.6: Explores, discovers, realizes, and discusses multiple solutions to a given movement problem.

Objective 2.7: Demonstrates the principles of contrast and transition.

Objective 2.8: Demonstrates the processes of reordering and chance.

Objective 2.9: Demonstrates the structures or forms of AB, ABA, cannon, call and response, and narrative.

Objective 2.10:   Choreographs a dance using choreographic principles, processes, and structures.

> **Sample Assessment**
> **Observation: Videotape**
> Students compare and contrast two videotaped dance compositions in terms of space, time, and force/energy. Students choose one of the following foci:
> 1) A critical review of one of the two dances using effective use of time, space, and force/energy as the criteria.
> 2) A checklist of movement elements for each of the two dances and a detailed description of the specific movements used.

Standard 4:	*Achieves and maintains a health-enhancing level of physical fitness.*

Objective 4.1:   Explains the relationship between a healthy lifestyle and dance proficiency.

> **Sample Assessment**
> **Student Report**
> Students prepare and present an oral report on healthy practices and lifestyle choices that enhance their ability to dance.

Objective 4.2:   Communicates effectively how lifestyle choices affect the dancer.

Standard 5:	*Demonstrates responsible personal and social behavior in physical activity settings.*

Objective 5.1:   Identifies areas of weakness and completes an action plan for improvement.

Objective 5.2:   Creates warm-ups and discusses the importance of preparing the body and mind for expressive purposes.

Objective 5.3:   Explains strategies for prevention of dance injuries.

Objective 5.4:   Demonstrates proper dance class procedure and etiquette.

Objective 5.5:   Demonstrates appropriate audience behavior during performances.

> **Sample Assessment**
> **Group Project**
> Students compile a list of appropriate audience behaviors
> and practice them while attending a dance performance
> within the community.

Standard 6:	*Demonstrates understanding and respect for differences among people in physical activity settings.*

Objective 6.1:   Reviews dance steps/movements from a variety of cultures and historical time periods.

Objective 6.2:   Discusses folk and/or classical dance from various cultures and describe similarities and differences in steps and movement styles.

Objective 6.3:   Describes the role of dance in two (2) different cultures or time periods.

> **Sample Assessment**
> **Written Report**
> Students submit a one-page paper on the significance of a
> folk or social dance to its culture or time period.

Standard 7:	*Understands that physical activity provides opportunities for enjoyment, challenge, self-expression, and social interaction.*

Objective 7.1:   Formulates and answers aesthetic questions.

Objective 7.2:   Demonstrates/explains how different forms of accompaniment can affect the meaning of a dance.

Objective 7.3:   Demonstrates/explains how the role of lighting and costume contribute to the meaning of a dance.

Objective 7.4:   Describes the effect of personal experience on the interpretation of a dance.

Objective 7.5:   **Creates a dance that communicates a topic of personal significance.**

> Sample Assessment
> **Student Project**
> Students create and perform a dance that successfully
> communicates a topic of personal significance for an audience
> of peers. After performing, the students facilitate an audience
> discussion concerning their interpretation/reactions to the
> dance and personal insights concerning the chosen topic.

Objective 7.6:   **Demonstrates confidence and maturity while performing a self-selected dance.**

Objective 7.7:   **Participates in a student performance.**

Objective 7.8:   **Participates in dance classes and/or dance experiences within the community.**

Objective 7.9:   **Attends dance performances within the community.**

> Sample Assessment
> **Summative Group Project**
> Students work in small groups to choose an idea, topic or theme, research it,
> create and solve movement problems using the research, and finally create an
> original piece of choreography. Students discuss the use of appropriate
> costumes, music and lighting for their dance and implement, if possible, these
> performance elements in their choreography. Completed pieces are performed
> before an audience of peers. Students should experiment with a variety of
> choreographic principles, processes, and structures and document the various
> steps of their choreographic process on videotape. All students establish a set
> of aesthetic criteria and apply it in evaluating their works and those of others.

Module and assessments contributed by:

Susan McGreevy-Nichols
Roger Williams Middle School

References:

Consortium of National Arts Associations. (1994). National standards for arts education: What every young American should know and be able to do in the arts. Reston, VA: Music Educators National Conference.

McGreevy-Nichols, S. & Scheff, H. (1995). Building-a-dance. Champaign, IL: Human Kinetics Publishers.

National Dance Association. (1991). Dance curricula guidelines K-12. Reston, VA: AAHPERD.

Seaton, D. C., Clayton, I., Howard, L., & Messersmith, L. (1974). Physical education handbook. Englewood Cliffs, NJ: Prentice Hall, Inc.

Sherbon, E. (1990). One the count of one. Chicago, IL: A Capella Books.

FITNESS/WELLNESS MODULES

Recommended Percentage of Program: 33%

Recommended Number of Modules: 8 ContentModules (required)
                                        4 Activity Modules (required)

Note: Fitness activity modules differ from other activity modules. The intent of the fitness activity modules is to improve specific elements of fitness through participation in an activity in which the student has already demonstrated competency.

Module One
Aerobic Fitness

Standard 2:	*Applies movement concepts and principles to the learning and development of motor skills.*

Objective 2.1:   Reviews the following terms:

> Target Heart Rate
> VO$_2$ Max
> Overload
> Duration
> Intensity
> Frequency
> Specificity of Exercise

Objective 2.2:   **Lists and describes five (5) guidelines for beginning an aerobic training program.**

Objective 2.3:   **Identifies benefits associated with aerobic fitness.**

Objective 2.4:   **Describes aerobic metabolism and training effect.**

Objective 2.5:   **Identifies risk factors related to various levels of aerobic fitness.**

> Sample Assessment
> **Written Test**
> Students complete a short, objective test of understanding of aerobic metabolism and training.

Standard 3:	*Exhibits a physically active lifestyle.*

Objective 3.1:   **Participates in various aerobic fitness activities and evaluates the value of each activity as it relates to aerobic fitness.**

Objective 3.2:   **Participates in a self-selected activity appropriate for improving cardiovascular fitness at least three (3) times a week.**

Standard 4:	*Achieves and maintains a health-enhancing level of physical fitness.*

Objective 4.1:   Completes an aerobic fitness profile.

Sample Assessment
Aerobic Fitness Test
Students participate in at least one of the following tests and complete a profile of cardiovascular fitness.

Harvard Step Test
Cooper 12 minute walk/jog
1.5 mile run
Modified Step Test
Bicycle Ergometer Test

Objective 4.2:   Demonstrates knowledge of the factors involved in planning and evaluating a fitness program.

Objective 4.3:   Sets and achieves a short term aerobic fitness goal.

Objective 4.4:   Monitors weekly progress towards achieving a fitness goal by maintaining an aerobic physical activity log.

Objective 4.5:   Describes and participates in the following aerobic training techniques: continuous, circuit, and Fartlek.

Standard 5:	*Demonstrates responsible personal and social behavior in physical activity settings.*

Objective 5.1:   Creates safety guidelines for participation in aerobic fitness activities.

Sample Assessment
Group Project
Students work in small groups to identify rules for safe participation in aerobic fitness activities. After each group has had an opportunity for input, the consolidated list is displayed as a safety poster in the classroom/gymnasium.

125

Module Two
Skill-Related Fitness

Standard 2:	*Applies movement concepts and principles to the learning and development of motor skills.*

Objective 2.1:   Differentiates between health- and skill-related fitness and identifies measures for each.

Objective 2.2:   Differentiates between anaerobic and aerobic training.

Objective 2.3:   Analyzes various sports and determines the skill-related components required for success in these sports.

Objective 2.4:   Defines the following terms:

Power	Reaction Time
Speed	Balance
Agility	Rhythm
Response time	Coordination

> **Sample Assessment**
> **Group Project**
> Students work in small groups to analyze two (2) individual and two (2) team sports relative to fitness components required for success. Students present an oral report of conclusions to the class.

Objective 2.5:   Contrasts energy expenditures between aerobic and anaerobic activities.

Standard 3:	*Exhibits a physically active lifestyle.*

Objective 3.1:   Participates in selected activities appropriate for improving 2 or 3 components of skill-related fitness such as agility, power, and speed.

Objective 3.2:   Participates in various activities, games, and sports requiring specific skill-related fitness components such as juggling, jump roping, or an obstacle course.

Standard 4:	*Achieves and maintains a health-enhancing level of physical fitness.*

Objective 4.1:   Describes and participates in the following anaerobic training techniques: plyometric and interval.

Objective 4.2:   Maintains a student log of physical activity for four (4) weeks and identifies the key skill-related fitness components in the various activities.

Standard 5:	*Demonstrates responsible personal and social behavior in physical activity settings.*

Objective 5.1:   **Creates safety guidelines for participation in skill-related fitness activities.**

Objective 5.2:   **Identifies risk factors associated with various skill-related training techniques.**

> Sample Assessment
> **Group Project**
> Students identify potential risk factors for specific skill-related training programs. For each risk factor, students develop a specific exercise protocol designed to reduce the potential adverse effects of training.

Module Three
Aerobic Activity

Standard 3:	*Exhibits a physically active lifestyle.*

Objective 3.1:   **Participates in one of the following aerobic activities:**

        Walking
        Cycling
        Jogging
        Aerobic Dance
        Step Aerobics
        Water Aerobics
        Swimming (must have Red Cross skill of intermediate or above)

These activities are designed to improve cardiovascular fitness through participation and will not focus on skill acquisition.

128

Module Four
Muscular Strength/Endurance

Standard 2:	*Applies movement concepts and principles to the learning and development of motor skills.*

Objective 2.1:   Reviews the differences between muscular strength and muscular endurance.

Objective 2.2:   Analyzes the effectiveness of various muscular strength and endurance programs.

Objective 2.3:   Identifies and explains the function of the following muscle groups:

Quadriceps	Gastrocnemius
Triceps	Deltoids
Pectoralis Major	Hip Flexors
Trapezius	Biceps
Brachialis	Latissimus Dorsi
Soleus	Abdominals
Hamstrings	Gluteals

> Sample Assessment
> **Group Project**
> Students work in small groups to analyze the function of several specific muscle groups. Students report their conclusions to the class by demonstrating the movements produced by each of the muscle groups.

Objective 2.4:   Differentiates between isometric and isotonic exercise.

Objective 2.5:   Analyzes the different effects that weight training has on men and women.

> Sample Assessment
> **Written Report**
> Students write a report summarizing the research findings relative to the differential effects of weight training on men and women. The teacher develops a scoring rubric to assess content and organization of the report.

Objective 2.6:   Describes the relationship between muscular strength and power, agility, and flexibility.

Objective 2.7:   Differentiates between weight training and weight lifting.

Objective 2.8:   **Identifies exercises or activities that will increase muscular strength/endurance of the following muscle groups:**

Quadriceps	Gastrocnemius
Triceps	Deltoids
Pectoralis Major	Hip Flexors
Trapezius	Biceps
Brachialis	Latissimus Dorsi
Soleus	Abdominals
Hamstrings	Gluteals

Standard 3:   *Exhibits a physically active lifestyle.*

Objective 3.1:   **Participates in self-selected activities appropriate for improving muscular strength/endurance at least three (3) times per week and records results.**

> **Sample Assessment**
> **Student Log**
> Students record the frequency, intensity, and duration of muscular strength/endurance training activities over a period of three (3) weeks.

Standard 4:   *Achieves and maintains a health-enhancing level of physical fitness.*

Objective 4.1:   **Completes a muscular strength/endurance profile.**

Objective 4.2:   **Sets and achieves a short term muscular strength/endurance goal.**

Objective 4.3:   **Plans and implements a program to maintain or increase muscular strength/endurance based on her/his fitness profile.**

> **Sample Assessment**
> **Fitness Tests**
> Students participate in one or more of the following tests of muscular strength/endurance:
>
> | | |
> |---|---|
> | Push ups | Pull ups |
> | Sit ups | Bench jumps |
> | Dips | Hand grip |
> | Flexed arm hang | dynamometer |

Standard 5:	Demonstrates responsible personal and social behavior in physical activity settings.

Objective 5.1:   Identifies risk factors associated with weight training and weight lifting.

Objective 5.2:   Creates safety guidelines for muscular strength/endurance training.

Module Five
Flexibility/Body Composition

Standard 2:	*Applies movement concepts and principles to the learning and development of motor skills.*

Objective 2.1:   Identifies activities appropriate for maintaining flexibility.

Objective 2.2:   Analyzes the effectiveness of various exercises for increasing flexibility.

Objective 2.3:   Explains the function of antagonistic and agonist muscle groups as they relate to flexibility.

Objective 2.4:   Differentiates between ballistic and static stretching.

Objective 2.5:   Identifies flexibility requirements for various dances, games, and sports.

Objective 2.6:   Identifies flexibility/stability exercises for the following parts of the body:

Neck   Knee

Shoulder   Ankle

Lower & Upper back   Elbow

Hip   Wrist

> Sample Assessment
> **Group Project**
> Students work in small groups to prepare a bulletin board illustrating appropriate flexibility/stability exercises for two (2) major joints of the body.

Objective 2.7:   Describes the relationship between body composition and nutrition, genetic predisposition, and exercise.

> Sample Assessment
> **Oral Report**
> Students present an oral report summarizing the research findings relative to the relationship between body composition and genetics.

Objective 2.8:   Analyzes the effectiveness of various diet programs on weight control.

> Sample Assessment
> **Role Playing**
> Students portray individuals attempting to control their weight through various diet programs. Students portray the positive and negative reactions to and effects of the diet program.

Objective 2.9:   Analyzes the impact of various activities on body composition.

Objective 2.10:   Identifies contraindicated exercises related to flexibility.

Objective 2.11:   Describes the relationship between flexibility and injury prevention, lower back pain, and strength.

Objective 2.12:   Identifies risk factors associated with too little or too much body fat.

Standard 3:	*Exhibits a physically active lifestyle.*

Objective 3.1:   Participates in stretching before and after activity.

Objective 3.2:   Keeps a log of caloric intake and caloric expenditure for one week.

> **Sample Activity**
> **Student Log**
> Students record food intake and physical activity for a one-week period. Both records are analyzed relative to caloric values.

Standard 4:	*Achieves and maintains a health-enhancing level of physical fitness.*

Objective 4.1:   Plans and implements a program based on her/his fitness profile to maintain or improve flexibility.

Objective 4.2:   Sets and achieves a short-term flexibility goal.

Objective 4.3:   Plans and implements a program of weight reduction, maintenance, or gain based on her/his body composition.

Standard 5:	*Demonstrates responsible personal and social behavior in physical activity settings.*

Objective 5.1:   Creates safety guidelines for flexibility training.

Module Six
Muscular Strength/Endurance/Flexibility Activity

Standard 3:	*Exhibits a physically active lifestyle.*

Objective 3.1:   Participates in activities to improve muscular strength/endurance and flexibilitysuch as:

> Weight-training
> Gymnastics
> Dance
> Mountain Biking
> Self-Defense
> Rock Climbing
> Roller Blading

These activities are designed to improve muscular strength/endurance and flexibility through participation and will not focus on skill acquisition.

Module Seven
Cardiovascular Risk Factors

Standard 2:	*Applies movement concepts and principles to the learning and development of motor skills.*

Objective 2.1:   Identifies appropriate activities for maintaining cardiovascular wellness.

Objective 2.2:   Compares and contrasts aerobic training programs and their impact on cardiovascular fitness.

Objective 2.3:   Describes the role of hypertension, body composition, smoking, family history, age, nutrition, and estrogen in cardiovascular wellness.

Objective 2.4:   Describes the difference between "good" cholesterol and "bad" cholesterol.

Objective 2.5:   Defines the following terms:

> Triglycerides   Blood Pressure
> Diabetes   HDL-Cholesterol
> LDL-Cholesterol

Objective 2.6:   Identifies types of food harmful to cardiovascular health.

Objective 2.7:   Completes a risk management profile for cardiovascular wellness and aerobic fitness.

Objective 2.8:   Describes the relationship between cardiovascular wellness and aerobic fitness.

> Sample Activity
> **Written Report**
> Students complete a
> Health-Risk Survey
> and identify the
> factors over which
> they have no control.

Standard 3:	*Exhibits a physically active lifestyle.*

Objective 3.1:   Participates in self-selected aerobic fitness activities at least three (3) times a week.

> Sample Activity
> **Student Log**
> Students record the frequency, intensity, and
> duration of aerobic training activities over a
> period of three (3) weeks.

Standard 4:	*Achieves and maintains a health-enhancing level of physical fitness.*

Objective 4.1:   Sets long- and short- term goals to improve aerobic fitness based on a fitness profile.

> **Sample Assessment**
> **Student Project**
> Students complete an action plan for improving or maintaining cardiovascular wellness. The plan should include specific behaviors related to diet, lifestyle choices, and physical activity.

Standard 5:	*Demonstrates responsible personal and social behavior in physical activity settings.*

Objective 5.1:   Identifies common aerobic activity injuries and describes how these injuries could be prevented.

Module Eight
Stress/Nutrition

Standard 2:	*Applies movement concepts and principles to the learning and development of motor skills.*

Objective 2.1:   Identifies the primary source and function of essential nutrients.

Objective 2.2:   Identifies the effect of diet on aerobic fitness, body composition, and long term health.

Objective 2.3:   Describes the relationships between diet, exercise, and body composition.

Objective 2.4:   Defines the following terms: metabolism, basal metabolic rate, calorie, and Setpoint Theory

Objective 2.5:   Analyzes the effectiveness of various diet programs.

Objective 2.6:   Differentiates between "Type A" and "Type B" personalities.

> **Sample Activity**
> **Role Playing**
> Students portray the reaction of individuals characterized as Type A and Type B personalities to specific stressful situations in school, at home, and in social settings.

Objective 2.7:   Analyzes and compares various relaxation training programs.

Objective 2.8:   Identifies the impact of stress on physiological wellness.

> **Sample Activity**
> **Student Project**
> Students complete a life experience survey to identify the sources of stress in their lives.

Objective 2.9:   Describes the risk factors involved in being overweight.

Standard 3:	Exhibits a physically active lifestyle.

Objective 3.1:   **Plans a balanced diet based on daily recommended U.S. dietary goals. Follows and records her/his planned diet for one week.**

> Sample Assessment
> **Student Project**
> Students use a computerized program such as DINE, to record and analyze their one-week diet plans.

Standard 4:	Achieves and maintains a health-enhancing level of physical fitness.

Objective 4.1:   **Designs a weight reduction, maintenance, or gain program that combines exercise with diet.**

Objective 4.2:   **Participates in various stress reduction programs including relaxation training and physical exercise.**

Module Nine
Aerobic Activity II

Standard 3:	*Exhibits a physically active lifestyle.*

Objective 3.1:   **Participates in one of the following aerobic activities.**

> Walking
> Cycling
> Jogging
> Aerobic Dance
> Step Aerobics
> Water Aerobics
> Swimming (must have Red Cross skill of intermediate or above)

These activities are designed to improve cardiovascular fitness through participation and will not focus on skill acquisition. Students must select an activity different from the one selected for participation in Module Three.

Module Ten
Wellness

Standard 2:	*Applies movement concepts and principles to the learning and development of motor skills.*

Objective 2.1:   Describes the relationship between physical fitness and wellness.

Objective 2.2:   Identifies behaviors or lifestyle choices that may impact negatively on wellness.

Objective 2.3:   Identifies appropriate activities for maintaining wellness.

Objective 2.4:   Evaluates her/his lifestyle and identifies inherent risk factors.

> **Sample Assessment**
> **Student Project**
> Students complete a personal wellness profile.

Standard 3:	*Exhibits a physically active lifestyle.*

Objective 3.1:   Maintains a wellness log that includes eating patterns, sleep and rest patterns, and activity patterns for a four (4) week period.

Standard 4:	*Achieves and maintains a health-enhancing level of physical fitness.*

Objective 4.1:   Designs, implements, and modifies a personal fitness program based on a personal wellness profile.

Objective 4.2:   Sets long- term and several short- term goals to improve wellness.

Objective 4.3:   Maintains a fitness portfolio, which includes an activity log, updates on health-related fitness assessments, and long- and short- term goals for a specific program plan.

> **Sample Assessment**
> **Student Journal**
> Students record their perceptions relative to success and failures in the attempt to achieve a health-enhancing level of physical fitness.

Module Eleven
Self-Selected Fitness Activity

Standard 2:	*Applies movement concepts and principles to the learning and development of motor skills.*

Objective 2.1:   Demonstrates knowledge of the factors involved in planning and evaluating a fitness program.

Standard 3:	*Exhibits a physically active lifestyle.*

Objective 3.1:   Improves personal fitness.

Standard 4:	*Achieves and maintains a health-enhancing level of physical fitness.*

Objective 4.1:   Demonstrates a commitment to personal fitness/wellness.

Sample Assessment
Final Student Project

Each student serves as a personal trainer for a peer, relative or teacher for a period of four (4) weeks. The student completes the following activities:

1. Administer a test of fitness and develop a fitness profile to include all elements of health-related fitness.
2. Complete a wellness profile to include sleep habits, stress evaluation, eating habits, and family health history.
3. Plan a fitness program for any identified area of concern.
4. Plan a program of changes in diet or lifestyle to improve overall wellness.
5. Develop a method of tracking progress.
6. Post-test the individual and evaluate the effectiveness of the programs.
7. Analyze what was and was not successful in the programs.
8. Provide information on what should be changed in the training programs, and how these changes would be made.
9. Write a summary of this experience.

Standard 5:	*Demonstrates responsible personal and social behavior in physical activity settings.*

Objective 5.1:   Understands the risk factors and safety issues in dance, games, and sports.

Module Twelve
Personalized Fitness

Standard 3:	*Exhibits a physically active lifestyle.*

Objective 3.1:   Participates in self-selected cross training activities such as:

Weight training	Rollerblading
Jogging	Step Aerobics
Biking	Walking
Swimming	Ultimate frisbee
Water Aerobics	Spinning

These activities are designed to improve various health-related or skill-related fitness components and will not focus on skill acquisition. Students must select activities different from the ones selected in Modules 3 and 9.

All Fitness Modules and Assessments contributed by:

Steveda Chepko
Springfield College

INDIVIDUAL/DUAL SPORTS MODULES

Recommended Percentage of Program: 22%

Recommended Number of Modules: 6 Level A
2 Level B

Note: It is recommended that:

a.   modules in grades 9 and 10 be prescribed (teacher-selected) for all students
b.   modules in grades 11 and 12 be elective (student-selected) within required activity categories
c.   modules not be repeated by an individial student

Wellness-Related Activity
Archery

Standard 1:	*Demonstrates competency in many movement forms and proficiency in a few movement forms.*

Objective 1.1:   Demonstrates the following skills:

REVIEW	DEMONSTRATE	ATTEMPT
	Brace/Unbrace	
	Stance	
	Nock	
	Draw	
	Anchor	
	Aim	
	Release	
	Follow-through	

Sample Assessment
The teacher could use checklists, scoring rubrics, rating scales, skill tests, verbal quizzes, and/or written tests to evaluate student progress in achieving competency in archery. Samples of the various types of assessments listed above are provided in the appendix at the end of this document.

Objective 1.2:   **Shoots at targets of varying size from various distances.**

Standard 2:	*Applies movement concepts and principles to the learning and development of motor skills.*

Objective 2.1:   **Evaluates the following skills for a peer using a checklist: draw, anchor, and aim.**

Sample Assessment
Checklist : Draw
Criteria:
* Three finger tips   Yes   No
* Thumb and pinkie in palm   Yes   No
* Draw hand relaxed   Yes   No
* Draws string to nose   Yes   No
* Comes to full draw with draw
  arm horizontal   Yes   No

Objective 2.2:   Discusses the effect of distance on the point of aim.

Objective 2.3:   Describes arrow trajectory at three (3) distances when other factors remain constant.

> Sample Assessment
> **Written Test**
> Students diagram arrow trajectory resulting from common shooting errors, such as: "creeping", canting, etc.

Objective 2.4:   Describes common rounds in archery.

Objective 2.5:   Recognizes the effects of consistency of movement patterns, force, and distance on optimal performance.

Standard 4:	*Achieves and maintains a health-enhancing level of fitness.*

Objective 4.1:   Designs a personal fitness program to increase upper body strength.

Standard 5:	*Demonstrates responsible personal and social behavior in physical activity settings.*

Objective 5.1:   Uses the proper technique for bracing/unbracing a bow.

Objective 5.2:   Determines proper arrow selection for self and two (2) other performers.

Objective 5.3:   Selects a bow with a draw that is consistent with upper body strength.

Objective 5.4:   Discusses the dangers inherent in improper nocking (i.e. direction, arrow placement).

> Sample Assessment
> **Group Project**
> Students work in small groups to compile a list of safety issues related to bow and arrow selection. The lists are displayed in the equipment area and are reviewed before each class.

Objective 5.5:   Identifies the effects of under- and overdrawing a bow.

Objective 5.6:   Shoots and retrieves on command.

Objective 5.7:   Self-scores results of at least three (3) ends of archery.

Objective 5.8:   Scores and compares the performance of a team of three (3) shooters at two (2) different distances.

> **Sample Assessment**
> **Group Project**
> Students work in small groups to develop and present an archery activity involving shooting at targets comprised of seasonal symbols (e.g., ornaments on a holiday tree).

Standard 6:	*Demonstrates understanding and respect for differences among people in physical activity settings.*

Objective 6.1:   Participates in activity simulating various handicapping conditions such as wheelchair archery or providing feedback to a "blind" shooter.

Objective 6.2:   Selects the appropriate equipment and shooting distance for optimal performance by a partner.

Objective 6.3:   Participates in a tournament using a handicapping system of scoring.

> **Sample Assessment**
> **Event Task**
> Students work in small groups to calculate team handicaps.

Standard 7:	*Understands that physical activity provides opportunities for enjoyment, challenge, self-expression, and social interaction.*

Objective 7.1:   Participates on a co-ed team.

Objective 7.2:   Identifies her/his level of potential in archery.

Objective 7.3:   Participates in intramural or recreational activity.

> **Sample Assessment**
> **Student Log**
> Students record instances of participation in archery over a four (4) week period, including number of arrows shot and total score.

Modules and Assessments contributed by:

Barbara Hemink
Clarkstown Senior High School

References:

Haywood, K.M. & Lewis, C.F. (1989). Archery: Steps to success. Leisure Press.

Haywood, K.M. & Lewis, C.F. (1989). Teaching archery: Steps to success. Leisure Press.

McKinney, W.C. (1980). Archery. Dubuque, Iowa: W.C. Brown Co.

Wellness-Related Activity
Badminton [A]

Standard 1:	*Demonstrates competency in many movement forms and proficiency in a few movement forms.*

Objective 1.1:   Reviews, demonstrates, or attempts the following skills:

REVIEW	DEMONSTRATE	ATTEMPT
Grips Forehand Backhand		

Strokes
Clear
  Fore underhand
  Back underhand
	Strokes
	Clear
	  Fore overhead
	  Back overhead
	Drop
	  Fore underhand
	  Fore overhead
	Smash
	  Forehand
		Strokes
		Drive
		  Forehand
		  Backhand
		Drop
		  Back underhand
		  Back overhead
		Smash
		  Backhand
		  Forehand block
		  Hair-pin

Serves Long	**Serves** Short	**Serves** Drive

	Offensive Skills
	  Forehand down-the-line
	  Forehand cross-court
		Offensive Skills
		  Backhand down-the-line
		  Backhand cross-court

	Defensive Skills
	  Return of serve
		Defensive skills
		  Return of smash

Sample Assessment
The teacher could use checklists, scoring rubrics, rating scales, skill tests, verbal quizzes, and/or written tests to evaluate student progress in achieving competency in badminton. Samples of the various types of assessments listed above are provided in the appendix at the end of this document.

Objective 1.2:   **Utilizes a variety of offensive and defensive strategies in a doubles game.**

Standard 2:	*Applies movement concepts and principles to the learning and development of motor skills.*

Objective 2.1: **Evaluates four (4) of the following skills using a checklist:**
Forehand & backhand grips
Forehand drive
Long serve
Forehand underhand clear
Forehand overhand clear

Sample Assessment
Checklist: Long Serve
Criteria:
• Contacts shuttle below waist   Yes No
• Weight shift from back to
  front foot   Yes No
• Observable wrist snap   Yes No
• Shuttle flight high & deep   Yes No
• Shuttle lands in proper
  service box   Yes No

Objective 2.2: **Describes the effect of changing the length of a 3rd class lever on striking skills.**

Objective 2.3: **Identifies the importance of weight transfer in striking.**

Objective 2.4: **Utilizes a variety of shots during game play.**

Sample Assessment
Peer Observation
Students observe a peer during a singles game and keep a tally sheet of all shot selections. Where possible, students indicate the outcome of the shot and provide feedback to the peer regarding skills that were over-utilized and under-utilized, as well as strokes/skills that are deficient.

Standard 4:	*Achieves and maintains a health-enhancing level of physical fitness.*

Objective 4.1: **Participates in drills and games that require agility and rapid response times.**

Objective 4.2: **Participates in drills and games that require aerobic fitness, flexibility, and muscular strength/endurance.**

Objective 4.3: **Identifies the health-related and skill-related fitness components inherent in competitive badminton.**

Standard 5:	*Demonstrates responsible personal and social behavior in physical activity settings.*

Objective 5.1: **Completes a safety inspection of the playing surface and equipment prior to activity.**

Objective 5.2: **Maintains safe distances while using a racquet.**

Objective 5.3:   Discusses the importance of maintaining body control while playing with a racquet.

Objective 5.4:   Demonstrates basic knowledge of the game including care of equipment, etiquette, basic rules, and definition of terms.

Objective 5.5:   Self-officiates a game.

Objective 5.6:   Serves as a linesperson and/or official for a singles game.

Objective 5.7:   Discusses the origins of badminton.

> Sample Assessment
> **Written Test**
> The student completes an objective test requiring application of rules to descriptions of game situations, and matching of badminton terms and definitions.

Standard 6:	*Demonstrates understanding and respect for differences among people in physical activity settings.*

Objective 6.1:   Engages in "cooperative shuttle placement" with a partner.

Objective 6.2:   Modifies her/his play in practice situations to facilitate optimum learning of a skill by an opponent.

Objective 6.3:   Participates in doubles and mixed doubles with partners of varying skill levels.

Standard 7:	*Understands that physical activity provides opportunities for enjoyment, challenge, self-expression, and social interaction.*

Objective 7.1:   Attends a competitive badminton match.

Objective 7.2:   Identifies her/his level of potential in badminton.

Objective 7.3:   Plays badminton on her/his own with friends.

SEE REFERENCES AT THE END OF LEVEL B

Wellness-Related Activity
Badminton [B]

Standard 1:	*Demonstrates competency in many movement forms and proficiency in a few movement forms.*

Objective 1.1:   Reviews, demonstrates, or attempts the following skills:

REVIEW	DEMONSTRATE	ATTEMPT
Strokes	**Strokes**	
Clear	Drive	
Fore underhand	Forehand overhead	
Back underhand	Backhand	
Drop	Drop	
Fore underhand	Back underhand	
Fore overhand	Back overhand	
Smash	Smash	
Forehand	Backhand	
	Forehand block	
	Hair-pin	
Serves	**Serves**	**Serves**
Long	Drive	Backhand
Short		Flick
Offensive Skills	**Offensive Skills**	
Forehand down-the-line	Backhand down-the-line	
Forehand cross-court	Backhand cross-court	
Defensive Skills	**Defensive skills**	
Return of serve	Return of smash	

Sample Assessment
The teacher could use checklists, scoring rubrics, rating scales, skill tests, verbal quizzes, and/or written tests to evaluate student progress in achieving proficiency in badminton. Samples of the various types of assessments listed above are provided in the appendix at the end of this document.

Objective 1.2:   **Evaluates and discusses the selection of offensive and defensive shots used in a singles game.**

Objective 1.3:   Discusses with her/his partner the options of offensive and defensive positioning for doubles play.

Objective 1.4:   Identifies how a variety of shots can be used strategically to "out-play" an opponent.

> **Sample Activity**
> **Group Project**
> Students work with a doubles partner to identify specific positioning and shots to be attempted in the following situations:
> (a) opponents in up and back positions
> (b) both opponents in up position
> (c) both opponents in back position

Standard 2:	Applies movement concepts and principles to the learning and development of motor skills.

Objective 2.1:   Evaluates four (4) of the following skills for a peer using a checklist:
Backhand, flick, drive or short serve
Forehand overhand drop
Forehand block
Backhand underhand drop
Backhand drive
Hair-pin drop
Return of smash

> **Sample Assessment**
> **Checklist: Forehand Overhand Drop Shot**
> Criteria:
> • Prepatory movement identical to overhead clear   Yes   No
> • No wrist snap; shuttle is blocked   Yes   No
> • Shuttle drops within three (3) feet of the net   Yes   No

Objective 2.2:   Describes the importance of ballistic movement in achieving maximum limb velocity and maximum transfer of force to an object.

Standard 4:	Achieves and maintains a health-enhancing level of physical fitness.

Objective 4.1:   Plans and implements a program designed to maximize the fitness component most lacking in her/his game.

Standard 5:	Demonstrates responsible personal and social behavior in physical activity settings.

Objective 5.1:   Creates a safety checklist for badminton.

Objective 5.2:   Plans and implements a program for maintaining equipment.

> Sample Activity
> **Student Project**
> Students work in small groups to design a computer spreadsheet which will display an inventory of equipment and a schedule for repair and/or replacement.

Objective 5.3:   Demonstrates knowledge of all rules of the game including scoring for both singles and doubles.

Objective 5.4:   Explains service rotation and setting the score for singles and doubles.

Objective 5.5:   Plans and supervises a six (6) team tournament.

> Sample Activity
> **Student Project**
> Students work in partners to select a specific type of tournament appopriate to the skill level of classmates, design draw sheets, implement the tournament, and record results.

Standard 6:	Demonstrates understanding and respect for differences among people in physical activity settings.

Objective 6.1:   Recognizes and appreciates the finesse involved in badminton by congratulating a peer on a well executed shot.

Objective 6.2:   Participates with players of varying abilities.

Standard 7:	Understands that physical activity provides opportunities for enjoyment, challenge, self-expression, and social interaction.

Objective 7.1:   Participates in an intramural or recreational badminton program.

Modules and Assessments contributed by:

> Linda Delano
> Springfield College
>
> Barbara Hemink
> Clarkstown Senior High School

References:

Ballou, R. B. (1992). <u>Badminton for beginners.</u> Englewood, CO: Morton Publishing Co.

Krotee, M. L. (1984). <u>Innovative theory and practice of badminton.</u> Dubuque, Iowa: Kendall/Hunt Pub. Co.

Wellness-Related Activity
Bowling

Standard 1:	*Demonstrates competency in many movement forms and proficiency in a few movement forms.*

Objective 1.1: Reviews, demonstrates, or attempts the following skills:

REVIEW	DEMONSTRATE	ATTEMPT
Aiming at a target	1 and 4 step approach	Hook ball
Rolling a ball	Grips for straight & hook balls	Converting splits
	Release & follow-through	
	Straight ball	
	Non-split spares	
	Spot bowling	
	Pin bowling	
	Line bowling	

Sample Assessment
The teacher could use checklists, scoring rubrics, rating scales, skill tests, verbal quizzes, and/or written tests to evaluate student progress in achieving competency in bowling. Samples of the various types of assessments listed above are provided in the appendix at the end of this document.

Objective 1.2: Identifies the most effective strategies for converting various spares.

Objective 1.3: Analyzes various strategies for converting splits using straight and hook balls.

Objective 1.4: Describes and demonstrates various alignments for converting spares and splits.

Objective 1.5: Differentiates between the grips used for rolling straight and hook balls.

Objective 1.6: Demonstrates the ability to score a line of bowling.

Student Activity
Event Task
Students compute their scoring average for three (3) lines of bowling.

155

Standard 2:	*Applies movement concepts and principles to the learning and development of motor skills.*

Objective 2.1:   Compares the effectiveness of pin, spot, and line techniques of aiming.

> **Sample Assessment**
> **Peer Observation**
> Students evaluate the effectiveness of a peer's use of different points of aim. Ten balls are rolled using each aiming technique and the results are recorded. A specific situation should be selected for the assessment; that is, strike ball or a specific spare.

Objective 2.2:   Describes the relationship between point of application of force and ball spin.

Objective 2.3:   Defines and uses correct bowling terminology.

Objective 2.4:   Identifies key issues to consider in selecting a bowling ball, including size, weight, and composition.

> **Sample Assessment**
> **Written Test**
> Students respond to ten (10) fill-in-the-blank questions related to bowling terminology.

Objective 2.5:   Describes the effect of various lane conditions on the path of a bowling ball.

Standard 4:	*Achieves and maintains a health-enhancing level of physical fitness.*

Objective 4.1:   Plans and implements a fitness program to improve upper body strength and flexibility.

Standard 5:	*Demonstrates responsible personal and social behavior in physical activity settings.*

Objective 5.1:   Identifies risk factors associated with lane conditions, pin-setting machines, and ball returns.

Objective 5.2:   Uses appropriate footwear and proper size and weight of bowling ball.

Objective 5.3:   Remains a safe distance behind other students who are bowling.

Objective 5.4:   Sets short- and long-term goals and charts progress toward achieving these goals.

> **Sample Assessment**
> **Student Log**
> Students record the number of frames bowled, scores, and cumulative average over a four (4) week period.

Standard 6:	*Demonstrates understanding and respect for differences among people in physical activity settings.*

Objective 6.1:   Recognizes differences in ability when setting-up four-person bowling teams.

Objective 6.2:   Modifies scoring to accomodate players of varying skill levels.

Standard 7:	*Understands that physical activity provides opportunities for enjoyment, challenge, self-expression, and social interaction.*

Objective 7.1:   Plans a tournament for young players.

Objective 7.2:   Participates in recreational bowling.

Module contributed by:

        Pat O'Leary Proseus
        Bishop Ford High School

        Colleen O'Leary
        Our Lady of Perpetual Help High School

References:

Strickland, R. (1989). Bowling: Steps to success. Leisure Press.

Strickland, R. (1989). Teaching bowling: Steps to success. Leisure Press.

Wellness-Related Activity
Golf [A]

Standard 1:	*Demonstrates competency in many movement forms and proficiency in a few movement forms.*

Objective 1.1:   Reviews, demonstrates, or attempts the following skills:

REVIEW	DEMONSTRATE	ATTEMPT
	Grips Overlapping Interlocking	
	Stances Square Open Closed	**Stances** Open - slice or fade Closed - hook or pull Sidehill lies - feet above or below ball
	Swings ¼ swing iron ½ swing iron ¾ swing iron Full swing iron ¾ swing wood	**Swings** Full swing 3 or 5 wood
	Strokes Putting - short Chip shot (¼ - ½ swing) Long iron shot flat lie	**Strokes** Putting long and lag with a break Medium iron shot uphill lie downhill lie Long iron shot fairway rough

Sample Assessment
The teacher could use checklists, scoring rubrics, rating scales, skill tests, verbal quizzes, and/or written tests to evaluate student progress in achieving competency in golf. Samples of the various types of assessments listed above are provided in the appendix at the end of this document.

Standard 2:	Applies movement concepts and principles to the learning and development of motor skills.

Objective 2.1:   Self-evaluates the following skills using a checklist: grip, stance, and swing.

> **Sample Assessment**
> **Checklist: Swing**
> Criteria:
> * Stance width appropriate for
>   length of club   Yes   No
> * Back swing smooth and legs
>   remain bent   Yes   No
> * Head remains down throughout   Yes   No
> * Weight transfers back to front   Yes   No
> * Non-dominant arm remains
>   straight   Yes   No
> * Ball contacted   Yes   No

Objective 2.2:   Plans a program of skill improvement based on her/his self-evaluation.

Objective 2.3:   Evaluates and modifies the play of her/his round of golf on a par-three golf course.

Objective 2.4:   Discusses the following strategies for 3, 4, and 5 par holes:

Club selection
Shot selection
Reading the green
Teeing up

> **Sample Assessment**
> **Video Analysis**
> Students view a videotape of three (3) golfers playing 2 or 3 holes of golf. Students record and evaluate the strategies employed by each golfer.

Objective 2.5:   Describes the relationship between point of application of force and ball spin.

Objective 2.6:   Describes the effect of changing the length of a 3rd class lever on striking skills.

Standard 4:	Achieves and maintains a health-enhancing level of physical fitness.

Objective 4.1:   Participates in drills and modified games that require agility, balance, flexibility, and strength.

Objective 4.2:   Participates in drills and modified games that require anaerobic fitness.

Standard 5:	Demonstrates responsible personal and social behavior in physical activity settings.

Objective 5.1:   Identifies the general safety rules of golf.

Objective 5.2:   Discusses safety at the practice range.

Objective 5.3:   Discusses safety on the golf course.

Objective 5.4:   Discusses the safe use of a motorized golf cart.

Objective 5.5:   Discusses the rules and regulations of golf.

Objective 5.6:   Identifies the rules governing tied scores and handicapping for Match Play and Medal Play.

Objective 5.7:   Discusses rules of etiquette when playing a round of golf.

Standard 6:	Demonstrates understanding and respect for differences among people in physical activity settings.

Objective 6.1:   Encourages others on the golf course.

Objective 6.2:   Participates in one round of golf with a simulated disabling condition.

Objective 6.3:   Participates in a round of golf using her/his handicap to equalize play/scoring.

> **Sample Assessment**
> **Debate**
> Students debate both sides of the issue of the use of a golf cart by a disabled player.

Standard 7:	Understands that physical activity provides opportunities for enjoyment, challenge, self-expression, and social interaction.

Objective 7.1:   Recognizes movement patterns that exhibit fundamentally sound biomechanics for a golf shot.

> **Sample Assessment**
> **Student Observation**
> Students compare and contrast the biomechanics of two (2) videotaped professional golfers.

Objective 7.2:   Attends a high school, college, or local golf tournament.

Objective 7.3:   Identifies school or local golfing opportunities in which s/he will feel comfortable participating.

SEE REFERENCES AT THE END OF LEVEL B

Wellness-Related Activity
Golf [B]

Standard 1:	*Demonstrates competency in many movement forms and proficiency in a few movement forms.*

Objective 1.1:   Reviews, demonstrates, or attempts the following skills:

REVIEW	DEMONSTRATE	ATTEMPT
Grips		
Overlapping		
Interlocking		
Stances	**Stances**	
Square	Open - slice and fade	
Open	Closed - hook or pull	
Closed	Side hill lies - feet above ball	
	feet below ball	
Swings	**Swings**	
¼ swing iron	Full swing 3 or 5 wood	
½ swing iron		
¾ swing iron		
Full swing iron		
¾ swing 3 or 5 wood		
Strokes	**Strokes**	**Strokes**
Putting - short	Putting - long and	Deep rough shots
Chip shot	lag with a "break"	Sand trap shots
(¼ to ½ swing)	Medium iron shot	explosions
Long iron shot	uphill lie	chips
flat lie	downhill lie	Planned hook with
	Long iron shot	wood
	fairway	Planned slice with
	rough	wood

Sample Assessment
The teacher could use checklists, scoring rubrics, rating scales, skill tests, verbal quizzes, and/or written tests to evaluate student progress in achieving proficiency in golf. Samples of the various types of assessments listed above are provided in the appendix at the end of this document.

Standard 2:	Applies movement concepts and principles to the learning and development of motor skills.

Objective 2.1: Evaluates the following skills for a peer, using a checklist:

Basic swing
Putting from a distance of 10 feet, "read the green"
Approach shot with seven, eight, or nine iron
3 wood shot
Chip shot using ¼, ½, or ¾ swing

Sample Assessment
Checklist : Short Approach Shot (nine iron)
Criteria:
- Stance open   Yes   No
- Backswing short   Yes   No
- Ball lofted   Yes   No
- Head down   Yes   No
- Follow through
  height comparable to backswing Yes   No

Objective 2.2: Plans a program of skill improvement based on her/his self-evaluation.

Objective 2.3: Evaluates and modifies the play of her/his round of golf on a par-three golf course.

Objective 2.4: Implements the following strategies for 3, 4 and 5 par holes:

Club selection
Shot selection
Reading the green
Teeing up

Sample Assessment
Event Task

Students play a round of golf and record scores for each of 9 holes. In addition, students cite the strategies employed for each hole.

Objective 2.5: Describes the relationship between and among timing, sequencing, and summation of forces in striking.

Objective 2.6: Describes the importance of ballistic movements in achieving maximum limb velocity and maximum transfer of force to an object.

Standard 4:	Achieves and maintains a health-enhancing level of physical fitness.

Objective 4.1: Plans a program to maximize her/his agility, balance, flexibility, and strength.

Objective 4.2:	Plans a program designed to improve anaerobic fitness.

Standard 5:	*Demonstrates responsible personal and social behavior in physical activity settings.*

Objective 5.1:	Applies general safety rules of golf when practicing at a practice range or playing on a golf course.

Objective 5.2:	Applies safe use of motorized carts when participating in a round of golf on a golf course.

Objective 5.3:	Follows proper etiquette when participating in a round of golf on a golf course.

> **Sample Assessment**
> **Interview**
> Students interview a groundskeeper at a local golf course and compile a list of the most common breeches of golf etiquette.

Objective 5.4:	Implements the rules and regulations of golf.

Standard 6:	*Demonstrates understanding and respect for differences among people in physical activity settings.*

Objective 6.1:	Modifies golf stroke fundamentals for peers with disabling conditions.

Objective 6.2:	Modifies rules to ensure parity among golfers with varying abilities.

> **Sample Assessment**
> **Event Task**
> Students compute handicaps for each classmate based on their scores in a 9-hole game.

Standard 7:	*Understands that physical activity provides opportunity for enjoyment, challenge, self-expression, and social interaction.*

Objective 7.1:   Recognizes movement patterns that exhibit proper solutions to various golf shot situations.

Objective 7.2:   Devises creative and unique solutions to various golf shot situations such as: hitting uphill, hitting downhill, hitting when the ball is below the feet, hitting when the ball is above the feet, and playing from the rough.

Objective 7.3:   Participates in a school or local golf tournament.

Sample Assessment
Student Journal

Students record participation in golf competition, including scores, perceptions regarding the course, and other reflections about the personal value of the experience.

Modules and Assessments contributed by:

Doris E. Wooledge
Delaware State University

Gretchen Brockmeyer
Springfield College

Barbara Hemink
Clarkstown Senior High School

References:

Owens, D. & Bunker, L. K. (1992). Advanced golf: Steps to success. Leisure Press.

Owens, D. & Bunker, L. K. (1989). Golf: Steps to success. Leisure Press.

Owens, D. & Bunker, L. K. (1989). Teaching golf: Steps to success. Leisure Press.

Wellness Related Activity
Gymnastics

Standard 1:	*Demonstrates competency in many movement forms and proficiency in a few movement forms.*

Objective 1.1   Reviews, demonstrates, or attempts the following skills:

REVIEW	DEMONSTRATE	ATTEMPT
Tumbling	**Tumbling**	**Floor Exercise**
Forward Roll	Jumps in combination	Turns in combination
Backward Roll	Body waves	Leaps in combination
Cartwheel		Balances
Headstand		Kip up
Handstand		Stunts
Round Off		Back handspring
Bridge		
Turns		
Leaps		
Back extension		
Handstand forward roll		
Vaulting	**Vaulting**	**Vaulting**
Squat	Flank ½ turn	Handspring
Flank		Pike
Bent hip squat		Headspring
Straddle		
Beam	**Beam**	**Beam**
Front support mount	Straddle mount	Running approach mount
Front and side scale	Kick turn	Locomotor mvmts. in
Knee scale	Shoulder roll back	combination
V-seat		Shoulder roll front
Shoulder stand		Roundoff dismount
Turns - full		
Squat ½ turn dismount		
Backward walking		

REVIEW	DEMONSTRATE	ATTEMPT
Uneven Bars	**Uneven Bars**	**Uneven Bars**
Double leg	Cast	Mount - Kip up
Stem rise	Back hip circle	Cast wrap
Mount - back pullover	Single leg stem rise	Front hip circle
Sole circle		Single leg shoot through
		Double leg stem rise
		Swing
		Back pullover from low
		to high bar
		Dismount - swinging
Parallel Bars	**Parallel Bars**	**Parallel Bars**
Hand walk	Mount	Mount single leg cut off
L-seat	Single leg cut-off	Cross support move
Straddle seat	Dismount front	Shoulder stand
Dismount flank		Inverted move
		Dismount
		Pommel Horse
		Mount
		On horse moves
		Leg circles
		Dismount
Rings	**Rings**	**Rings & Horizontal Bar**
Dismount	Bird's nest	Hang
Skin-the-cat		Support move (L-seat)
Inverted hang		Follow roll/hip circle
		Dismount swinging

Sample Assessment

The teacher could use checklists, scoring rubrics, rating scales, skill tests, verbal quizzes, and/or written tests to evaluate student progress in achieving competency in gymnastics. Samples of the various types of assessments listed above are provided in the appendix at the end of this document.

Standard 2:	Applies movement concepts and principles to the learning and development of motor skills.

Objective 2.1:   **Demonstrates competency in at least two self-selected gymnastic events.**

> Sample Assessment
> **Checklist : Straddle Vault**
> Criteria:
> - Approach and take off fluid   Yes   No
> - Take-off provides adequate height   Yes   No
> - Hips high   Yes   No
> - Head up   Yes   No
> - Legs straight, toes pointed   Yes   No
> - Sticks landing   Yes   No

Objective 2.2:   **Identifies skills that can be used in combination.**

> Sample Assessment
> **Scoring Rubric**
>
> Students create a basic floor routine from a list of tumbling skills provided by the teacher. A scoring rubric is used to assess performance.
> **Level 3:** Performance fluid; skills appropriately combined; over-all quality of performance above average.
> **Level 2:** Performance somewhat fluid; some skills appropriately combined; overall quality of performance average.
> **Level 1:** Performance not fluid; skills inappropriately combined; over-all quality of performance below average.

Objective 2.3:   **Identifies common performance errors for several gymnastics skills.**

Objective 2.4:   **Modifies gymnastics moves by using different leg and arm positions, as appropriate.**

Objective 2.5:   **Describes the relationships between center of gravity, line of gravity, and base of support for maintaining stability.**

Objective 2.6:   **Describes the relationship between radius of rotation and rotational velocity.**

Objective 2.7:   Identifies the importance of force absorption in landing.

Objective 2.8:   Describes the contribution of factors such as timing, flow, and line, to successful performance.

Objective 2.9:   Identifies skills that logically flow from one to another.

Objective 2.10:   Performs skills that represent a variety of speeds, heights, and directions.

Objective 2.11:   Identifies the relationship between body type and the selection/performance of gymnastics skills and events.

Objective 2.12:   Identifies the relationship of power, speed, muscular strength, and flexibility to the selection/performance of gymnastic skills and events.

Standard 4:	*Achieves and maintains a health-enhancing level of physical fitness.*

Objective 4.1:   Participates in drills and activities that develop flexibility, muscular strength/endurance, and power.

Objective 4.2:   Plans and implements a fitness program specific to the events s/he has selected to demonstrate.

Standard 5:	*Demonstrates responsible personal and social behavior in physical activity settings.*

Objective 5.1:   Discusses the safety guidelines of the United States Gymnastics Federation for participation in gymnastics activities.

Objective 5.2:   Adheres to the safety guidelines for each event.

Objective 5.3:   Identifies risk factors inherent to participation in gymnastic activities.

Objective 5.4:   Describes the role of warm-up, cool-down, and event-specific conditioning in prevention of injury.

Sample Assessment
Group Project
Students work in small groups to develop and demonstrate three (3) event-specific warm-ups or cool-downs.

168

Objective 5.5:   **Identifies the United States Gymnastics Federation System for scoring the events s/he has selected to demonstrate.**

Sample Assessment
Event Task
Students individually score videotaped performances in a competitive gymnastics event, and compare results with the scores given by USGF judges.

Objective 5.6:   **Plans and performs a routine, including a move from each required category, for the events s/he has selected to demonstrate.**

Standard 6:	*Demonstrates understanding and respect for differences among people in physical activity settings.*

Objective 6.1:   **Identifies the progress and accomplishments of peers.**

Standard 7:	*Understands that physical activity provides opportunities for enjoyment, challenge, self-expression, and social interaction.*

Objective 7.1:   **Identifies her/his potential in gymnastics.**

Objective 7.2:   **Identifies event preference in gymnastics.**

Objective 7.3:   **Participates in an in-class or school gymnastics demonstration.**

Objective 7.4:   **Attends a gymnastics meet.**

Modules and assessments contributed by:

> Gail Reiken
> Montclair, NJ
>
> Barbara Hemink
> Clarktown Senior High School

References:

Williams, A. (1987). Curriculum gymnastics: A teacher's guide to theory and practice. London: Hodder and Stoughton.

Wellness-Related Activity
Racquetball [A]

Standard 1:	*Demonstrates competency in many movement forms and proficiency in a few movement forms.*

Objective 1.1:   **Reviews, demonstrates, or attempts the following skills:**

REVIEW	DEMONSTRATE	ATTEMPT
Grips		
Forehand		
Backhand		
Strokes	**Strokes**	**Strokes**
Forehand	Forehand	Overhand drive
Backhand	Forehand off backwall	Volley
Volley	Backhand	Short hop
forehand	Backhand off backwall	Drop shot
backhand	Forehand ceiling ball	
	Backhand ceiling ball	
	Backwall shot	
	Serves	**Serves**
	Drive serve	Jam serve
	Lob serve	Angle lob
	Z serve	Wraparound serve
	Defensive skills	**Defensive skills**
	Pass shot return	Drive return
	Ceiling ball return	
	Court position	
	Offensive skills	**Offensive skills**
	Passing shots	Pinch shot
	Down the line	Around the world
	Cross court	
	Kill shot	

Sample Assessment

The teacher could use checklists, scoring rubrics, rating scales, skill tests, verbal quizzes, and/or written tests to evaluate student progress in achieving competency in racquetball. Samples of the various types of assessments listed above are provided in the appendix at the end of this document.

Objective 1.2:   Discusses with a student coach various strategies or shots to implement in a singles match.

Objective 1.3:   Identifies her/his level of skill in racquetball as a novice, D, or C classification.

Standard 2:	Applies movement concepts and principles to the learning and development of motor skills.

Objective 2.1:   Self-evaluates match play.

Sample Assessment Rating Scale : Match Play			
Criteria:	Always	Sometimes	Never
• Anticipates opponents shots	___	___	___
• Uses a variety of strokes and shot angles	___	___	___
• Moves to an appropriate covering position	___	___	___
• Uses more than one type of serve	___	___	___

Objective 2.2:   Self-evaluates two (2) of the following skills, using a checklist:

Forehand
Backhand
Ceiling ball

Sample Assessment Checklist : Forehand		
Criteria:		
• Early racquet preparation	Yes	No
• Side to front wall	Yes	No
• Contact with ball	Yes	No
• Able to hit ball off front foot	Yes	No
• Racquet face perpendicular to floor for the following shots:		
- shots off front wall	Yes	No
- shots off backwall	Yes	No
- angled shots	Yes	No
- kill shots	Yes	No

Standard 4:	Achieves and maintains a health-enhancing level of physical fitness.

Objective 4.1:   Participates in drills and matches that emphasize reaction time, agility, and explosive movements.

Objective 4.2:   Participates in drills and matches that require anaerobic fitness, flexibility, and endurance.

Objective 4.3:   Identifies the health-related fitness components required in racquetball.

Standard 5:	*Demonstrates responsible personal and social behavior in physical activity settings.*

Objective 5.1:   Identifies safety issues associated with the design of protective eye wear and tethers.

Objective 5.2:   Compares various types of hinders (court, avoidable, safety, hold-up, player hinders, screens, and contact hinders).

Sample Assessment Event Task
Students serve as an official or linesperson for a match.

Objective 5.3:   Identifies responsibilities of officials and lines people.

Objective 5.4:   Discusses the origins of racquetball.

Standard 6:	*Demonstrates understanding and respect for differences among people in physical activity settings.*

Objective 6.1:   Serves as a partner in drills which require cooperation in dropping, tossing, or hitting.

Objective 6.2:   Recognizes differences in ability when determining doubles teams.

Standard 7:	*Understands that physical activity provides opportunities for enjoyment, challenge, self-expression, and social interaction.*

Objective 7.1:   Plays racquetball outside of class.

Objective 7.2:   Participates in an intramural tournament.

SEE REFERENCES AT END OF LEVEL B

Wellness-Related Activity
Racquetball [B]

Standard 1:	*Demonstrates competency in many movement forms and proficiency in a few movement forms.*

Objective 1.1:   Reviews, demonstrates, or attempts the following skills:

REVIEW	DEMONSTRATE	ATTEMPT
Strokes	**Strokes**	**Strokes**
Forehand	Overhand drive	Overhand kill
Forehand off	Volley	
backwall	Short hop	
Backhand	Drop shot	
Backhand off		
backwall		
Forehand ceiling ball		
Backhand ceiling ball		
Backwall shot		
Serves	**Serves**	**Serves**
Drive serve	Jam serve	Backspin
Lob serve	Angle lob	Topspin
Z serve	Wraparound	
Defensive Skills	**Defensive Skills**	
Pass shot return	Drive return	
Ceiling ball return		
Court position		
Offensive Skills	**Offensive Skills**	**Offensive Skills**
Passing shots	Pinch shot	Splat
Down the line	Around the world	Z ball
Cross court		Jam shot
Kill shot		

Sample Assessment

The teacher could use checklists, scoring rubrics, rating scales, skill tests, verbal quizzes, and/or written tests to evaluate student progress in achieving proficiency in racquetball. Samples of the various types of assessments listed above are provided in the appendix at the end of this document.

Objective 1.2:   **Discusses with a partner when to use various types of shots or strategies in singles and doubles play.**

Standard 2:	*Applies movement concepts and principles to the learning and development of motor skills.*

Objective 2.1:   **Evaluates two (2) of the following skills for a peer, using a checklist:**

Overhand kill
Topspin serve
Z-ball

> Sample Assessment
> **Checklist : Overhand Kill**
> Criteria:
> * Racquet up, side to front wall   Yes   No
> * Nondominant hand extended
>   towards ball   Yes   No
> * Weight shift from back to front   Yes   No
> * Racquet face over the ball   Yes   No
>   at contact
> * Follow through to low target   Yes   No

Objective 2.2:   **Provides feedback to peers.**

> Sample Assessment
> **Peer Observation**
> Students mark a partner's serve placement on a court diagram.

Objective 2.3:   **Applies strategies during game play.**

> Sample Assessment
> **Event Task**
> Students coach a doubles team during a match and give pointers at time-outs and between games.

Standard 4:	*Achieves and maintains a health-enhancing level of physical fitness.*

Objective 4.1:   **Designs a program to improve a self-selected fitness component.**

Standard 5:	*Demonstrates responsible personal and social behavior in physical activity settings.*

Objective 5.1:   **Discusses special safety considerations for doubles and cut-throat play.**

Objective 5.2:   **Organizes and directs a class tournament.**

Objective 5.3:   **Describes modifications necessary for one-wall racquetball.**

Objective 5.4:   Sets goals to improve two (2) skills and charts her/his progress toward those goals.

Sample Assessment   **Student Log**   Students chart or record progress in achieving self-set goals. Personal level of skill is identified as C or B.

Standard 6:   *Demonstrates understanding and respect for differences among people in physical activity settings.*

Objective 6.1:   Investigates the rules for wheelchair racquetball.

Objective 6.2:   Modifies rules to participate with individuals of varying ability in games such as no serve or 2-bounce.

Standard 7:   *Understands that physical activity provides opportunities for enjoyment, challenge, self-expression, and social interaction.*

Objective 7.1:   Attends a professional match or open level match in a tournament.

Objective 7.2:   Participates in a local tournament.

Modules and Assessments contributed by:

> Lynn Couturier
> Springfield College

References:

Allsen, P. E. (1988). Racquetball. Dubuque, Iowa: W.C. Brown

Kittleson, S. (1992). Racquetball: Steps to success. Leisure Press.

Kittleson, S. (1994). Teaching racquetball: Steps to success. Champaign, IL: Human Kinetics Pub. Inc.

Turner, E. T. (1988). Skills & strategies for winning racquetball. Champaign, IL: Leisure Press.

Wellness-Related Activity
Tennis [A]

Standard 1:	*Demonstrates competency in many movement forms and proficiency in a few movement forms.*

Objective 1.1:   **Reviews, demonstrates, or attempts the following skills:**

REVIEW	DEMONSTRATE	ATTEMPT

Grips
   Forehand
   Backhand
   Serve		

Strokes
   Forehand
   Backhand
   Volley
      forehand & backhand
	Strokes
	   Lob
	   Overhead
	   Drop shot
		Strokes
		   Topspin
		      forehand & backhand

		Offensive Skills
		   Cross-court forehand & backhand
		   Down-the-line forehand & backhand
		   Approach shots
		   Serve & volley
		   Serve placement

	Defensive Skills
	   Return of serve
	   Return of lob
		Defensive Skills
		   Return of overhead

Serves
   Drop
	Serves
	   Flat
		Serves
		   Slice

Sample Assessment
The teacher could use checklists, scoring rubrics, rating scales, skill tests, verbal quizzes, and/or written tests to evaluate student progress in achieving competency in tennis. Samples of the various types of assessments listed above are provided in the appendix at the end of this document.

Standard 2:	*Applies movement concepts and principles to the learning and development of motor skills.*

Objective 2.1:   **Self-evaluates two (2) of the following skills using a checklist: serve, overhead, or lob.**

> ### Sample Assessment
> ### Checklist: Serve
> Criteria:
> - Toss high   Yes   No
> - Toss in front of body   Yes   No
> - Toss on dominant side   Yes   No
> - Weight shift from back
>   to front   Yes   No
> - Racquet arm extended on
>   contact   Yes   No
> - Follow through across body   Yes   No
> - Ball lands in proper service
>   box   Yes   No

Objective 2.2:   **Plans and implements a program of skill improvement based on her/his self-evaluation.**

> ### Sample Assessment
> ### Student Log
> Students warm up in activities that include 10 trials of a specified skill such as serve, volley, backhand, or the like. Students maintain a record of individual student success in each skill. For example, students chart progress in serving by recording the number of successful serves in 10 attempts for several warm-up sessions. Periodically, students submit a graph of their performance over time (Radford, K. W., Schincariol, L., Hughes, A. S. (1995). Enhance performance through assessment. Strategies, Mar./Apr., 5-9.).

Objective 2.3:   **Describes the relationship between point of application of force and ball spin.**

Objective 2.4:   **Describes the effect of changing the length of a 3rd class lever on striking skills.**

Objective 2.5:   **Identifies the importance of weight transfer in striking.**

Standard 4:	*Achieves and maintains a health-enhancing level of physical fitness.*

Objective 4.1:   **Participates in drills and games that require agility, rapid response time, anaerobic fitness, and muscular strength/endurance.**

177

Objective 4.2:   Identifies the fitness component(s) most lacking in her/his game.

Standard 5:	*Demonstrates responsible personal and social behavior in physical activity settings.*

Objective 5.1:   Maintains safe distances while using a racquet.

Objective 5.2:   Discusses the importance of inspecting equipment and playing surface.

Objective 5.3:   Engages in proper warm-up prior to play.

Objective 5.4:   Demonstrates knowledge of etiquette and the basic rules of tennis, including scoring of game, set, match, and tie-break.

> **Sample Assessment**
> **Video Analysis**
> Students view a videotape of a professional match during class time, and prepare written answers to questions regarding strategies and techniques observed, strengths and weaknesses of players, conduct of players and spectators, and scoring procedures.

Objective 5.5:   Officiates a singles or a doubles game for her/himself.

Standard 6:	*Demonstrates understanding and respect for differences among people in physical activity settings.*

Objective 6.1:   Engages in "cooperative tennis ball placement" with a partner.

Objective 6.2:   Modifies her/his play in practice situations to facilitate optimum learning of skills by an opponent.

Standard 7:	*Understands that physical activity provides opportunities for enjoyment, challenge, self-expression, and social interaction.*

Objective 7.1:   Attends a competitive tennis match.

Objective 7.2:   Identifies her/his potential in tennis.

Objective 7.3:   Plays tennis matches with friends outside of class.

SEE REFERENCES AT THE END OF LEVEL B

Wellness-Related Activity
Tennis [B]

Standard 1:	*Demonstrates competency in many movement forms and proficiency in a few movement forms.*

Objective 1.1:   Reviews, demonstrates, or attempts the following skills.

REVIEW	DEMONSTRATE	ATTEMPT
Strokes	**Strokes**	**Strokes**
Lob	Topspin forehand	Topspin backhand
Overhead		Backspin forehand &
Drop shot		backhand
		Topspin lob
	Offensive Skills	**Offensive Skills**
	Down-the-line forehand	½ volley
	Cross court fore & backhand	
	Approach shots	
	Serve & volley	
	Serve placement	
Defensive Skills		**Defensive Skills**
Return of serve		Return of overhead
Return of lob		
Serves	**Serves**	**Serves**
Flat	Slice	Topspin

Sample Assessment

The teacher could use checklists, scoring rubrics, rating scales, skill tests, verbal quizzes, and/or written tests to evaluate student progress in achieving proficiency in tennis. Samples of the various types of assessments listed above are provided in the appendix at the end of this document.

Standard 2:	Applies movement concepts and principles to the learning and development of motor skills.

Objective 2.1: Evaluates two (2) of the following skills for a peer, using a checklist:

Down-the-line forehand
Cross-court backhand
Serve

Sample Assessment
Checklist : Cross-court backhand
Criteria:
• Early racket preparation .... Yes   No
• Turns dominant side to net .... Yes   No
• Reaches for ball .... Yes   No
• Contacts ball ahead of body ..... Yes   No
• Follows through across body to ear level .... Yes   No
• Ball lands cross court .... Yes   No

Objective 2.2: Describes the relationships between ball spin, trajectory, and rebound.

Sample Assessment
Student Project
Students work in small groups to apply biomechanical principles to tennis, including spin, trajectory, levers, and limb velocity. Students demonstrate the application of principles and discuss appropriate situations for use in a game.

Objective 2.3: Describes the importance of ballistic movement in achieving maximum limb velocity and maximum transfer of force to an object.

Standard 4:	Achieves and maintains a health-enhancing level of physical fitness.

Objective 4.1: Plans and implements a program designed to maximize the fitness component most lacking in her/his game.

Standard 5:	Demonstrates responsible personal and social behavior in physical activity settings.

Objective 5.1: Creates a safety checklist for tennis.

Objective 5.2: Evaluates the level of safe play involved in a doubles' game.

Objective 5.3: Develops a conditioning program for injury prevention.

Objective 5.4:   Demonstrates appropriate tennis etiquette.

Objective 5.5:   Plans and implements an in-class tournament using an appropriate ranking and seeding system.

Objective 5.6:   Serves as a line or net judge for a doubles match.

Standard 6:	*Demonstrates understanding and respect for differences among people in physical activity settings.*

Objective 6.1:   Participates in a teaching session involving students with various handicapping conditions.

Objective 6.2:   Participates in doubles with partners of both greater and lesser ability.

Standard 7:	*Understands that physical activity provides opportunities for enjoyment, challenge, self-expression, and social interaction.*

Objective 7.1:   Participates in an intramural or recreational tennis program.

Student Assessment
Student Journal
Student records participation in tennis matches, including scores, perceptions of opponents' ability, and reflections about personal enjoyment and value of the experience.

Sample Assessment
Event Task
Students work in computer lab to obtain information from the Internet on topics such as Grand Slam winners, current player rankings, Davis cup competition, and/or new equipment and products. Students present a written and/or oral report of findings.

Module & Assessments contributed by:

Barbara Hemink
Clarkstown Senior High School

References:

Brown, J. (1989). <u>Tennis: Steps to success.</u> Champaign, IL: Leisure Press.

Brown, J. (1989). <u>Teaching tennis: Steps to success.</u> Champaign, IL: Leisure Press.

Clark, J. F. (1989). <u>Seven lifetime sports: A handbook for skill development.</u> Dubuque, Iowa: Eddie Bowers Pub. Co.

Gould, D. (1993). <u>Tennis anyone?</u> Mountain View, CA: Mayfield Pub. Co.

Wellness-Related Activity
Track and Field

Standard 1:	*Demonstrates competency in many movement forms and proficiency in a few movement forms.*

Objective 1.1:   **Reviews, demonstrates, or attempts the following skills:**

REVIEW	DEMONSTRATE	ATTEMPT
Running Events	**Running Events**	**Running Events**
Starts Standing	**Starts** Sprint Bunched Medium	**Starts** Elongated
Relays Sprint Visual exchange	**Relays** Sprint Verbal exchange	**Relays** Long distance or sprint Non-verbal exchange
Sprints 60m.	**Sprints** 100m. 200m.	**Sprints** 400m.
Hurdles "mini"	**Hurdles** low	**Hurdles** high
	Mid-Distance 800m.	**Mid-Distance** 1500m.
Distance	**Distance** 1600m.	**Distance** 3000m.

Jumping Events	**Jumping Events**
	Long Jump
	High Jump
	  scissor kick
	  straddle roll
		Jumping Events
		Triple Jump
		High Jump
		  Fosbury flop

Throwing Events	**Throwing Events** (select one) Shot put Discus	**Throwing Events** (select new) Shot put Discus

> **Sample Assessment**
> The teacher could use checklists, scoring rubrics, rating scales, skill tests, verbal quizzes, and/or written tests to evaluate student progress in achieving competency in track and field. Samples of the various types of assessments listed above are provided in the appendix at the end of this document.

Standard 2:	*Applies movement concepts and principles to the learning and development of motor skills.*

Objective 2.1:   **Evaluates two (2) of the following event skills for a peer using a checklist:**

Throwing Events	**Running Events**	**Jumping Events**
Grip	Start	Approach
Footwork	Arm action	Take-off
Release	Leg action	Flight
Follow through	Stride	Landing
	Pace	
	Finish	

> **Sample Assessment**
> **Checklist : Hurdling**
>
> Criteria:
> **Start:**
> * Eyes focused slightly ahead on "set"   Yes   No
> * First step & arm in opposition   Yes   No
> * Gradually rises to running form   Yes   No
>
> **Arm Action:**
> * Upper body relaxed while running   Yes   No
> * Lead leg and opposite arm extended
>   while hurdling   Yes   No
>
> **Leg Action:**
> * Trail leg "steps out" after lead leg lands   Yes   No
>
> **Stride:**
> * Same number of steps between hurdles   Yes   No

Objective 2.2:   **Identifies the various strategies used in distance running.**

Objective 2.3:   **Identifies the various strategies used in relay racing.**

Objective 2.4:   **Identifies common performance errors for specific events and techniques.**

Objective 2.5:   **Describes the relationships between timing, sequencing, and summation of forces in throwing.**

Objective 2.6:   Describes the importance of ballistic movement in achieving maximum limb velocity and maximum transfer of force to an object.

Objective 2.7:   Describes the relationships between center of gravity, line of gravity, and base of support in maintaining stability.

Objective 2.8:   Describes the relationship between radius of rotation and rotational velocity.

Objective 2.9:   Identifies the importance of force absorption in landing.

Objective 2.10:   Describes the contribution of factors such as timing, flow, and movement efficiency to successful performance.

Objective 2.11:   Identifies the relationship between body type and the selection/performance of track and field events.

Standard 4:	*Achieves and maintains a health-enhancing level of physical fitness.*

Objective 4.1:   Plans and implements a fitness program specific to the events s/he has selected to demonstrate.

Objective 4.2:   Participates in drills and activities that require speed, power, endurance, agility, balance, coordination, and rapid response time.

Objective 4.3:   Identifies the relationship between skill-related fitness attributes and success in specific track and field events.

Standard 5:	*Demonstrates responsible personal and social behavior in physical activity settings.*

Objective 5.1:   Describes the role of warm-up, cool-down, and event-specific conditioning in prevention of injury.

Objective 5.2:   Maintains safe distances while participating in the various events.

Objective 5.3:   Identifies rules, regulations, and scoring techniques for each event.

Objective 5.4:   Sets and meets individual short-term goals.

> **Sample Assessment**
> **Event Task**
> Students serve as an official during a peer's practice session for a specific event.

Standard 6:	*Demonstrates understanding and respect for differences among people in physical activity settings.*

Objective 6.1:   Participates in appropriate events and tasks for an in-class or inter-class track and field meet.

> **Sample Assessment**
> **Group Project**
> Students work as a group to assign event participants, scorekeepers, lane judges, starters, timers, field judges, and coaches for an interclass track and field meet. All students must participate in at least one event and serve in one other capacity.

Standard 7:	*Understands that physical activity provides opportunities for enjoyment, challenge, self-expression, and social interaction.*

Objective 7.1:   Attends a local track and field meet.

> **Sample Assessment**
> **Student Journal**
> Students attend a track and field meet and record their reflections about "team" vs. "individual" sporting events. For example: Does track and field lend itself to both types of competition? Are the competitors out for themselves or the team? Is there a difference between individual and team sport? Does a "personal best" override the team outcome?

Module contributed:

         Keri Camarigg
         Northampton High School

References:

     Bowerman, W. J. (1991). <u>High performance training for track and field.</u> Champaign, IL: Leisure Press.

     Carr, G. A. (1991). <u>Fundamentals of track and field.</u> Champaign, IL: Leisure Press.

RECREATIONAL ACTIVITIES MODULES

Recommended Percentage of Program: 22%

Recommended Number of Modules: 8 (Any Combination of Levels A and B)

Note 1:   In some recreational activity modules, such as New Games, behavioral objectives are concentrated under Content Standards 5-7. In other recreational activity modules, such as Cross-Country Skiing, behavioral objectives focus more on development of competency or proficiency in specific motor skills.

Note: It is recommended that:

a.   modules in grades 9 and 10 be prescribed (teacher-selected) for all students
b.   modules in grades 11 and 12 be elective (student-selected) within required activity categories
c.   modules not be repeated by an individual student

Wellness-Related Activity
Floor Hockey

Standard 1:	*Demonstrates competency in many movement forms and proficiency in a few movement forms.*

Objective 1.1:   Reviews, demonstrates, or attempts the following skills:

REVIEW	DEMONSTRATE	ATTEMPT
	Stick Handling	
	Grip	
	Dominant hand dribble	
	Non-domin. hand dribble	
	Speed/direction control	
	Stop puck	
	Passing	
	Push	
	Slap	
	Drive	
	Flick/scoop	
	Shooting	**Shooting**
	Wrist	Backhand
	Slap	Flick
	Offensive Skills	
	Spacing	
	Give & go	
	Follow shot	
	Screen	
	Pick	
	Fake/Dodge	
	Face-off	
	Defensive Skills	
	Clearing	
	Covering	
	Backing up	
	Player to player	
	Zone	

REVIEW	DEMONSTRATE	ATTEMPT
	Goalie Skills	
	Positioning	
	Stick control	
	Catching	
	Clearing	
	Covering the puck	

Sample Assessment

The teacher could use checklists, scoring rubrics, rating scales, skill tests, verbal quizzes, and/or written tests to evaluate student progress in achieving competency in floor hockey. Samples of the various types of assessments listed above are provided in the appendix at the end of this document.

Objective 1.2:   **Describes and demonstrates basic strategies of game play.**

Sample Assessment
Peer Observation

Students work in partners. One member of the pair observes the play of the partner. The observer records the number of picks, fakes, dodges, and clears that are utilized in a game situation. The student observer informs the partner of the data collected. The students then reverse roles and repeat the process.

Standard 2:	*Applies movement concepts and principles to the learning and development of motor skills.*

Objective 2.1:   **Evaluates the following skills for a peer, using a checklist: dribble, push pass, slap shot, and drive.**

Sample Assessment
Checklist: Slap shot

Criteria:

• Wide grip	Yes	No
• Backswing to waist height	Yes	No
• Weight-shift to non-dominant foot	Yes	No
• Dominant arm extended at contact	Yes	No
• Follow through to waist height	Yes	No

Objective 2.2:   Describes the effect of changing the length of a third class lever on striking skills.

Objective 2.3:   Identifies the importance of weight transfer in striking.

Objective 2.4:   Identifies the importance of force absorption in receiving an object.

Objective 2.5:   Describes and demonstrates the principles for reducing the angles for various shots on goal while playing goalie.

Objective 2.6:   Identifies the importance of fluidity, creativity, and spatial awareness in the game.

Standard 4:	*Achieves and maintains a health-enhancing level of physical fitness.*

Objective 4.1:   Participates in activities and games that will develop speed, agility, and hand-eye coordination.

Objective 4.2:   Participates in activities and games that require anaerobic fitness.

Standard 5:	*Demonstrates responsible personal and social behavior in physical activity settings.*

Objective 5.1:   Identifies safety equipment and its proper use.

> Sample Assessment
> **Group Project**
> Students work in small groups to identify safety factors that are pertinent to game play. The list is put in poster form and displayed in the gymnasium area where instruction takes place. One poster is reviewed prior to each instructional period.

Objective 5.2:   Discusses the impact of rough play and fouls on personal injury.

Objective 5.3:   Sets penalties for rules infractions and rough play.

Objective 5.4:   Discusses the importance of teamwork and cooperation to successful participation in the game.

Objective 5.5:   Officiates, interprets rules, and imposes penalties for students in a game situation.

Standard 6:	*Demonstrates understanding and respect for differences among people in physical activity settings.*

> **Sample Assessment**
> **Event Task**
> Students serve as captains for an intraclass team and make decisions regarding lineup, positions, and length of participation time of their teammates.

Objective 6.1:   Develops plays and patterns to utilize individual and team talents.

Objective 6.2:   Modifies rules to ensure participation of all students including those with special needs.

Objective 6.3:   Participates in drills and games with students of varying abilities.

Objective 6.4:   Maintains equal playing time for members of a team.

Standard 7:	*Understands that physical activity provides opportunities for enjoyment, challenge, self-expression, and social interaction.*

Objective 7.1:   Identifies her/his potential and personal goals in floor hockey.

Module & Assessments contributed by:
Marlene Kelly
Anne Arundel County Schools

References:

Calgary Board for Health and Physical Education Curriculum Action Project. (1980). Floor hockey-type games. Canada: Canadian association for health, physical education and recreation.

Wellness-Related Activity
Mountain Biking

Standard 1:	*Demonstrates competency in many movement forms and proficiency in a few movement forms.*

Objective 1.1:   Demonstrates appropriate handling techniques for the following skills: cornering, jumping/hopping, descending, ascending, braking/stopping.

> Sample Assessment
> **Rating Scale: Cornering**
> Criteria:
> 3 = Cranks horizontal, leans into turn, accelerates out of the turn
> 2 = Cranks not horizontal, brakes through turn
> 1 = Touches down in turn

Objective 1.2:   Maintains correct body and hand positioning during bike rides of varying lengths/difficulties.

Objective 1.3:   Demonstrates appropriate shifting sequences for varying terrain.

Standard 2:	*Applies movement concepts and principles to the learning and development of motor skills.*

Objective 2.1:   Evaluates her/his body position and balance while riding and modifies positioning when appropriate.

Objective 2.2:   Uses a checklist to evaluate the position of a peer riding on a short section of trail.

Objective 2.3:   Describes the relationships between center of gravity, line of gravity, and base of support in maintaining stability.

Objective 2.4:   Identifies the reciprocal effects of centripetal and centrifugal forces.

> Student Assessment
> **Checklist: Body Position**
> Criteria:
> **Level Position**
> • Body balanced and relaxed, anticipates obstacle   Yes   No
> **Downhill Position**
> • Pedals level, weight off saddle, elbows and knees loose   Yes   No
> **Climbing Position**
> • Bent forward at hip, back straight, buttocks back on saddle   Yes   No

192

Objective 2.5:   Identifies and describes the function of each mechanical component of a mountain bike.

Standard 4:	*Achieves and maintains a health-enhancing level of physical fitness.*

Objective 4.1:   Plans and implements a fitness program to increase upper and lower body strength/endurance.

Objective 4.2:   Plans and implements a program to increase anaerobic and aerobic fitness.

Standard 5:	*Demonstrates responsible personal and social behavior in physical activity settings.*

Objective 5.1:   Demonstrates safe bike-riding techniques.

Objective 5.2:   Identifies the necessary equipment for safe participation in mountain biking.

Objective 5.3:   Completes a bike safety check.

Objective 5.4:   Obeys all trail riding rules and etiquette.

> Sample Assessment
> **Checklist: Safety Check**
> Criteria:
> • Correct tire pressure   Yes   No
> • Shifts smoothly   Yes   No
> • Front and rear brakes
>   engage properly   Yes   No
> • Helmets fastened
>   properly   Yes   No

> Sample Assessment
> **Group Project**
> Students design and produce a safety and
> etiquette poster to hang in the meeting area.

Objective 5.5:   Yields to hikers and equestrians during trail riding.

Objective 5.6:   Demonstrates the following environmentally appropriate trail-riding techniques:

> Riding on the outside edge of the trail
> Portage on brooks and streams

Standard 6:	*Demonstrates understanding and respect for differences among people in physical activity settings.*

Objective 6.1:   Evaluates strengths and weaknesses of a team of riders and assigns each to a portion of a trail.

Standard 7:	*Understands that physical activity provides opportunities for enjoyment, challenge, self-expression, and social interaction.*

Objective 7.1: Demonstrates creative ways to maneuver over/around obstacles encountered during trail rides.

Objective 7.2: Identifies her/his level of potential in mountain biking.

Objective 7.3: Participates in mountain biking outside of class.

> **Student Assessment**
> **Student Log**
> Students record the date, time, and length of trail rides over a period of three (3) weeks.

Module and Assessments contributed by:

Bob Acorsi
Springfield College

Steveda Chepko
Springfield College

Strickland, B. (ed.) (1996). Mountain Biking Skills. Emmaus, PA: Rodale Press.

Wellness-Related Activity
New Games

Standard 1:	*Demonstrates competency in many movement forms and proficiency in a few movement forms.*

Objective 1.1:   **Participates in activities that require the use of non-traditional styles of throwing, catching, and striking.**

Objective 1.2:   **Participates in traditional activities using unique equipment and modified rules.**

Standard 2:	*Applies movement concepts and principles to the learning and development of motor skills.*

Objective 2.1:   **Defines and describes the difference between product and process.**

Objective 2.2:   **Compares the outcome of non-traditional and traditional styles of throwing, catching, and striking for self or a peer.**

Standard 4:	*Achieves and maintains a health-enhancing level of physical fitness.*

Objective 4.1:   **Participates in new games that require agility, balance, and flexibility.**

Objective 4.2:   **Participates in new games that require muscular strength/endurance.**

Standard 5:	*Demonstrates responsible personal and social behavior in physical activity settings.*

Objective 5.1:   **Identifies the key elements of successful group processing:**
Listening Skills
Offering Ideas
Cooperation
Trust
Risk Taking (Positive)
Shared Leadership

Objective 5.2:   **Identifies "roadblocks" to group processing:**
Poor attitude
Lack of risk taking
Lack of communication

195

Objective 5.3:   Reflects on her/his behavior and how this behavior impacts on the group.

Objective 5.4:   Evaluates the attitude of the group during various activities.

Objective 5.5:   Participates in group problem-solving activities that require cooperation and creativity.

Sample Assessment
Scoring Rubric
Students work in small groups to demonstrate as many solutions as possible for each activity.
Criteria:
Level 4: more than 2 solutions, all members actively involved.
Level 3: 2 solutions, all involved
Level 2: 1 solution, many but not all involved
Level 1: "copies" other group's solutions

Sample Activities:
5.5a: Moonball
5.5b: Group Juggle
5.5c: Warp Speed
5.5d: Trolley's
5.5e: Bridges

Objective 5.6:   Identifies key elements of a supportive environment:

Warm (positive) Feedback
Help Others
Lack of Peer Pressure
Acceptance of Individual Differences

Objective 5.7:   Sets operating procedures for the group to establish physical and psychological safety.

Objective 5.8:   Discusses the positive effect of a supportive environment on group participation.

Objective 5.9:   Evaluates her/his participation level during various activities.

Sample Assessment
Rating Scale: Participation
Criteria:
4 = participates fully
3 = participates with encouragement
2 = participates with great reservation
1 = no participation

Objective 5.10:   Explores various strategies for solving movement problems and evaluates the potential effectiveness of the proposed solutions.

Objective 5.11:   Acknowledges the existence of more than one effective solution for various movement problems.

Objective 5.12:   Participates in activities that require combining others' ideas in reaching the best strategy for solving a movement problem.

Objective 5.13:   Identifies the numerous roles that individuals play within the group process.

Objective 5.14:   Identifies contributions s/he makes to the group in order to successfully complete tasks, compete in an appropriate manner, or effectively function as a team member.

Objective 5.15:   Participates in activities that offer physical and psychological risks within a safe environment.

Objective 5.16:   Participates in setting group goals and attempts to help the group meet these goals.

Objective 5.17:   Integrates elements of effective group processing into experiences outside of the classroom.

> Sample Assessment
> **Student Journal**
> Students record participation in, results of, and feelings about group processing in every day life.

Standard 6:	*Demonstrates understanding and respect for differences among people in physical activity settings.*

Objective 6.1:   Demonstrates knowledge of the names of group members.

Sample Activities:
        6.1a: Peeka Who
        6.1b: Group Juggle
        6.1c: Adjective or Action Name Game

Objective 6.2:   Demonstrates behaviors that reflect a concern for fair play:

Involving others in the activity
Self-monitoring of violations of the rules
Resolving conflicts in an appropriate manner.

Objective 6.3:   **Attempts to give warm (positive) and cool feedback to others in the group.**

Sample Assessment
Checklist: Feedback
Criteria:
- Comments are confined to
  issues of group processing   Yes   No
- Criticism is constructive   Yes   No
- Effective contributions are
  reinforced   Yes   No
- Comments are distributed
  among group members   Yes   No

Objective 6.4:   **Cooperates with others in small and large group activities to achieve a common goal.**

Sample Activities:
6.4a:	Hog Call
6.4b:	Moonball
6.4c:	Warp Speed
6.4d:	Speed Rabbit
6.4e:	Other beginner level initiatives

Objective 6.5:   **Creates a caring environment for all members in the group.**

Objective 6.6:   **Analyzes and makes use of the physical, social, and psychological strengths and weaknesses of individual members of the group.**

Objective 6.7:   **Attempts to solve movement problems based on the strengths and weaknesses of group members.**

Sample Assessment
Peer Observation
Students create a checklist of skills/abilities needed for successful completion of several movement problems. Students assess the abilities of members of the group using the checklist, and assign appropriate roles to each member of the group for each of the movement problems.

Standard 7:	*Understands that physical activity provides opportunities for enjoyment, challenge, self-expression, and social interaction.*

Objective 7.1:   **Participates in self-testing activities.**

Objective 7.2:   **Participates in activities that require her/him to "trust" others and for others to "trust" her/him.**

Sample Activities:
7.2a:	Everybody's Up
7.2b:	Back to Back
7.2c:	Two Person Trust Fall
7.2d:	Three Person Trust Fall
7.2e:	Willow in the Wind
7.2f:	Levitation
7.2g:	Cookie Machine/Car Wash
7.2h:	Trust Fall from a Height

Objective 7.3:   **Expresses her/his needs based on self-evaluation of participation in various activities.**

Objective 7.4:   **Participates in individual problem-solving activities that require unique and creative movement solutions.**

Sample Activities:
7.4a:	Tension Traverse
7.4b:	Swinging Tires
7.4c:	Catwalk
7.4d:	Criss Crotch
7.4e:	Low Two Line Bridge
7.4f:	Hour Glass
7.4g:	Tag Games with Creative Movement

Objective 7.5:   **Discusses elements of play that make activities fun and exciting for everyone.**

Objective 7.6:   **Sets various individual challenges and attempts to meet these challenges.**

Objective 7.7: **Reports her/his reflections on participation in activities requiring physical and psychological risks.**

> **Sample Assessment**
> **Student Journal**
> Students establish two (2) long-term goals. Goals may be physical, social, or psychological in nature. Students reflect on individual progress in the form of journal entries.

Objective 7.8: **Participates in recreational programs outside of the classroom.**

Module contributed by:

Ted France
Springfield College

References:

Fluegelman, A. (1981). More new games. Englewood Cliffs, NJ: Prentice-Hall.

Fluegelman, A. (1976). The new games book. Garden City, NY: Doubleday.

Orlick, T. (1982). The second comparative sports and games book. New York: Pantheon/Random.

Rohnke, K. (1981). Silver bullets: A guide to initiative problems, adventure games, and trust activities. Hamilton, MA: Project Adventure.

Rohnke, K. (1989). Cowstails and cobras II: A guide to games, initiatives, ropes courses, and adventure curriculum. Dubuque, IA: Kendall/Hunt.

Wellness-Related Activity
Orienteering [A]

Standard 1:	*Demonstrates competency in many movement forms and proficiency in a few movement forms.*

Objective 1.1:   **Reviews, demonstrates, or attempts the following skills:**

REVIEW	DEMONSTRATE	ATTEMPT
Map Skills	**Map Skills**	**Map Skills**
Identify and locate symbols on a simple map (hand drawn without features of elevation)	Identify and locate symbols on a topographical map	Prepare a map for an orienteering activity
Orient a simple map of a given area	Orient a topographical map of the terrain in a given area	Transfer master map controls to a personal map
Orient a street map of a given area	Correctly classify (5 D's) symbols on a topographical map	
Place control points correctly on a map after finding them in a given area	Describe the features of a given area, using the symbols of a topographical map	
	Locate a map section on a larger topographical map, based on a description of the section	
	Calculate the elevation of different points on a topographical map	
Compass Skills		
Identify the parts of an orienteering compass		
Place the names of the cardinal and intercardinal points on a compass rose		
Adjust the compass housing to reflect specific compass bearings		
Identify the bearing of a previously-adjusted compass		

REVIEW	DEMONSTRATE	ATTEMPT
Identify specific objects at given bearings Take and relate/identify bearings to specific objects (intercardinal/degree), standing at a designated spot(s)		
Pacing and Measuring Measure distances on a map Estimate a distance walked, using the concept of pacing Convert simple distances to be traveled into personal pace steps		**Pacing and Measuring** Identify how changes in terrain and degree of steepness affect accuracy when pacing
Orienteering Draw a diagram on graph paper, given cardinal directions and simple distances List the appropriate cardinal directions and simple distances in order for another student to correctly replicate the diagram Identify and use control markers, cards, and control punches	**Orienteering** Grid a simple map according to the declination of the compass Identify compass, map, true, magnetic, and grid north Use a back reading (azimuth) to circumvent an obstacle Apply map reading in the field Use triangulation to locate position on a single map Run and/or walk an orienteering course while map reading by thumb	**Orienteering** Place given compass readings and distances on a topographical map Take compass readings and distances from a topographical map Select the best route to an objective and identify the handrails, catching features, points for aiming, and attack points to be used (cunning running) Identify escape routes for each orienteering exercise or competition area

Sample Assessment

The teacher could use checklists, scoring rubrics, rating scales, verbal quizzes, and/or written tests to evaluate student progress in achieving competency in orienteering. Samples of the various types of assessments listed above are provided in the appendix at the end of this document.

Objective 1.2:   Discusses the pros and cons of a selected route.

Objective 1.3:   Participates in activities such as Silver Dollar Hunt, Three-legged Compass Walk, Compass Competition, Mini-Orienteering Walk, Star Orienteering, and Clover Leaf Orienteering.

Standard 2:	*Applies movement concepts and principles to the learning and development of motor skills.*

Objective 2.1:   Identifies areas of personal difficulty in orienteering skills.

Objective 2.2:   Identifies and evaluates alternate detours for various orienteering courses.

> Sample Activity
> **Event Task**
> Students compare two (2) detours to a target destination relative to length, steepness, obstacles, and estimated time to traverse.

Standard 4:	*Achieves and maintains a health-enhancing level of physical fitness.*

Objective 4.1:   Participates in orienteering courses of various lengths/difficulties that require aerobic and/or anaerobic fitness.

Objective 4.2:   Identifies the relationship between higher levels of personal fitness and speed during participation in orienteering race activities.

Standard 5:	*Demonstrates responsible personal and social behavior in physical activity settings.*

Objective 5.1:   Identifies potentially dangerous obstructions and features shown on a map.

> Sample Activity
> **Event Task**
> Students compile a "pack list" of items to be taken on a specific course.

Objective 5.2:   Selects appropriate clothing for participation in orienteering activities.

Objective 5.3:   Identifies appropriate articles that increase safety and ease of participation in orienteering activities.

Objective 5.4:   Demonstrates respect for private property and responsibility in use of the environment during map and compass activities.

Standard 6:	Demonstrates understanding and respect for differences among people in physical activity settings.

Objective 6.1: Identifies appropriate orienteering exercises for individuals of various age/experience levels.

Standard 7:	Understands that physical activity provides opportunities for enjoyment, challenge, self-expression, and social interaction.

Objective 7.1: Identifies her/his potential in orienteering.

Objective 7.2: Applies map and compass skills to other recreational pursuits.

> Sample Activity
> **Student Project**
> Students plan, organize, and implement an appropriate "Family Outing" requiring map and compass skills.

SEE REFERENCES AT END OF LEVEL B

Wellness-Related Activity
Orienteering [B]

Standard 1:	*Demonstrates competency in many movement forms and proficiency in a few movement forms.*

Objective 1.1:   **Reviews, demonstrates, or attempts the following skills:**

REVIEW	DEMONSTRATE	ATTEMPT
Map Skills	**Map Skills**	
Identify and locate symbols on a topographical map	Prepare a map for an orienteering activity	
Orient a topographical map of the terrain in a given area	Transfer master map controls to a personal map	
Correctly classify (5 D's) symbols on a topographical map		
Describe the features of a given area, using the symbols of a topographical map		
Locate a map section on a larger topographical map, based on a description of the section		
Calculate the elevation of different points on a topographical map		
	Pacing and Measuring	
	Identify how changes in terrain and degree of steepness affect accuracy when pacing	
Orienteering	**Orienteering**	
Grid a simple map according to the declination of the compass	Place given compass readings and distances on a topographical map	
Identify compass, map, true, magnetic, and grid north	Take compass readings and distances from a topographical map	
Use a back reading (azimuth) to circumvent an obstacle	Select the best route to an objective and identify the handrails, catching features, points for aiming,	
Apply map reading in the field	and attack points to be used	

REVIEW	DEMONSTRATE	ATTEMPT
Use triangulation to locate position on a single map Run and/or walk an orienteering course while map reading by thumb	Identify escape routes for each orienteering exercise or competition	

Sample Assessment

The teacher could use checklists, scoring rubrics, rating scales, verbal quizzes, and/or written tests to evaluate student progress in achieving proficiency in orienteering. Samples of the various types of assessments listed above are provided in the appendix at the end of this document.

Objective 1.2:   Discusses the pros and cons of a selected route.

Objective 1.3:   Participates in activities such as: Line Orienteering, Route Orienteering, Project Orienteering, Score Orienteering, and an Orienteering Race.

Standard 2:	Applies movement concepts and principles to the learning and development of motor skills.

Objective 2.1:   Identifies areas of difficulty for a peer.

Sample Activity
Checklist: Orienteering Skills

Criteria:

- Places compass reading on a topographical map correctly   Yes   No
- Reads distances on a topographical map correctly   Yes   No
- Identifies effective escape routes for an exercise   Yes   No

Standard 4:	Achieves and maintains a health-enhancing level of physical fitness.

Objective 4.1:   Identifies the aerobic and anaerobic demands of participation in orienteering activities.

Objective 4.2:   Plans and implements a program of aerobic and anaerobic fitness.

Standard 5:	Demonstrates responsible personal and social behavior in physical activity settings.

Objective 5.1:   Identifies escape routes for each orienteering exercise or competition area.

Objective 5.2:   Transfers marked danger areas from a master map to a personal map.

Objective 5.3:   Adjusts speed to conditions of weather and terrain.

Objective 5.4:   Demonstrates respect for wildlife and vegetation.

Objective 5.5:   Demonstrates respect for private property and responsibility in use of the environment during map and compass activities.

Sample Assessment
Checklist: Respect for Environment
Criteria:
- Carries out litter   Yes   No
- Shows consideration for wildlife   Yes   No
- Shows consideration for vegetation   Yes   No

Standard 6:	Demonstrates understanding and respect for differences among people in physical activity settings.

Objective 6.1:   Complies with the orienteering Code of Conduct.

Objective 6.2:   Creates an orienteering exercise for individuals with various handicapping conditions.

Standard 7:	Understands that physical activity provides opportunities for enjoyment, challenge, self-expression, and social interaction.

Objective 7.1:   Creates alternative solutions to orienteering problems.

Objective 7.2:   Attempts to achieve her/his potential in orienteering.

Objective 7.3:   **Participates in recreational activities requiring orienteering skills.**

> **Sample Activity**
> **Student Report**
> Students attend a lecture by a park ranger or environmentalist on wilderness safety and write a summary of the presentation.

Modules and Assessments contributed by:

Mary Ellen Evans
Castleton State College

Willie Cerauskis
Swanton Elementary and
Executive Secretary VAHPER

Ree Arnold
Montclair State University

References:

Blomberg, I. (1984). It's easy to find your way. Clifton Hill, Australia: Orienteering service of Australia.

Disley, J. (1973). Orienteering. Harrisbury, PA: Stackpole Books.

Gilchrist, J. (1975). Teaching Orienteering. Willowdale, Canada: Orienteering Services.

Kjellstrom, D. (1976). Be an expert with map and compass: The complete "orienteering" handbook. New York, NY: Charles Scribner's Sons.

Orienteering Service of Australia. (1986). Lesson plan - orienteering. Clifton Hill, Australia: Orienteering Service of Australia.

Tonkin, G. (1984). Lesson plans - maps and navigation. Clifton Hill, Australia: Orienteering service of Australia.

TEAM SPORTS MODULES

Recommended Percentage of Program: 17%

Recommended Number of Modules: 4 Level A
2 Level B

Note: It is recommended that:

a.   modules in grades 9 and 10 be prescribed (teacher-selected) for all students
b.   modules in grades 11 and 12 be elective (student-selected) within required activity categories
c.   modules not be repeated by an individial student

Wellness-Related Activity
Basketball [A]

Standard 1:	*Demonstrates competency in many movement forms and proficiency in a few movement forms.*

Objective 1.1:   Reviews, demonstrates, or attempts the following skills:

REVIEW	DEMONSTRATE	ATTEMPT
Dribbling	**Dribbling**	**Dribbling**
Speed	Change of pace	Behind the back
Dominant & Non-dominant	Crossover	Between the legs
	Spin	
Passing	**Passing**	**Passing**
Chest	Overhead	Baseball
Bounce	Flip	Behind the back
	Outlet	
Shooting	**Shooting**	**Shooting**
Layup dominant	Layup non-dominant	Reverse layup
Set	Jump	Baby hook
	Offensive Skills	**Offensive Skills**
	Give & go	Pick & roll
	Front door cut	Double screen
	Back door cut	Combining 2 or more
	Jab step	offensive
	Screen	movements in a
	Pick	sequence
	Fakes	Rebound - ball up
		and shoot
	Defensive Skills	**Defensive Skills**
	Player to player	Denial player to
	Boxing out	player
	Rebound - outlet pass	Match-up zone
	Zone principles	

Sample Assessment
The teacher could use checklists, scoring rubrics, rating scales, skill tests, verbal quizzes and/or written tests to evaluate student progress in achieving competency in basketball. Samples of the various types of assessments listed above are provided in the appendix at the end of this document.

Standard 2:	Applies movement concepts and principles to the learning and development of motor skills.

Objective 2.1:   Self-evaluates two (2) of the following skills using a checklist: jump shot, foul shot, and/or layup.

Objective 2.2:   **Plans a program of skill improvement based on her/his self-evaluation.**

> Sample Assessment
> **Scoring Rubric**
> The teacher uses a scoring rubric to assess the student's self-evaluation. Examples of teacher scoring rubrics are in Appendix A.

Objective 2.3:   **Describes the relationship between point of application of force and ball spin.**

Objective 2.4:   **Identifies movement patterns that exhibit optimal temporal sequences, range, and force.**

Objective 2.5:   **Serves as a coach for classmates during 3 on 3 play.**

Standard 4:	Achieves and maintains a health-enhancing level of physical fitness.

Objective 4.1:   **Participates in drills and modified games that require agility, speed, and quick response time.**

Objective 4.2:   **Participates in drills and modified games that require anaerobic fitness.**

Standard 5:	Demonstrates responsible personal and social behavior in physical activity settings.

Objective 5.1:   **Identifies the most common injuries in basketball and plans a program of prevention.**

Objective 5.2:   **Discusses the risks factors involved with intentional fouls.**

Objective 5.3:   **Creates guidelines for safe 3 on 3 play.**

Objective 5.4:   **Self-officiates 2 on 2 and/or 3 on 3 games.**

Objective 5.5:   **Identifies the duties and responsibilities of each official.**

Standard 6:	Demonstrates understanding and respect for differences among people in physical activity settings.

Objective 6.1:   Modifies rules to ensure parity in 3 on 3 play.

Objective 6.2:   Participates in at least one game in which various handicapping conditions are stimulated.

Objective 6.3:   Supports teammates during practice and game play.

> **Sample Assessment**
> **Teacher Observation**
> The teacher uses an anecedotal record to assess the extent to which students support teammates during practice.

Objective 6.4:   Discusses the effects of "trash talking" on teammates and opponents.

Standard 7:	Understands that physical activity provides opportunities for enjoyment, challenge, self-expression, and social interaction.

Objective 7.1:   Participates in intramural or pick-up games outside of class.

Objective 7.2:   Identifies her/his level of potential in basketball.

SEE REFERENCES AT THE END OF LEVEL B

Wellness-Related Activity
Basketball [B]

Standard 1:	*Demonstrates competency in many movement forms and proficiency in a few movement forms.*

Objective 1.1:   Reviews, demonstrates, or attempts the following skills:

REVIEW	DEMONSTRATE	ATTEMPT
Dribbling	**Dribbling**	**Dribbling**
Change of pace	Behind the back	Between the legs
Crossover		
Spin		
Passing	**Passing**	**Passing**
Overhead	Baseball	Behind the back bounce
Flip	Behind the back	
Outlet		
Shooting	**Shooting**	**Shooting**
Layup non-dominant	Reverse layup	Baby hook
Jump		
Offensive Skills	**Offensive Skills**	**Offensive Skills**
Give & go	Pick & roll	Motion offense
Front door cut	Double screen	
Back door cut	Combining 2 or more offensive	
Jab step	movements in a sequence	
Screen	Rebound - ball up and shoot	
Pick		
Fakes		
Defensive Skills	**Defensive Skills**	**Defensive Skills**
Boxing out	Denial player to player	Zone press
Player to player	Match-up zone	Trapping
Zone principles		
Rebound - outlet pass		

Sample Assessment
The teacher could use checklists, scoring rubrics, rating scales, skill tests, verbal quizzes and/or written tests to evaluate student progress in achieving proficiency in basketball. Samples of the various types of assessments listed above are provided in the appendix at the end of this document.

Standard 2:	Applies movement concepts and principles to the learning and development of motor skills.

Objective 2.1:   Evaluates two (2) of the following skills for a peer using a checklist: jump shot, foul shot, reverse layup, and/or baby hook.

Objective 2.2:   Evaluates the offensive and defensive play of her/his team.

Objective 2.3:   Describes the relationship between ball spin, trajectory, and rebound.

Standard 4:	Achieves and maintains a health-enhancing level of physical fitness.

Objective 4.1:   Plans a program to maximize her/his agility, speed, and response time.

Objective 4.2:   Plans a program designed to improve anaerobic fitness.

Standard 5:	Demonstrates responsible personal and social behavior in physical activity settings.

Objective 5.1:   Plans an injury prevention program for her/his youth sport team.

Objective 5.2:   Modifies rules to lower the physiological and psychological risk factors in youth sport play.

Objective 5.3:   Serves as a coach for a youth league team.

Objective 5.4:   Identifies overuse injuries associated with youth sport play.

> **Sample Assessment**
> **Interview**
> Students interview a parent, a medical doctor, or athletic trainer to identify incidences and causation of injury to youth sport participants.

Objective 5.5:   Officiates full court 5 on 5 games in class or during intramural play.

> **Sample Assessment**
> **Written Test**
> Students complete a sample officiating test in basketball.

Standard 6:	*Demonstrates understanding and respect for differences among people in physical activity settings.*

Objective 6.1:   Includes all players on her/his team in drills, scrimmages, and games.

Objective 6.2:   Maintains a rotation on her/his youth sport team that gives all players equal playing time.

Objective 6.3:   Discusses with her/his team issues of diversity and differences in sport.

Standard 7:	*Understands that physical activity provides opportunities for enjoyment, challenge, self-expression, and social interaction.*

Objective 7.1:   Participates in organized play through a recreational league or school team.

Objective 7.2:   Attempts to achieve her/his potential in basketball.

Sample Assessment
Portfolio
Students prepare a written self-evaluation of current skill level and individual goals, and chart daily practice/play performance on major basketball skills. Materials are maintained in students' portfolios.

Modules and Assessments contributed by:

Stevie Chepko
Springfield College

References:

Philip, J. A. & Wilkerson, J.D. (1990). Teaching team sports: A coeducational approach. Human Kinetics: Champaign, IL.

Summit-Head, P. & Jennings, D. (1991). Basketball. Wm C. Brown Publishers.

Wissel, H. (1994). Steps for success: Basketball. Human Kinetics: Champaign, IL.

Wellness-Related Activity
Lacrosse [A]

Standard 1:	*Demonstrates competency in many movement forms and proficiency in a few movement forms.*

Objective 1.1:   Reviews, demonstrates, or attempts the following skills:

REVIEW	DEMONSTRATE	ATTEMPT
	Throwing	**Throwing**
	Overarm	Sidearm
	Underarm	Non-dominant overarm
	Catching	**Catching**
	Straight-on	High
	Strong Side	Low
	Backhand	Non-dominant hand
	Cradling	**Cradling**
	Protected	Change of level
	Strong side	Non-dominant hand
	Backhand	Switch between dominant & non-dominant
	Scooping	
	Ball rolling towards	
	Ball rolling away	
	Shooting	**Shooting**
	Overarm	Non-dominant hand
	Underarm	High reverse
		Rising
		Sidearm
Offensive Skills	**Offensive Skills**	**Offensive Skills**
Stutter step	V-cut	Head, body, & stick fake
Give & Go	Pivot	Pick & roll
Front door cut	Scissor cut	Sealing off a defender
Back door cut	Roll the crease	
	Defensive Skills	**Defensive Skills**
	Player to player	Double teaming
	Communication	Crease defense
	Player down	Denial defense

> **Sample Assessment**
> The teacher could use checklists, scoring rubrics, rating scales, verbal quizzes and/or written tests to evaluate student progress in achieving competency in lacrosse. Samples of the various types of assessments listed above are provided in the appendix at the end of the document.

Standard 2:	*Applies movement concepts and principles to the learning and development of motor skills.*

Objective 2.1: Self-evaluates two (2) of the following skills using a checklist: cradling, throwing, and/or ground ball pickups.

> Sample Assessment
> **Scoring Rubric**
> The teacher uses a scoring rubric to assess student's achievement of the self-evaluation objective. Examples of teacher scoring rubrics are in Appendix A.

Objective 2.2: Plans a program of skill improvement based on her/his self-evaluation.

Objective 2.3: Describes the effect of changing the length of a 3rd class lever on throwing skills.

Objective 2.4: Identifies the importance of weight transfer in throwing.

Objective 2.5: Identifies the importance of force absorption in receiving an object.

Standard 4:	*Achieves and maintains a health-enhancing level of physical fitness.*

Objective 4.1: Participates in drills and modified games that require agility, speed, and explosive movement.

Objective 4.2: Participates in drills and modified games that require anaerobic fitness.

Standard 5:	*Demonstrates responsible personal and social behavior in physical activity settings.*

Objective 5.1: Discusses the safety issues associated with the design of protective equipment for men's and women's lacrosse.

Objective 5.2: Creates guidelines for safe 6 on 6 play.

Objective 5.3: Identifies the risk factors that have been reduced by the modification of rules for coed lacrosse.

Objective 5.4: Discusses examples of dangerous use of the stick and possible ramifications.

Objective 5.5:   Self-officiates 2 on 2 and/or 3 on 3 games.

Objective 5.6:   Identifies the responsibilities and basic signals of the officials.

Objective 5.7:   Identifies at least five differences between the men's and women's game of lacrosse.

Standard 6: *Demonstrates understanding and respect for differences among people in physical activity settings.*

Objective 6.1:   Recognizes the cultural origins of lacrosse as a game developed and played by native peoples.

Sample Assessment   **Written Report**   Students investigate and report on one of the following aspects of the heritage of lacrosse: - significance of the game to native peoples   - original name of the game, origin of the name "la crosse"   - how the game was played and became established in the U.S.

Objective 6.2:
Maintains a rotation system for her/his team to ensure equal playing time for all members.

Objective 6.3:   Is supportive of teammates in game play and drills.

Standard 7: *Understands that physical activity provided opportunities for enjoyment, challenge, self-expression, and social interaction.*

Objective 7.1:   Participates in intramural or recreational play outside of class.

SEE REFERENCES AT THE END OF LEVEL B

Wellness-Related
Lacrosse [B]

Standard 1:	*Demonstrates competency in many movement forms and proficiency in a few movement forms.*

Objective 1.1:   Reviews, demonstrates, or attempts the following skills:

REVIEW	DEMONSTRATE	ATTEMPT
Throwing	**Throwing**	
Overarm	Sidearm	
Underarm	Non-dominant overarm	
Catching	**Catching**	
Straight-on	High	
Strong Side	Low	
Backhand	Non-dominant hand	
Cradling	**Cradling**	
Protected	Change of level	
Strong side	Non-dominant hand	
Backhand	Switch between dominant & non-dominant	
Scooping		
Ball rolling towards		
Ball rolling away		
Shooting	**Shooting**	
Overarm	Non-dominant hand	
Underarm	High reverse	
	Rising	
	Sidearm	
Offensive Skills	**Offensive Skills**	**Offensive Skills**
V-cut	Head, body, & stick fakes	Fast break
Pivot	Sealing off a defender	Pick & roll
Scissor Cut	Combination of 2 or more moves	
Roll the crease		
Defensive Skills	**Defensive Skills**	
Player to player	Double teaming	
Communication	Crease defense	
Player down	Denial defense	

> **Sample Assessment**
> The teacher could use checklists, scoring rubrics, rating scales, verbal quizzes and/or written tests to evaluate student progress in achieving proficiency in lacrosse. Samples of the various types of assessments listed above are provided in the appendix at the end of this document.

Standard 2:	Applies movement concepts and principles to the learning and development of motor skills.

Objective 2.1: Evaluates two (2) of the following skills for a peer using a checklist: cradling, throwing, and/or ground ball pickups.

> **Sample Assessment**
> **Checklist: Teacher Observation**
> The teacher uses a checklist to assess student's achievement of the evaluation objective. Examples of teacher checklists are included in Appendix A.

Objective 2.2: Evaluates the play of her/his team (6 on 6) and, at half-time, makes recommendations and modifications for second half.

Objective 2.3: Describes the relationships between timing, sequencing, and summation of forces in throwing.

Objective 2.4: Describes the importance of ballistic movement in achieving maximum limb velocity and maximum transfer of force to an object.

Objective 2.5: Describes centrifugal and centripetal forces as they apply to the skill of cradling.

Standard 4:	Achieves and maintains a health-enhancing level of physical fitness.

Objective 4.1: Designs a program to maximize her/his agility, speed, and explosive movements.

> **Sample Assessment**
> **Student Report**
> Students submit a written report of a personal fitness program. Criteria for assessment of the report include accuracy of analysis of fitness status, application of principles of training, and appropriateness of program.

Objective 4.2: Designs a program to improve cardiovascular endurance.

Standard 5:	Demonstrates responsible personal and social behavior in physical activity settings.

Objective 5.1:   Discusses appropriate modifications in equipment and rules for youth sport play.

Objective 5.2:   Identifies common injuries associated with lacrosse and possible prevention techniques.

Objective 5.3:   Develops appropriate warm-up and cool-down activities for lacrosse.

Objective 5.4:   Works as a volunteer at a youth sport clinic or tournament or serves as an assistant coach for a youth sport team.

> **Sample Assessment**
> **Student Journal**
> Students record the frequency and nature of volunteer participation in youth sports, as well as, feelings and reflections about happenings and results.

Objective 5.5:   Officiates 3 on 3 games.

Standard 6:	Demonstrates understanding and respect for differences among people in physical activity settings.

Objective 6.1:   Modifies a 6 on 6 game to ensure that all participants will be able to compete successfully.

Standard 7:	Understands that physical activity provides opportunities for enjoyment, challenge, self-expression, and social interaction.

Objective 7.1:   Identifies her/his level of potential in lacrosse.

Objective 7.2:   Participates in organized play through intramurals, summer leagues, summer camps, or school teams.

> **Sample Assessment**
> **Student Log**
> Students record the frequency and nature of out-of-class participation in lacrosse.

Modules and Assessments contributed by:

Lynn Couturier
Springfield College

References:

Green, T. S. & Kurtz, A. B. (1989). Modern women's lacrosse. Hanover, NH: ADB Publications.

USWLA. (1992). Women's lacrosse coaching manual - Level 1. Hamilton, NY: USWLA.

Wellness-Related Activity
Soccer [A]

Standard 1:	*Demonstrates competency in many movement forms and proficiency in a few movement forms.*

Objective 1.1:   **Reviews, demonstrates, or attempts the following skills:**

REVIEW	DEMONSTRATE	ATTEMPT
Passing	**Passing** Outside of foot Chip	**Passing**
Receive/Prepare Ground balls outside of foot	**Receive/Prepare**	**Receive/Prepare**
Bouncing balls outside of foot chest	Bouncing balls inside of foot ½ volley	Bouncing balls outside of foot ½ volley
Flighted balls instep		Flighted balls outside of foot inside of foot ½ volley chest
Dribbling Combinations	**Dribbling** Moves/Feints/Fakes	**Dribbling**
Shooting/Instep Moving off a dribble	**Shooting/Instep**	**Shooting/Instep**
	Heading Stationary	**Heading** Jump

Sample Assessment
The teacher could use checklists, scoring rubrics, rating scales, skill tests, verbal quizzes and/or written tests to evaluate student progress in achieving competency in soccer. Samples of the various types of assessments listed above are provided in the appendix at the end of this document.

Objective 1.2:   Reviews, demonstrates or attempts the following goalie skills:

REVIEW	DEMONSTRATE	ATTEMPT
Ground Balls Moving forward/back/side	**Ground Balls**	**Ground Balls**
Catch/Bounce Stationary	**Catch/Bounce** Moving forward/back/side	**Catch/Flighted** Moving forward/back/side
Redirect	**Redirect**	**Redirect** Parry
Distribution Windmill throw	**Distribution**	**Distribution** Drop Kick

Objective 1.3:   Identifies the reasons for utilizing as much of the available space on a field as possible in a game.

Objective 1.4:   Describes the purpose of width and depth as strategy in soccer.

Objective 1.5:   Discusses the pattern of movement used in both types of diagonal runs as well as the penetrating run.

Standard 2:	*Applies movement concepts and principles to the learning and development of motor skills.*

Objective 2.1:   Self-evaluates three (3) of the following skills using a checklist: inside of the foot pass, instep pass, outside of the foot pass, and/or chip pass.

Objective 2.2:   Describes the relationship between point of application of force and resultant ball spin.

Objective 2.3:   Provides corrective feedback to participants in 4 on 1 and 3 on 1 drills.

Sample Assessment
Checklist: Feedback
Criteria:
* Correctly identifies most important performance error   Yes   No
* Provides appropriate correction for identified error   Yes   No
* Provides feedback in an appropriate manner   Yes   No

Objective 2.4:   Identifies the importance of weight transfer in kicking.

224

Objective 2.5:   Identifies the importance of force absorption in receiving an object.

Standard 4:	*Achieves and maintains a health-enhancing level of physical fitness.*

Objective 4.1:   Participates in drills, activities, and modified games that require strength, agility, flexibility, and speed.

Objective 4.2:   Participates in drills, activities, and modified games that require both aerobic and anaerobic fitness.

Standard 5:	*Demonstrates responsible personal and social behavior in physical activity settings.*

Objective 5.1:   Identifies risk factors associated with body contact in soccer.

Objective 5.2:   Identifies risk factors associated with the ball being kicked or redirected.

Definition
Identifies
Implies that the teacher will have students do such things as design bulletin boards, list, and/or verbally respond to questions about issues such as risk factors associated with playing soccer.

Objective 5.3:   Identifies risk factors associated with the potential of coming in contact with the goal.

Objective 5.4:   Identifies risk factors associated with dangerous play in and around the goal and the possible ramifications.

Objective 5.5:   Discusses the safety issues associated with the design of protective equipment for the lower leg.

Objective 5.6:   Self-officiates 1 on 1 play.

Objective 5.7:   Officiates 2 on 2 games played by peers.

Sample Assessment
Checklist: Officiating
Criteria:
- Maintains proper positioning   Yes   No
- Correctly calls violations   Yes   No
- Correctly calls fouls   Yes   No
- Properly aligns teams for penalty kicks   Yes   No
- Properly aligns team for corner kicks   Yes   No
- Maintains control of the game   Yes   No

225

Objective 5.8:   Recognizes the two common systems of officiating in soccer.

Objective 5.9:   Creates scoring systems for modified games that reward the use of specific skills.

Standard 6:	*Demonstrates understanding and respect for differences among people in physical activity settings.*

Objective 6.1:   Discusses reasons for the worldwide popularity of soccer.

Objective 6.2:   Identifies the importance of parity in ensuring quality play.

Objective 6.3:   Participates in at least one game in which various handicapping conditions are simulated.

Objective 6.4:   Provides encouragement and positive feedback to classmates in drills, activities, and games.

Standard 7:	*Understands that physical activity provides opportunities for enjoyment, challenge, self-expression, and social interaction.*

Objective 7.1:   Identifies her/his level of potential in soccer.

Objective 7.2:   Participates in intramural or recreational games outside of class.

> **Sample Assessment**
> **Student Log**
> Students record the frequency and nature of out-of-class participation in soccer.

REFERENCES AT THE END OF LEVEL B

Wellness-Related Activity
Soccer [B]

Standard 1:	*Demonstrates competency in many movement forms and proficiency in a few movement forms.*

Objective 1.1:   Reviews, demonstrates, or attempts the following skills:

REVIEW	DEMONSTRATE	ATTEMPT
Passing Outside of foot Chip	**Passing**	**Passing**
Receive/Prepare Bouncing balls inside of foot 1/2 volley	**Receive/Prepare** Bouncing balls outside of the foot Flighted balls outside of the foot inside of the foot chest	**Receive/Prepare** Bouncing balls outside of foot 1/2 volley Flighted balls 1/2 volley
Dribbling Moves/Feints/Fakes	**Dribbling**	**Dribbling**
Shooting/Instep Moving Off a dribble	**Shooting/Instep**	**Shooting/Instep**
Heading Stationary	**Heading** Jump	**Heading**

Sample Assessment
The teacher could use checklists, scoring rubrics, rating scales, skill tests, verbal quizzes and/or written tests to evaluate student progress in achieving proficiency in soccer. Samples of the various types of assessments listed above are provided in the appendix at the end of this document.

Objective 1.2:   Reviews, demonstrates or attempts the following goalie skills:

REVIEW	DEMONSTRATE	ATTEMPT
Catch/Bounce Moving forward/back/side	**Catch/Flighted** Moving forward/back/side	**Catch/Flighted**
Redirect	**Redirect** Parry	**Redirect** Box
Distribution	**Distribution** Drop kick	**Distribution**

Standard 2:	*Applies movement concepts and principles to the learning and development of motor skills.*

Objective 2.1:   Evaluates three (3) of the following skills for a peer, using a checklist: inside of the foot pass, instep pass, outside of the foot pass, and/or inside of the foot ½ volley reception.

Objective 2.2:   Describes the relationship between timing, sequencing, and summation of forces in kicking.

Objective 2.3:   Identifies offensive skills/concepts during game play.

> **Sample Assessment**
> **Student Observation**
> Students observe an in-class game and a) discuss the success or failure of each team in using open space, and b) identify diagonal or penetrating runs.
> Students should be provided with a rating scale to facilitate their observations.

Standard 4:	*Achieves and maintains a health-enhancing level of physical fitness.*

Objective 4.1:   Plans and implements a program to improve her/his strength, agility, flexibility, and speed.

Objective 4.2:   Plans and implements a program to improve her/his aerobic and anaerobic fitness levels.

Standard 5:	*Demonstrates responsible personal and social behavior in physical activity settings.*

Objective 5.1:   Identifies the most common injuries associated with soccer and plan an injury-prevention program for a youth soccer team.

Objective 5.2:   Develops and implements an appropriate warm-up and cool-down program for her/his personal use.

Objective 5.3:   Develops appropriate rule modifications for small-sided games to decrease risk factors.

Sample Assessment Checklist: Game Modification		
Criteria:		
• Modification is appropriate for skill level	Yes	No
• Modification reduces contact in game	Yes	No
• Modification maintains essential elements of the game	Yes	No
• Modification requires all individuals to actively participate	Yes	No

Objective 5.4:   Identifies differences and similarities in the two systems of officiating.

Objective 5.5:   Identifies hand signals used in officiating.

Standard 6:	*Demonstrates understanding and respect for differences among people in physical activity settings.*

Objective 6.1:   Discusses the social and emotional significance of the World Cup to countries of the world.

Objective 6.2:   Plans and integrates modifications in rules that provide parity for modified and small-sided games.

Objective 6.3:   Adapts and modifies small-sided and modified games to meet individual and team differences.

Objective 6.4:   Modifies and adapts rules to ensure equal playing time for all players.

Standard 7:	*Understands that physical activity provides opportunities for enjoyment, challenge, self-expression, and social interaction.*

Objective 7.1:   Attempts to achieve her/his potential in soccer.

Objective 7.2:   Participates in organized play through recreational leagues, summer sports camps, or school teams.

Modules and Assessments contributed by:

Peter Haley
Springfield College

References:

Benedek, E., Palfai, E., & Palfai, J. (1978). 600 games for soccer training. Corvina.

Chyzowych, W. (1979). The official soccer book of the United States federation. Rand McNally

Coerver, W. (1986). Soccer fundamentals for players and coaches. Prentice Hall.

Lurbacher, J. A. (1991). Steps to success: Teaching soccer. Leisure Press.

Whitehead, N. & Cook, M. (1984). Games, drills and fitness practices for soccer coaching. A&C Black Publishers Limited.

Wellness-Related Activity
Slow Pitch Softball [A]

Standard 1:	*Demonstrates competency in many movement forms and proficiency in a few movement forms.*

Objective 1.1:   Reviews, demonstrates, or attempts the following skills.

REVIEW	DEMONSTRATE	ATTEMPT
Throwing	**Throwing**	**Throwing**
Underhand	Full to ¾ motion	Force plays
Overhand from infield	(short & long distance)	Tag Plays
Overhand from outfield	Sidearm	Cut-off
	Underhand feed	Double play feed
Catching	**Catching**	**Catching**
With glove	Above the waist	Deep fly ball
	Below the waist	Drop step left/right
	Backhand	Short fly ball
	Midline	(basket catch
		on the move)
Fielding	**Fielding**	**Fielding**
Ground ball	Ground ball	Ground ball
Fly balls	straight on	right/left
One hop		charge
Line drive		backhand
Hitting	**Hitting**	**Hitting**
Grip	Positioning	Pitched balls at
Stance	Stance	various
Pivot	open	trajectories &
Weight shift	closed	locations
Place hitting	squared	high/low
		in/outside
	Pitching	**Pitching**
	5' to 8' arc	6' to 12' arc
		Inside/outside of
		plate

REVIEW	DEMONSTRATE	ATTEMPT
Offensive Skills	**Offensive Skills** Baserunning Rocker step Tagging up Over running Rounding base	**Offensive Skills** Baserunning Figure 4 slide Bent leg slide

Defensive Skills	**Defensive Skills**
	Force Play
	Tag Play
		Defensive Skills
		Stretch to catch
		Blocking bag/ plate
		Backing up
		  outfield/bases/plate
		Double Play
		  footwork at 2nd

Sample Assessment

The teacher could use checklists, scoring rubrics, rating scales, skill tests, verbal quizzes and/or written tests to evaluate student progress in achieving competency in softball. Samples of the various types of assessments listed above are provided in the appendix at the end of this document.

Standard 2:	*Applies movement concepts and principles to the learning and development of motor skills.*

Objective 2.1:   Self-evaluates two (2) of the following skills using a checklist: throwing, catching, hitting, and/or fielding.

Sample Assessment
Video Analysis
Students self-evaluate skill performance from a video-tape.

Objective 2.2:   Plans and implements a program of skill improvement based on her/his self-evaluation.

Objective 2.3:   Identifies the importance of weight transfer in striking and throwing.

Objective 2.4:   Describes the relationship between point of application of force and ball spin.

Objective 2.5:   Describes the effect of changing the length of a 3rd class lever on throwing and striking skills.

Objective 2.6:   Analyzes the interaction of mass and angular velocity for optimal bat selection.

Standard 4:	Achieves and maintains a health-enhancing level of physical fitness.

Objective 4.1:   Participates in drills and modified games that require anaerobic fitness.

Objective 4.2:   Participates in drills and modified games that require muscular strength.

Standard 5:	Demonstrates responsible personal and social behavior in physical activity settings.

Objective 5.1:   Identifies the most common injuries in softball and plans a program of prevention.

Objective 5.2:   Creates guidelines for safe play and equipment.

Objective 5.3:   Maintains safe playing distances while hitting and throwing.

Objective 5.4:   Identifies the responsibilities, basic signals, and verbal calls of the umpire.

Sample Assessment Checklist: Umpiring		
Criteria:		
• Calls balls and strikes correctly	Yes	No
• Calls infield fly and dead ball when appropriate	Yes	No
• Maintains proper positioning in the field	Yes	No
• Calls "safe" and "out" correctly	Yes	No
• Demonstrates overall knowledge of the rules	Yes	No
• Uses proper hand signals	Yes	No

Objective 5.5:   Umpires behind the plate for two (2) innings and in the field for two (2) innings.

Objective 5.6:   Identifies four (4) differences between the games of slow pitch and fast pitch softball.

Objective 5.7:   Identifies two (2) modifications of rules for coed slow pitch softball.

Sample Assessment Event Task
Students score a slow pitch game in regulation score book.

233

Standard 6:	*Demonstrates understanding and respect for differences among people in physical activity settings.*

Objective 6.1:   Modifies rules to ensure parity during class play.

Objective 6.2:   Participates in at least one (1) game in which various handicapping conditions are simulated.

Objective 6.3:   Offers encouragement and positive feedback to teammates in game play and drills.

Standard 7:	*Understands that physical activity provided opportunities for enjoyment, challenge, self-expression, and social interaction.*

Objective 7.1:   Identifies her/his level of potential in softball.

Objective 7.2:   Participates in intramural or pick-up games outside of class.

SEE REFERENCES AT THE END OF LEVEL B

Wellness-Related Activity
Softball [B]

Standard 1:	*Demonstrates competency in many movements forms and proficiency in a few movement forms.*

Objective 1.2:   **Reviews, demonstrates, or attempts the following skills.**

REVIEW	DEMONSTRATE	ATTEMPT
Throwing Full to ¾ motion (short & long distance) Sidearm Underhand feed	**Throwing** Force play Tag Play Cut off Double play feed	**Throwing** Run down Relay
Catching Above the waist Below the waist Backhand Midline	**Catching** Deep fly ball Drop step left/right Short fly ball (basket catch on the move)	**Catching** Over the shoulder

Fielding
 Ground ball
  straight on
	Fielding
	 Ground ball
	  left/right
		Fielding
		 Ground ball
		  backhand
		  charge

Hitting
 Stance
  open
  closed
  squared
	Hitting
	 Pitched balls at various
	  trajectories and locations:
	   inside/outside
	   high/low
		Hitting
		 Pitched balls with spins

Pitching 5' to 8' arc	**Pitching** 6' to 12' arc In/outside plate	**Pitching** Various spins

REVIEW	DEMONSTRATE	ATTEMPT
Offensive Skills	**Offensive Skills**	**Offensive Skills**
Baserunning	Baserunning	Baserunning
Rocker step	Figure 4 slide	Pop-up slide
Tagging up	Bent leg slide	
Over running		
Rounding base		
Defensive Skills	**Defensive Skills**	**Defensive Skills**
Force Play	Stretch to catch	
Tag Play	Blocking bag/plate	
	Backing up outfield/bases/plate	
	Double Play - footwork at 2nd	

> **Sample Assessment**
>
> The teacher could use checklists, scoring rubrics, rating scales, skill tests, verbal quizzes and/or written tests to evaluate student progress in achieving proficiency in softball. Samples of the various types of assessments listed above are provided in the appendix at the end of this document.

Objective 1.2:   **Develops modified softball games designed to improve specific skills used in the game.**

Objective 1.3:   **Differentiates between the skills needed for slow pitch and fast pitch softball.**

Objective 1.4:   **Coaches three (3) innings of a game, evaluating and recommending modifications in the play of her/his team.**

> **Sample Assessment**
> **Checklist: Coaching**
>
> Criteria:
>
> | | | |
> |---|---|---|
> | • Exhibits knowledge of rules | Yes | No |
> | • Positions the fielders correctly | Yes | No |
> | • Directs base runners correctly | Yes | No |
> | • Prepares an effective lineup | Yes | No |
> | • Makes modifications based on skill level of players | Yes | No |

Standard 2:	Applies movement concepts and principles to the learning and development of motor skills.

Objective 2.1: Evaluates two (2) or more of the following skills for a peer, using a checklist: pitching, base running, and/or backing up the play.

Objective 2.2: Identifies activities to improve areas of skill deficiency.

Objective 2.3: Describes the relationships between timing, sequencing, and summation of forces in striking.

Sample Assessment
Student Project
Students design specific drills and practice conditions for a classmate, based on the evaluation of the classmate's skills.

Objective 2.4: Describes the importance of ballistic movement in achieving maximum limb velocity and maximum transfer of force to an object.

Standard 4:	Achieves and maintains a health-enhancing level of physical fitness.

Objective 4.1: Plans and implements a program designed to maximize agility, speed, upper body strength, and flexibility.

Objective 4.2: Plans and implements an anaerobic fitness program.

Standard 5:	Demonstrates responsible personal and social behavior in physical activity settings.

Objective 5.1: Identifies protocols for handling various injuries.

Objective 5.2: Develops pre-season and post-season fitness programs designed to prevent injuries.

Objective 5.3: Identifies overuse injuries associated with youth sport play.

Sample Assessment
Interview
Students interview a medical doctor, school nurse, or athletic trainer to identify common injuries in softball and appropriate treatment protocols.

Standard 6:	Demonstrates understanding and respect for differences among people in physical activity settings.

Objective 6.1: Participates with classmates of various abilities.

Objective 6.2: Implements practice conditions and game strategies to ensure equal playing time for all members of her/his team.

Standard 7:	*Understands that physical activity provides opportunities for enjoyment, challenge, self-expression, and social interaction.*

Objective 7.1:   Attempts to achieve her/his potential in softball.

Objective 7.2:   Participates in organized play through a recreational league or school team.

Modules and Assessments contributed by:

Lesley Wilson
Northhampton High School

Kathy Mangano
Springfield College

Diane Potter
Springfield College

Barabara Hemick
Clarkstown Senior High School

References:

Orlick, T. (1978). Winning through cooperation. Acropolis Books.

Potter, D. L. & Brockmeyer, G. A. (1989). Softball: Steps to success. Leisure Press.

Potter, D. L. & Brockmeyer, G. A. (1989). Teaching softball: Steps to success. Leisure Press.

Wellness-Related Activity
Volleyball [A]

Standard 1:	*Demonstrates competency in many movement forms and proficiency in a few movement forms.*

Objective 1.1:   Reviews, demonstrates, or attempts the following skills:

REVIEW	DEMONSTRATE	ATTEMPT
Serving Underhand	**Serving** Overhand floater	**Serving** Topspin
Ball Control Overhead Forearm pass	**Ball Control**	**Ball Control** Quick set Back set
Offensive Skills Creating topspin Dominant hand hit	**Offensive Skills** Down ball 4-2 system Modified 4-2 system	**Offensive Skills** Quick hit Tip shot Roll shot Non-dom. hand hit Back row attack skills 5-1 system 6-2 system
Defensive Block	**Defensive** Dig	**Defensive** Sprawl Cover

Sample Assessment
The teacher could use checklists, scoring rubrics, rating scales, skill tests, verbal quizzes and/or written test to evaluate student progress in achieving competency in volleyball. Samples of various types of assessments listed above are provided in the appendix at the end of this document.

Objective 1.2:   Demonstrates transition from "free ball" on offense.

Objective 1.3:   Identifies movement patterns in low, mid, and high zones.

Objective 1.4:   Identifies movement patterns that display tempo, speed, and power.

Objective 1.5:   Identifies one (1) basic defensive coverage and the responsibilities of each team member in that coverage.

Standard 2:	Applies movement concepts and principles to the learning and development of motor skills.

Objective 2.1:   Self-evaluates two (2) of the following skills using a checklist: set, forearm pass, and/or overhead serve.

Objective 2.2:   Evaluates the defensive play of a team and makes modifications based on this evaluation.

Objective 2.3:   Describes the relationship between the point of applications of force and ball spin.

Standard 4:	Achieves and maintains a health-enhancing level of physical fitness.

Objective 4.1:   Participates in drills and modified games that require speed, power, rapid response time, and agility.

Objective 4.2:   Participates in drills and modified games that require aerobic fitness.

Objective 4.3:   Identifies appropriate strength training activities for volleyball.

> **Sample Assessment**
> **Student Project**
> Students analyze specific strength requirements for volleyball and identify principles of training appropriate to strength improvement.

Objective 4.4   Identifies an appropriate warm-up program for volleyball.

Standard 5:	Demonstrates responsible personal and social behavior in physical activity.

Objective 5.1:   Exhibits exemplary social behavior during drills and games by making honor calls.

Objective 5.2:   Identifies the most common injuries in volleyball and plans a program of prevention.

Objective 5.3:   Identifies safety concerns in the volleyball facility.

> **Sample Assessment**
> Checklist: Self-officiating
> Criteria:
> * Calls net violations correctly   Yes No
> * Calls lines correctly Yes No
> * Calls illegal hits correctly   Yes No

Objective 5.4:   Self-officiates 3 on 3 games.

Objective 5.5:   Serves as a lines person for a 6 on 6 game.

Objective 5.6:   Identifies the duties of the 1st and 2nd referee.

Objective 5.7:   Identifies sanctions involved with yellow and red card violations.

Objective 5.8:   Serves as a coach for classmates during 6 on 6 play.

Standard 6:	Demonstrates understanding and respect for differences among people in physical activity settings.

Objective 6.1:   Modifies rules to ensure parity in 4 on 4 play.

Objective 6.2:   Offers encouragement and positive fedback to teammates in game play and drills.

Objective 6.3:   Participates in at least one game in which various handicapping conditions are simulated.

Objective 6.4:   Discusses etiquette in volleyball and the effects of "trash talking" on teammates and opponents.

> **Sample Assessment**
> **Role Playing**
> Students portray members of rival volleyball teams. They act out the situation in which members of one team continually exhibit poor etiquette, including "trash talking". Students summarize reactions to and perceptions of the situation.

Objective 6.5:   Discusses the topic of "honoring your opponent" as it relates to fair play.

Standard 7:	Understands that physical activity provides opportunities for enjoyment, challenge, self-expression, and social interaction.

Objective 7.1:   Attends a high school or Junior Olympic match.

Objective 7.2:   Plays reverse coed doubles.

SEE REFERENCES AT THE END OF LEVEL B

Wellness-Related Activity
Volleyball [B]

Standard 1:	Demonstrates competency in many movement forms and proficiency in a few movement forms.

Objective 1.1:   Reviews, demonstrates, or attempts the following skills:

REVIEW	DEMONSTRATE	ATTEMPT
Serving	**Serving**	**Serving**
Overhand floater	Topspin	Jump Serve
Ball Control	**Ball Control**	**Ball Control**
	Quick set	Jump set
	Back set	Covering attacker
Offensive Skills	**Offensive Skills**	**Offensive Skills**
Down ball	Quick hit	
4-2 system	Tip shot	
Modified 4-2 system	Roll shot	
	Back row attack skills	
	Non-dominant hand hit	
	5-1 system	
	6-2 system	
Defensive Skills	**Defensive Skills**	**Defensive Skills**
Dig	Sprawl	
	Cover	

Sample Assessment

The teacher could use checklists, scoring rubrics, rating scales, skill tests, verbal quizzes and/or written test to evaluate student progress in achieving proficiency in volleyball. Samples of various types of assessments listed above are provided in the appendix at the end of this document.

Objective 1.2:   Reviews "free ball" transition.

Objective 1.3:   Identifies the advantages/disadvantages of at least two (2) defensive coverages and the specific responsibilities of each tean member in the coverage.

Standard 2:	Applies movement concepts and principles to the learning and development of motor skills.

Objective 2.1:   Evaluates three (3) of the following skills for a peer, using a checklist:

Topspin serve	Back set
Quick set	Quick 1 hit
Block	Sprawl

Objective 2.2:   Describes the relationships between ball spin, trajectory, and rebound.

> **Sample Assessment**
> **Group Project**
> Students form groups of four (4) to demonstrate, assess, and record the relationships between ball spin, trajectory, and rebound of a spike. Students submit graphs of the results.

Standard 4:	Achieves and maintains a health-enhancing level of physical fitness.

Objective 4.1:   Plans and implements a program designed to maximize speed, power, rapid response time, and agility.

Objective 4.2:   Plans and implements an aerobic fitness and muscular strength program.

Standard 5:	Demonstrates responsible personal and social behavior in physical activity settings.

Objective 5.1:   Prepares a guide for a stretching program for her/his youth sport or class team.

> **Sample Assessment**
> **Student Project**
> Students pre-test a team for flexibility, administer a program of stretching, and post-test on flexibility. Results of the pre/post comparison are graphed and discussed.

Objective 5.2:   Reviews the most common injuries in volleyball and plans an injury prevention program for her/his youth sport team or class team.

Objective 5.3:   Prepares a risk management checksheet for the volleyball facility.

Objective 5.4:   Participates in a training clinic for officials and serves as a member of an officiating team for a playday.

Standard 6:	*Demonstrates understanding and respect for differences among people in physical activity settings.*

Objective 6.1:   Includes all players in drills, modified games, and scrimmages.

Objective 6.2:   Establishes a rotational order that provides equal playing time for all.

Objective 6.3:   Ensures that all players play each position during a competition.

Objective 6.4:   Discusses with her/his team issues of diversity and individual differences as they relate to volleyball.

Standard 7:	*Understands that physical activity provides opportunities for enjoyment, challenge, self-expression, and social interaction.*

Objective 7.1:   Attends a college or high school match.

Objective 7.2:   Participates in organized play through a school, Junior Olympics or recreational league.

Objective 7.3:   Attempts to achieve her/his potential in volleyball.

> **Sample Assessment**
> **Student Project**
> Students prepare an analysis of a volleyball match including a description of offensive and defensive systems, substitution, and use of specific ball control and defensive skills.

Modules and Assessments contributed by:

Joel Dearing
Springfield College

References:

Neville, W. (1994). Serve it up: Volleyball for life. Mountain View, CA: Mayfield Press.

Viera, B. L. & Ferguson, B. J. (1989). Teaching volleyball: Steps to success. Leisure Press.

Glossary

Analysis of Curricular Content (NASPE, 1995)

Content Standard: Specifies "what students should know and be able to do," as a result of a quality physical education program.

Performance Standard: Indicates the level of achievement students are expected to attain in the content standards.

Performance Benchmark: Describes behavior that indicates progress toward a performance standard.

Student Achievement

Attempt: Implies that the skill will be taught, but the student will not master or show competency in the skill.

Demonstrate: Implies that the student will demonstrate competency in the skill.

Explore: Implies that the student has demonstrated competency in the skill and will explore variations of the movement in dimensions such as speed, flow, or direction.

Review: Implies the continual review of the skill and serves as a developmental checkpoint.

Competency: Implies that the student has mastered the fundamental skills of the activity and can apply these skills in game situations or performances. Demonstrating competency includes using fundamental game strategies or applying skills to solve advanced movement problems.

Proficiency: Implies that the learner has mastered advanced skills of the activity and can adapt these skills in game situations or performances. Demonstrating proficiency will include using advanced game strategies, creating movement patterns, or creating unique combinations of movements.

Curricular Design

Module: A self-contained unit of content, based on 15 days of class participation.

Level A Module: An activity module designed to develop competency in a variety of dance forms, activities, and sports.

Level B Module: An activity module designed to develop proficiency in selected dance forms, activities, and sports.

Assessment of Student Achievement

Authentic Assessment :	Determines the extent to which students can use or apply skill, knowledge, or behavior in a real-world environment. Includes demonstration of mature movement patterns in a game, application of strategy during game play, using principles of fitness to plan a personal training program, and the like.
Pre-Assessment:	Occurs at the beginning of a unit of instruction or of a school year, and allows for the planning of appropriate developmental sequences.
Formative Assessment:	Occurs throughout a unit, and provides feedback to students and teachers.
Summative Assessment:	Occurs at the end of a unit of instruction or grading period, and measures the student's progress and level of achievement.
Developmental Assessment:	Requires students to perform fundamental movement skills (running, jumping, kicking, throwing, catching, and striking) to assess progress in achieving developmental movement skills.
Performance-Based Assessment:	Requires students to perform a specific skill to assess the technique used to perform the skill.
Checklist:	Specifies whether or not criteria for successful performance of an activity are met.
Rating Scale:	Specifies the extent to which, or frequency with which, criteria for successful performance of an activity are met.
Scoring Rubric:	Specifies multiple criteria for successful performance of an activity and generally includes progressive levels of achievement.
Event Task:	Specifies a performance task to be completed by students for which multiple possible solutions exist.
Student Log:	Record of student behaviors over a period of time.
Student Journal:	Record of student perceptions, reflections, or feelings about participation in physical activity.
Student Portfolio:	A collection of student-selected documaentation of progress in achieving a specific goal.
Peer Observation:	Provision of feedback on performance to a peer, based on criteria supplied by the teacher.

Appendix A
Examples of Assessment Tools

Examples of specific assessment tools for selected activities are presented in this Appendix. The examples illustrate some of the many valid and authentic techniques that can be used to evaluate the extent to which students have accomplished specific behavioral objectives. The examples are intended as reference information; additional or alternate assessment tools can and should be developed as appropriate for a particular program.

The examples include the following assessment tools:

Dance
    Scoring rubrics for student log and group project
    Portfolio

New Games
    Contract
    Icebreaker games
    Deinhibitizer games

Archery
    Parameters and environment
    Rating scale
    Group project

Golf
    Checklists - peer or self observation
    Rating scales - instructor assessment
    Event task
    Scoring Rubrics: Student Journal

Floor Hockey
    Scoring rubric for skill assessment
    Student observation: video analysis - officiating

Softball
    Skills test
    Written test
    Rating scale
    Checklist

Tennis
    Skills test

Racquetball
    Written test
    Student Projects

Badminton
    Rating scale

Lacrosse
    Rating scales
    Student project
    Event task

Motor Development
    Standardized tests

Dance

Sample Scoring Technique for Assessment Tasks/Projects:
- Checklist of completion/inclusion of various steps of the project
- Rating scales for level/quality of performance
- Scoring rubric which addresses multiple criteria and level/quality. Note: when at all possible involve students in the development of criteria and rubrics

Sample Assessment Techniques
- Peer/self-evaluations/observations
- Student/teacher interviews to determine understanding of subject matter
- Anecdotal references from teachers and peers
- Formal tests

Scoring Rubric: Student Log
4 =   student submitted a "validated" practice log, indicating over 15 hours of practice on skills and a completed action plan for improvement
3 =   student submitted a "validated" practice log, indicating between 8 to 14 hours of practice on skills and a completed action plan for improvement
2 =   student submitted a "validated" practice log, indicating between 3 to 7 hours of practice on skills and an incomplete action plan for improvement
1 =   student did not submit a practice log or practiced less than 2 hours

Scoring Rubric: Group Choreography Project
4 =   combination contained all five skills, all skills were skillfully performed, student performed the combination to music with a finished performance quality
3 =   combination contained all five skills, however only 3 to 4 skills were skillfully performed, student had an over-all performance quality
2 =   combination did not contain all five skills, skills were poorly performed and over-all performance lacked quality
1 =   student did not attempt task

Portfolio Items
- Student's practice log
- Video of finished "Chance Dance"
- Peer and self-evaluations of the finished dance
- Teacher evaluation using scoring rubric
- A personal action plan for improvement of skills
- Proof of dance class(es) taken within the community
- Anecdotal references from the teacher concerning the understanding of proper class procedure and etiquette

Assessments contributed by:
Susan McGreevy-Nichols
Roger Williams Middle School

248

New Games

Assessment for New Games and Adventure activities can easily be dealt with if the teacher uses what Project Adventure calls the "Full Value Contract." The "Full Value Contract" is a document, created by the teacher and the students, which sets the ground rules for participation and the creation of a safe learning environment. Within this document the teacher identifies her/his minimum expectation for student participation. The students then develop the contract based on this minimum expectation. It is important for the students to have knowledge of the basic premise of the unit goals and objectives. For example, if the overriding goals are affective domain social skills, the students should have quantifiable objectives to create the contract. Throughout the unit, the teacher should evaluate each student on their individual progress and compliance with the contract.

The teacher may choose to create behavior and performance goals based on the contract designed by the students and the goals of the curriculum. These social behavior goals will probably be defined in the curriculum, but it is important to involve the students in the process of creating the contract in their own words. It is the responsibility of the teacher to ask questions which allow the students to construct a contract that includes the goals of the curriculum.

Sample Assessment for Icebreaker Games

Icebreaker games allow the students to meet others in their group and to form identity within their work groups. The teacher uses icebreakers to build a foundation that allows students to create a safe play atmosphere. As one form of assessment for these activities, the teacher may choose to have students complete a profile sheet on the members of their group. The teacher may provide an outline for the profile which the students follow. The type of outline provided is dependent on which games were played as icebreakers and the information that the students share with one another. The teacher may create and modify games which allow the students to share the appropriate information. The following is an example of a profile sheet.

Name
Age
Number of sisters and brothers
Favorite sport or game
Favorite class in school
Favorite animal
Favorite meal
Favorite Olympic sport
What is the best part of Physical Education?

The teacher may evaluate the accuracy and quality of the individual profile sheet and the information that the students complete and give points for the number of well-documented profiles complied by the students.

As a follow-up assessment for profiling, each student can be assigned to complete a more detailed interview with a member of the group. The activity may be structured for the student as follows: You are a reporter for the local newspaper. Your assignment is to take the information which has been supplied on the information sheet and create more detailed questions for a personal interview. Once you have created these questions, find this person and interview her/him. Upon completing the interview, write a short biography about this person. The teacher may now assess the student's ability to create more detailed questions designed to learn more about group members.

Sample Assessments for Deinhibitizer Games

Deinhibitizers are games which are played after icebreaker games. The purpose of deinhibitizer games is to help students become more comfortable being physically active in front of others. Deinhibitizers are structured to have the games progress quickly to keep all students are active at the same time, and to reduce non-activity time to a minimum. Assessment involves identifying the extent to which a student is participating.

For example:
4 = full participation
3 = moderate participation
2 = meets minimum expectation for participation
1 = does not participating

In some situations, students choose not to be involved in the beginning, but as the games progress, the students who have self-selected out become more involved. The teacher must continually remind the student of the minimum level of participation, as stated in the Full Value Contract, while offering the opportunity to enter the game.

Assessments contributed by:
Ted France
Springfield College

Archery

Assessment Parameters and Environment

The following Peer Observation utilizes a rating scale to assess present level of performance. Precede this activity with a class that allows each student to review the rating scale for the skill components being evaluated. Additionally, a "practice" rating scale, perhaps somewhat shorter, can be used by the entire class to evaluate a single performer.

When the actual observation is conducted, students can work in pairs or larger groups, depending upon class size and equipment. For example, use one or more evaluators per performer at each of "x" number of targets. Performers will rotate to as many targets as time will allow for them to shoot 3 - 6 arrows per target. If there is more than one evaluator per target, position them such that the performer can be seen from as many angles as possible. The performers will "shoot-on-command", so that the evaluators have sufficient time to evaluate and record each of the rating scale components. A scorer should also be present to record the results of each arrow, including direction and height of arrows not reaching the target.

A follow-up lesson should be included to provide feedback to each performer. The fact that each performer had been rated at several different targets by different evaluators should provide reasonably complete, reliable results for feedback purposes. Grading for the evaluators can be assigned by using rubrics. For example:

4 =   All aspects of performance rated by all evaluators
      All students worked together to accomplish the desired task
      Final evaluation submitted
      Suggestions for improvement submitted

Archery
Rating Scale: Peer Observation

Shooter:_____   Date: _____

Evaluator/s:_____

	ALWAYS	SOMETIMES	NEVER
Stance			
Straddles shooting line	☐	☐	☐
Posture erect	☐	☐	☐
Side towards target	☐	☐	☐
Nock			
Cock feather points away from bow	☐	☐	☐
Arrow on proper side of bow	☐	☐	☐
Arrow straight from arrow rest to string	☐	☐	☐
Draw			
Bow hand relaxed	☐	☐	☐
Bow elbow straight and rotated downward	☐	☐	☐
Shoulders relaxed	☐	☐	☐
3 fingers - distal tips	☐	☐	☐
Drawing straight	☐	☐	☐
Elbow of string hand at shoulder	☐	☐	☐
Thumb and little finger of string hand relaxed and in palm	☐	☐	☐
Shoulders level	☐	☐	☐
Anchor			
String index finger along bottom of jaw	☐	☐	☐
Thumb "hooked" at back of jaw	☐	☐	☐
String touches nose and chin	☐	☐	☐
Mouth closed	☐	☐	☐
Aim			
Stops breathing	☐	☐	☐
Drawing elbow remains parallel to ground	☐	☐	☐
Bow arm moves right, left, up, or down-but position remains vertical	☐	☐	☐
Release			
Only fingers move - no "plucking" or "creeping"	☐	☐	☐
Head remains still	☐	☐	☐
Bow remains vertical	☐	☐	☐
Follow through			
Position held until arrow reaches target	☐	☐	☐

Archery
Final Evaluation
(to be done in conjunction with the shooter)

1. **Compare the analysis of technique to the actual results of the performance.**

2. **Which component/s of shooting seem to have the most adverse affect on the scores of the performance?**

3. **Which component/s of shooting seem to have the most positive affect on the scores of the performance.**

4. **List three (3) suggestions for improved performance.**

Assessments contributed by:
Barbara Hemink
Clarkstown Senior High School

Badminton
Rating Scale: Peer Observation

Skill: Singles Serve/Underhand Clear   Evaluator:_____

Performer:_____

Preparation Phase:	Very Good	Good	Fair	Poor
1. Grip	☐	☐	☐	☐
2. Movement to shuttle	☐	☐	☐	☐
3. Pivot-side to net	☐	☐	☐	☐
4. Weight back	☐	☐	☐	☐
5. Racket back/high	☐	☐	☐	☐

Execution Phase:				
6. Focus on shuttle	☐	☐	☐	☐
7. Step to target	☐	☐	☐	☐
8. Shift weight to front foot	☐	☐	☐	☐
9. Contact shuttle low	☐	☐	☐	☐
10. Wrist snap @ contact	☐	☐	☐	☐
11. Low-high swing path	☐	☐	☐	☐

Follow-through Phase:				
12. Weight on front foot	☐	☐	☐	☐
13. Racket finish high	☐	☐	☐	☐
14. Racket to target	☐	☐	☐	☐
15. Move to ready position	☐	☐	☐	☐

RESULTS:				
1. Serve has good height	☐	☐	☐	☐
2. Serve has good distance	☐	☐	☐	☐
3. Clear-good height (def.)	☐	☐	☐	☐
4. Clear-good distance (def.)	☐	☐	☐	☐
5. Clear-approriate height/ distance (off.)	☐	☐	☐	☐
6. Clear used strategically	☐	☐	☐	☐

Assessments contributed by:

Dr. Diane Potter
Springfield College

Golf
Level A Checklist: Peer of Self Observation

Golfer:_____   Date:_____

Evaluator:_____

Skill	Demonstrates	Does Not Demonstrate
Grips (grasping the golf club)		
Overlapping grip	☐	☐
Interlocking grip	☐	☐
Stances (addressing the golf ball)		
Square stance	☐	☐
Open stance	☐	☐
Closed stance	☐	☐
Golf Swings (swinging the golf club)		
Backswing, downswing, & follow through (full swing)	☐	☐
Swing plane	☐	☐
Weight shift	☐	☐
Timing and tempo	☐	☐
¼ swing (clockface, 5-7)	☐	☐
½ swing (clockface, 3-9)	☐	☐
Golf Strokes (hitting the golf ball)		
Putting (short)	☐	☐
Chip shot (¼ - ½ swing)	☐	☐
Chip shot (distance short to long)	☐	☐
Target	☐	☐
Fairway irons (full shot, ¾ swing)	☐	☐

Assessments contributed by: Doris E. Wooledge
Delaware State University

Golf
Level B Checklist: Peer or Self Observation

Golfer:_____   Date:_____

Evaluator:_____

Objectives: 1.1, 2.1

<u>Skill</u>	<u>Demonstrates</u>	<u>Does Not Demonstrate</u>
Golf Swings:		
Putting:		
Long with a break	❐	❐
Lag with a break	❐	❐
Full Swings with long irons:		
On fairway	❐	❐
In rough	❐	❐
Full swing with long irons, employing:		
Varying distances, including approach shots with a 7,8, or 9 iron	❐	❐
Various target sizes	❐	❐
Fullswing with various woods, including the #3 wood	❐	❐
Full swing with woods, employing:		
Various size targets	❐	❐
Varying distances	❐	❐
Assorted lies (uphill and downhill)	❐	❐

Assessments contributed by: Doris E. Wooledge
                                       Delaware State University

Golf
Level A Rating Scale: Instructor Assessment

Golfer:_____   Date:_____

Assessment Key:
3 = good
2 = average
1 = needs improvement

<u>SKILL</u>   <u>ASSESSMENT</u>   <u>COMMENTS</u>

Grips (grasping the golf club)
    Overlapping grip
    Interlocking grip

Stances (addressing the golf ball)
    Square stance
    Open stance
    Closed stance

Golf Swings (swinging the golf club)
    Backswing, downswing, &
      follow through (full swing)
    Swing plane
    Weight shift
    Timing and tempo
    ¼ swing (clockface, 5-7)
    ½ swing (clockface, 3-9)

Golf Strokes (hitting the golf ball)
    Putting (short)
    Chip shot (¼ - ½ swing)
    Chip shot (distance short to long)
    Target
    Fairway irons (full shot, ¾ swing)

Total Points (48 possible)

Assessments contributed by: Doris E. Wooledge
                                   Delaware State University

Golf
Level B Rating Scale: Instructor Assessment

Golfer:_____   Date:_____

Assessment Key:
3 = good
2 = average
1 = needs improvement

Objectives: 1.1, 2.1

<u>**SKILL**</u>   <u>**ASSESSMENT**</u>   <u>**COMMENTS**</u>

Golf Swings:
Putting:
      Long with a break
      Lag with a break

Full Swings with long irons:
      On fairway
      In rough

Full swing with long irons, employing:
      Varying distances, including approach
          shots with a 7,8, or 9 iron
      Various target sizes

Fullswing with various woods, including the
 #3 wood

Full swing with woods, employing:
      Various size targets
      Varying distances
      Assorted lies (uphill and downhill)

Total Points (30 possible)

Assessments contributed by: Doris E. Wooledge
                             Delaware State University

Golf
Level B Rating Scale: Instructor Assessment

Golfer:_____   Date:_____

Assessment Key:
3 = good
2 = average
1 = needs improvement

Advanced Skill	**Assessment**	**Comments**

Golf Swings:

Stance:

    Open - slice or fade with wood and
        long irons

    Closed - hook or pull with wood and
        long irons

    Side hill lies - feet above ball and feet
        below ball

Strokes:

    Deep rough shots

    Sand Traps:

        Sand trap explosions

        Sand trap chips

    Planned hook with wood

    Planned slice with wood

Total Points (30 possible)

Assessments contributed by: Doris E. Wooledge
                             Delaware State University

Golf
Event Task: Mechanical Analysis

Criteria and Assessment

Respond to the following mechanical analysis tasks. Your score depends upon the number of tasks that are correctly completed.

1. Describe the relationship between point of application of force and ball spin.

2. Demonstrate the relationship between point of application of force and ball spin.

3. Describe the effect of changing the length of a third class lever on striking the ball.

4. Demonstrate the effect of changing the length of a third class lever on striking the ball.

5. Identify movement patterns involved in a fundamental golf shot.

6. Demonstrate movement patterns involved in a fundamental golf shot.

7. List the consequences of poor body mechanics while striking a golf ball.

Level One: Exemplary 35 points (Correctly respond to all of the tasks)

Level Two: Good 30 points (Correctly respond to tasks 1, 2, 4, 5, 7, and 8)

Level Three: Average 20 points (Correctly respond to tasks 1, 3, 5, and 7)

Assessments contributed by: Doris E. Wooledge
                                      Delaware State University

Golf

Scoring Rubric: Student Journal

Golfer: _____   Date: _____

Exemplary:

    A. Expresses positive attitudes toward participation in a mock disabling activity.
    B. Expresses positive views toward safety on the golf course and use of motorized vehicles.
    C. Attends three (3) or more local, high school or college golf tournaments or matches.
    D. Gives examples of correct club selection and strategies for golfing situations.
    E. Gives examples of consideration to others during golfing situations.
    F. Gives examples of self-correction of golf strokes or strategies.

Acceptable:

    A. Records participation in a mock disabling activity.
    B. List entries of motor vechile use on golf course with some regard toward others.
    C. Attends at least (2) local, high school or college golf tournaments or matches.
    D. List entries of occasional selection of correct clubs and strategies for golfing situations.
    E. Gives examples of requesting help for correcting improper golf swing and strategies.

Needs Improvement:

    A. Records presence at 1 golfing event
    B. Lists entries of unsafe use of motorized vehicles on a golf course.
    C. Records negative attitudes toward safety on a golf course.
    D. Has difficulty selecting and does not ask for help to choose correct strategies and clubs for golfing situations.

Unacceptable:

    A. Does not make journal entries.
    B. Records a lack of tolerance toward others with disabling conditions.
    C. Shows no evidence of attending local, school, or college golfing events.
    D. Records negative attitudes toward safety and proper etiquette on the golf course.

Assessments contributed by: Doris E. Wooledge
                                       Delaware State University

Golf
Scoring Rubric: Student Journal

Criteria for Scoring Journal Entries on Golf Safety and Etiquette	POSSIBLE POINT VALUES	ACTUAL POINT VALUES
1. Analyzes and expresses positive feelings about safety on a golf course.	1 - 5	
2. Analyzes and shows appreciation for safety concerning the use of motorized golf vehicles.	1 - 5	
3. Expresses positive attitudes toward participating in a simulated disabling game.	1 - 5	
4. Records presence and a positive attitude toward attendance of local, high school, or college/university golf matches or tournaments.	1 - 5	
5. Analyzes the use of strategy and rules for club selection, shot selection, teeing up and handicap for match and medal play.	1 - 5	
6. Records observations of televised and international golf tournaments.	1 - 5	
Total Points (30 Possible Points)		

Assessments contributed by: Doris E. Wooledge
                                                          Delaware State University

Racquetball
Written Test

Name _____   **Date** _____

What type of shot is a ceiling ball, offensive or defensive?
1. _____

When would you use it?
2. _____

List 3 technique points you would use when hitting a backwall shot to the front wall.
3. _____
4. _____
5. _____

If your second serve hits the ceiling first, the ref will call:
6. _____

If your first serve hits the ceiling first, the ref will call:
7. _____

The best time to hit a pinch shot is when:
8. _____

Is it legal to hit the ball on the fly on a return of serve?
9. _____

What is the restraining line (5 foot line) for?
10. _____

A serve which hits the back wall on the fly is called?
11. _____

A passing shot is used when your opponent is:
12. _____

Describe a passing shot.
13. _____

How many games must you win to win a match?
14. _____

How many points in a tiebreaker?

15. _____

In a doubles match, how many people serve the first time up?

16. _____

A loss of serve for the first person in the doubles team is called:

17. _____

When can the partner of the server leave the doubles box?

18. _____

A screen serve occurs when:

19. _____

List 2 points of a good ready position for racquetball.

20. _____

21. _____

Describe a z serve.

22. _____

Describe a cross-court shot.

23. _____

When would you use a down the line shot?

24. _____

What is a kill shot?

25. _____

Bonus:

What is a wrap around serve? or what is a jam serve?

Assessments contributed by:
>   Lynn Couturier
>   Springfield College

Racquetball
Student Projects

1. Officiate a match using a scorecard. Evaluate effectiveness.

2. Attend a professional or open level match and track type of shots used to end rallies.

3. Write a report on one of the following:

      A. the history of racquetball
      B. top players in the game
      C. safety considerations

4. Develop a fitness program for racquetball.

Assessments contributed by:
                        Lynn Couturier
                        Springfield College

Tennis Skills Test

Initial Assessment of Skill Level for Ability Grouping

Record student performance of basic strokes:

1.   Number of consecutive forehand strokes against a wall in one minute.

2.   Number of consecutive backhand strokes against a wall in one minute.

3.   Number of points scored in ten service attempts to forehand court.

SCORING:

```
                    I              I              I
                    I              I              I
                    I              I              I
                    I              I              I
        -           --------------------------------              X-
                    I  2  3  I                  I            (server)
                    I  1  2  I                  I
                    I  2  3  I                  I
                    I              I              I
```

O - rater

4.   Number of points scored in ten volley attempts. Partner must throw or hit ball to forehand
        side within one step of the performer.

SCORING:

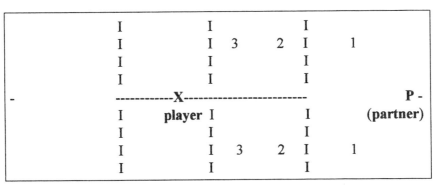

O - rater

Assessments contributed by:

Barbara Hemink
Clarkstown High School

Floor Hockey
Scoring Rubric: Skill Assessment

1.   The students work in a cooperative environment utilizing peer assessment of specific skills. The evaluator utilizes a three point scale as follows:

3 =   Student performs skill with success. Appropriate form is always exhibited and the outcome is achieved consistently.
2 =   Student performs skill with some success. Appropriate form is exhibited and outcome is achieved most of the time.
1 =   Student performs skill with little success. Form is not appropriate and, desired outcome is not achieved.

Student Observation: Video Analysis - Officiating

The teacher video tapes student officiating segments. The students view their officiating experience and write a critique including the following issues:

(1) positioning
(2) administration
(3) working cooperatively with their partner
(4) consistency in calls
(5) maintaining a safe environment of play

Assessments contributed by:

Marlene Kelly
Anne Arundel County Schools

Lacrosse
Rating Scale: Instructor Assessment

Name _____   Score _____

Five Trials Each Task:

1.   **Catching**
      5 =   Catches successfully on the move on both sides most of the time.
      4 =   Catches successfully on the move on the strong side most of the time, but
               inconsistent on the weak side.
      3 =   Catches on the move, but uses a basket catch most of the time.
      2 =   Uses a basket catch and stops to catch.
      1 =   Fails to catch most of the time.

2.   **Throwing**
      5 =   Throws on the move accurately to a moving target most of the time.
      3 =   Throws on the move accurately to a moving target some of the time.
      1 =   Stops to throw.

3.   **Scooping**
      5 =   Picks up the ball moving towards/away while moving, most of the time.
      3 =   Picks up the ball moving towards/away while moving some of the time.
      1 =   Has difficulty picking up the ball most of the time.

4.   **1 on 1 play**
      5 =   Executes basic skills and moves off the ball well while defended. Plays
               tight defense throughout the game.
      4 =   Executes basic skills and moves off the ball most of the time while defended.
      3 =   Plays defense inconsistently.
      2 =   Has difficultly executing basic skills while defended.Has difficultly losing defender.
      1 =   Plays defense loosely.

Assessments contributed by:
               Lynn Couturier
               Springfield College

Lacrosse
Rating Scale: Instructor Assessment

NAME_____

Scoring:

Drill 1	**x-**	**x**	**x+**	**Trial**	**1**	**2**	**3**
Pickup	miss	bobble	clean				
Cradle	drop	average	strong				
Shot	miss	in	in&creative				

Drill 2

Offense

Catch	misses+	on run	makes tough
Passing	off	accurate	both posts
Movement	dead	+first	recuts

Defense	loose	stays w/	intercepts

Drill 3

Game	little	average	aggress/smart

Assessments contributed by:
> Lynn Couturier
> Springfield College

Lacrosse
Student Project: Coed Lacrosse

Name _____   Score _____

Develop a set of rules for a coed lacrosse game with 7 players per team. You must consider the following factors (use diagrams if necessary):

1.   type of equipment for age
2.   how to score; goal cages or touch down lines (if goals, what about goalies?)
3.   fouls and penalties
      a. checking?
      b. rules for ground balls
      c. how to start play at the beginning of the game
      d. how to start play after a goal
      e. safety issues
4.   boundaries and boundary rules
5.   any other restrictions/limitations (# passes or # steps)

Assessments contributed by:
Lynn Couturier
Springfield College

Lacrosse
Event Task: Observation of Game

Name _____   **Date** _____

Observe one men's and one women's lacrosse game.
For each:
Describe the game.
How many players start the game?
How big is the playing field?
What type of equipment do the field players wear?
What is the out of bounds rule?
What is the procedure for a foul?
Is there off sides?

Game #1   Men's or   Women's   Date _____   Opponent _____

Game #2   Men's or   Women's   Date _____   Opponent _____

Reflect on the differences and similarities between the two games. What was the style of play like? Did you see anything the could be incorporated into coed lacrosse?

Assessments contributed by:
                    Lynn Couturier
                    Springfield College

Softball
Skills Test

Each player will be skill tested and evaluated on throwing, fielding ground balls, and hitting.

I. Throwing
Objective Assessment:
- **A. Objective:** To measure the ball throwing ability of the student.
- **B. Equipment:** Softballs, back stop/wall, stopwatch, drawn line, tape measure, tape and score sheets.
- **C. Description:** The student stands within the 5 ft by 10 ft throwing area. On the signal "Ready, Go!," the ball is thrown at the target using an overhand throw. The rebound is caught, either in the air or on the bounce, and the student continues throwing as many times as possible in 20 seconds. A 10 second practice trial is allowed. The student has two 20-sec trials.
- **D. Testing Area:** Back stop or wall with a 5 ft by 10 ft target area. A drawn line 25 ft away from target at least 10 ft wide.
- **E. Scoring:** The trial is the number of correct hits in 20 seconds. The test score is the best of two trials. A hit is not scored if the student steps on or over any one of the lines of the throwing area or if the ball lands outside one of the target lines.

Subjective Assessment

Based on throws made within the 20 seconds allotted time, rate the student's technique according to the items listed below on a scale of 1-3 (1 = least developed / 3= highly developed)

Mechanical Analysis:
- A. With 2 or 3 fingers
- B. Steps with glove side foot towards target
- C. Rotates glove shoulder towards target
- D. Watches target
- E. Extends throwing arm back
- F. Releases ball at eye level
- G. Snaps wrist
- H. Follows through with throwing side shoulder facing target

II. FIELDING
Objective Assessment:
- **A. Objective:** To measure the fielding ability of the student.
- **B. Equipment:** Softballs, playing field, bat, glove, drawn line, scoresheet.
- **C. Description:** The student will stand behind a 10 ft line placed in the infield area (near shortstop or second base) with glove on in ready position. A designated assistant/teacher will hit a self tossed ball or a thrown ball on the ground to the student. The student must field the ball under control behind the 10 ft line. The

student will receive 10 grounders by the designated assistant teacher. A practice trial is allowed with 3 grounders. The student will receive two - 10 grounders trial.

D. Testing Area: Infield area (skinned or grass infield) with a 10 ft line drawn in the shortstop or second base area. Tosser/hitter is positioned at home plate or at least 25 ft away from student.

E. Scoring: The student will receive 2 points if he/she fields the ball under control; 1 point if ball is bobbled, yet still playable; 0 points if unsuccessfully fielded.

Subjective Assessment

Based on grounders fielded within the 10 tosses/hits, rate the student's technique according to the items listed below on a scale of 1 - 3 (1 = least developed / 3 = highly developed)

Mechanical Analysis:

    A. Fingers pointing down - glove on ground
    B. Uses 2 hands - bare hand guides ball into glove
    C. Feet shoulder width apart, knees bent
    D. Watches ball into glove
    E. Brings ball into stomach area, then directly to throwing shoulder

III. Hitting/Striking

Objective Assessment:

A. Objective: To measure the hitting/striking ability of the student.

B. Equipment: Softballs, bat, playing area, tee, helmets, scoresheet.

C. Description: The student will hit/strike a ball that is tossed, pitched underhand, (by designated assistant/teacher) or hit off tee. The student will receive 10 swings. A practice trial is allowed with 3 swings. The student will receive to - 10 swing trials.

D. Testing Area: Playing field with batter at home plate.

E. Scoring: The student will receive 3 points for a line drive hit; 2 points for a fly ball; 1 point for a grounder; 0 points for a swing and miss

Subjective Assessment

Based on the 10 swings made, rate the student's technique according to the items listed below on a scale of 1 - 3 (1 = least developed / 3 = highly developed).

Mechanical Analysis:

    A. Middle knuckles of both hands lined up on grip
    B. Comfortable stance
    C. Knees slightly bent
    D. Bat angled back slightly
    E. Steps with front foot towards pitcher/ball

F. Rotates hips towards pitcher/pivots on ball of back foot
G. Pulls bat through with lead arm
H. Extends lead arm during swing
I. Turns wrists over on contact
J. Watches ball hit bat
K. Swings in a level plane
L. Follows through

Assessments contributed by:
                Kathy Mangano
                Springfield College

Slow Pitch Softball
Written Test

Name _____   **Date** _____

Part I: True and False. If the statement is true, write <u>TRUE</u>; if the statement is false write <u>FALSE</u>. (1pt each)

_____ 1. A pop up lands in fair territory between home and third base, rolls into foul territory
and is then touched by the catcher. The ball is a foul ball.

_____ 2. A runner is on second base with no outs. The batter hits a long fly ball to right field. After the right
fielder catches the fly ball, the runner on second tags up and advances to third base arriving before
the right fielder's throw. This is a legal play.

_____ 3. The strike zone is that space between the batter's shoulders and top of the knees.

_____ 4. Bunting is not permitted in the game of slow pitch.

_____ 5. There is no limit on the height of the pitch in slow pitch as long as it has an arc of at least three
feet.

_____ 6. A game of slow pitch involves 10 players for each team.

_____ 7. A runner may leave the base when the pitcher releases the ball.

_____ 8. A batter is out if he/she foul tips the ball that goes directly from the bat, not higher than the
batter's shoulders, into the catcher's glove.

_____ 9. A batter may step out of the batter's box to make contact with the ball during her/his swing.

_____10. A baserunner may only advance one base on an overthrown if the ball lands in fair territory.

Part II: Multiple Choice. Place the letter of the <u>BEST</u> answer in the space provided. (2pts each)

_____11. Which bases may be over run without liability of being put out?
      A. First and Second
      B. First and Third
      C. Third and Home
      D. First and Home

_____12. The distance between each base in slow pitch is:
        A. 60 feet
        B. 43 feet
        C. 65 feet
        D. 40 feet

_____13. A regulation softball game consists of how many innings?
        A. Six innings
        B. Seven innings
        C. Eight innings
        D. Nine innings

_____14. A baserunner in slow pitch may not lead off the base until:
        A. The ball leaves the pitcher's hand
        B. The ball reaches home plate
        C. The ball is touched by the catcher
        D. The pitcher is holding the ball on the pitcher's mound

_____15. In the picture below, which one has home plate facing the correct way?

     A.   B.

Assessments contributed by:
                    Kathy Mangano
                    Springfield College

Softball
Rating Scale: Self Observation

The following self-rating inventory is provided so that you can evaluate your overall performance. Read the statements carefully and respond to them thoughtfully.

I. Physical Skills

	Very Good	Good	Fair	Poor
1. Catching	____	____	____	____
2. Throwing Overhand	____	____	____	____
3. Throwing Underhand	____	____	____	____
4. Fielding Ground Balls	____	____	____	____
5. Fielding Fly Balls	____	____	____	____
6. Hitting Using Tee	____	____	____	____
7. Hitting Pitched Ball	____	____	____	____
8. Hitting a Soft Toss	____	____	____	____
9. Hitting Ground Balls with Fungo Bat	____	____	____	____
10. Hitting Fly Balls with Fungo Bat	____	____	____	____
11. Slow Pitching	____	____	____	____
12. Baserunning Over running the base	____	____	____	____
Rounding the base	____	____	____	____

II. Game Concept Skills

	Very Good	Good	Fair	Poor
1. Position Play as a Infielder Covering	_____	_____	_____	_____
2. Position Play as an Outfielder Covering	_____	_____	_____	_____
3. Force Play	_____	_____	_____	_____
4. Tag Play	_____	_____	_____	_____
5. Double Plays	_____	_____	_____	_____
6. Relays	_____	_____	_____	_____
7. Cutoffs	_____	_____	_____	_____
8. Rundowns(defensive)	_____	_____	_____	_____
9. Rundowns(offensive)	_____	_____	_____	_____
10. Rules of Play Do you know the rules?	_____	_____	_____	_____

III. Overall Softball Skills:

Considering all factors you rated above, how would you rate your softball performance?

_____Very Good

_____ Good

_____ Fair

_____ Poor

Assessments contributed by:
Kathy Mangano
Springfield College

278

Softball
Checklist: Peer Observation

Performer _____   Evaluator _____

DIRECTIONS:
1. Work in groups of three (3): one "Assessor", one "Performer", and one "Partner".
2. "Assessor" watches only the "Performer" and assesses her/his performance.
3. After the completion of each skill category rotate within your group so that your responsibility changes. Each person in the group has the responsibility of each "role" within each skill category
4. The "Assessor" reads each task before the "Performer" begins so that the criteria being assessed are clear.

I. Throwing:

A. The "performer" throws 5 balls to "partner". Overall, did the "performer":

	YES	NO
1. Use a two/three finger grip	_____	_____
2. Rotate non-throwing shoulder toward direction of throw	_____	_____
3. Transfer weight to back foot	_____	_____
4. Extend throwing arm back	_____	_____

Comments:

B. The "performer" throws 5 balls to "partner". Overall, did the "performer":

1. Step with glove side foot	_____	_____
2. Rotate hips and shoulders square to target	_____	_____
3. Lead with elbow (throwing side)	_____	_____
4. Snap wrist		

Comments:

C. The "performer" throws 5 balls to "partner". Overall, did the "performer".

1. Complete shift of weight to front foot	_____	_____
2. Follow through with throwing hand across body.	_____	_____
3. Follow through step with throwing side foot	_____	_____

Comments:

II. Fielding:

The "performer" fields 10 balls hit on the ground or thrown on the ground by the "partner". Overall, did the "performer":

	YES	NO
1. Have glove on ground with fingers pointing down	_____	_____
2. Use 2 hands - barehand guide ball into glove	_____	_____
3. Have feet comfortably apart, knees bent	_____	_____
4. Watch ball into glove	_____	_____
5. Bring ball into stomach area, then to throwing shoulder for return throw	_____	_____

Comments:

III. Hitting:

A. "Performer" stands in the "ready position of hitting". Did the performer:

1. Have middle knuckles lined up in grip	_____	_____
2. Stand in a comfortable stance	_____	_____
3. Have knees slightly flexed	_____	_____
4. Have bat angled back slightly	_____	_____

Comments:

B. The "performer" hits 5 balls tossed or pitched by partner, or hit off tee. Overall, did the performer:

1. Step towards ball	_____	_____
2. Rotate hips and shoulders towards pitcher	_____	_____
3. Pivot on ball of back foot	_____	_____
4. Finish swing with hips/shoulders facing pitcher	_____	_____

Comments:

C. The "performer" hits 5 balls tossed or pitched by partner or hit off tee. Overall, did the performer:

1. Pull bat through with lead arm	_____	_____
2. Extend lead arm during swing	_____	_____
3. Turn wrist on contact	_____	_____
4. Watch ball on contact	_____	_____
5. Have level swing	_____	_____
6. Swing "through the ball" - follow through	_____	_____

Comments:

Assessments contributed by:

Kathy Mangano
Springfield College

Motor Development
Standardized Tests

Assessment of students in adapted physical education may be formal or informal and no one procedure may be appropriate. Currently, most school personnel use a combination of norm-referenced tests and criterion-referenced tests, although the trend seems to be toward criterion-referenced tests and portfolios. Generally, norm-referenced instruments designed for a specific population of individuals with a disablility are difficult to find because testing of large numbers of subjects with the same disability is often impossible and therefore, validity and reliability may be compromised.

Bruininks-Oseretsky Test of Motor Proficiency (1978) is composed of 8 sub-tests which yield a Gross Motor Composite index of the ability to use small muscles in the hand and arm, and a Battery Composite which is a summary of performances on 8 sub-tests as an index of general motor proficiency. Gross motor skills include running speed and agility, balance items, bilateral coordination skills, and items evaluating strength. Fine motor skills are measured with items of response speed, visual-motor control, and upper-limb speed and dexterity. Sub-test 5 (upper-limb coordination) requires both gross and fine motor movements. The instrument has both a short and long form and is appropriate for children from 4 ½ to 14 ½ years of age.

Project UNIQUE (Winnick & Short, 1985) is a norm-referenced test designed to evaluate the physical fitness of students in four generic classifications: auditorily impaired, visually impaired, orthopedicly involved, able bodied. Orthopedic impairments are further subclassified as either amputee, cerebral palsied, congenital anomalies, or neuromuscular weakness with or without the use of assistive devices. Sub-tests measure body composition, muscular strength and endurance, flexibility, and cardio-respiratory endurance with certain items that can be substituted or modified. Percentile tables for both boys and girls ages 10 to 17 years are included.

Denver II (Frankenburg & Dodds, 1992) is a revision of the Denver Developmental Screening Test and is designed to compare a child's performance to that of well children of the same age (birth to 6 years). It consists of 125 items in four sections: Gross Motor (sitting, walking, jumping, and gross motor movement); Language (hearing, understanding, language use); Fine Motor-Adaptive (object manipulation, eye-hand coordination); Personal-Social (care of personal needs, interaction with others). Performance is compared to normal developmental stages and/or skill acquisition. The instrument is designed to quickly identify children who are likely to have significant delays in development.

Peabody Developmental Motor Scales (1983) were normed on children (birth through 7 years) in 20 states representing diverse social conditions. They were designed to assess both fine and gross motor development and may be used to identify children with abnormal and/or delayed motor development. The fine motor component (112 items) represents grasping, eye-hand coordination, hand use, and manual dexterity. The gross motor scales (170 items) represent balance, locomotion, nonlocomotion, reflexes, and receipt and propulsion of objects.

Test of Gross Motor Development (Ulrich, 1985) may be used/interpreted either as a criterion- or norm-referenced tool. Twelve items are divided into two components: Locomotor Skills (run, gallop, hop, leap, horizontal jump, skip, and slide) and Object Control Skills (two-hand strike, stationary bounce, catch, kick, overhand throw). They are designed to evaluate the gross motor functioning of skills most frequently taught to preschool, early elementary, and special education children. Norms are provided with developmental motor quotients and age equivalents.

Test of Lateral Awareness and Directionality (LAD) (Lockavitch & Mauser, 1980) may be administered individually or to a small group and is designed to measure left-right labeling ability. It is a

281

criterion-referenced test used to help identify students who have difficulty with lateral awareness and directionality yet be able to pass other tests on the basis of chance. Children will be classified as Level 1 (Underdeveloped), Level 2 (Moderately Developed) or Level 3 (Fully Developed). The test is especially useful to identify children with potential problems in academic areas. It is appropriate for students in the first grade and above.

Prudential FITNESSGRAM (Cooper Institute for Aerobics Research, 1994) utilizes one mastery standard for each age, gender, and fitness domain. Mastery standards are presented as a range of scores that indicate a healthy fitness zone from low to high for students aged 5 to 17+ years. Items include a 1 mile run, body mass index, curl-up, push-up, modified pull-up, pull-up, sit & reach, shoulder stretch, trunk lift, and flexed arm hang.

Physical Best and Individuals with Disabilities (AAHPERD, Seaman, ED., 1995) is a manual which details modifications of items on the Prudential FITNESSGRAM test. It includes safety considerations, contraindications, and methods to avoid aggravating specific conditions students with disabilities might have. It also offers alternative suggestions for measuring the fitness components of individuals with diverse disabilities who may be included in regular physical education programs. Program planning, strategies for inclusion, instructional strategies for teaching students with disabilities and activity modifications are detailed in Chapter 8.

Assessment contributed by:
>Dr. Elizabeth Evans
>Springfield College

REFERENCE LIST K-5

ELEMENTARY METHODS

Ashworth, S. & Mosston, M. (1994). Teaching physical education (4th ed.). Columbus: Charles E. Merril.

Corbin, C.B., & Pangrazi, R.P. (1994). Teaching strategies for improving youth fitness. Reston, VA: AAHPERD.

Cone, S.L., Purcell-Cone, T., Werner, P., & Woods, A.M. (1998). Interdisciplinary teaching through physical education. Champaign, IL: Human Kinetics.

Dauer, V.P. & Pangrazi, R.P. (1995). Dynamic physical education for elementary school children. Boston: Allyn and Bacon.

Ennis, C.D., & Silverman, S.J. (1996). Student learning in physical education: Applying research to enhance instruction. Champaign, IL: Human Kinetics.

Graham, G., Holt/Hale, S.A., & Parker, M. (1998). Children moving: A reflective approach to teaching physical education. (4th ed.). Mountain View, CA: Mayfield.

Hacker, P., Malmberg, E., & Nance, J. (1996). Gymnastics fun and games. Champaign, IL: Human Kinetics.

Hellison, D.R. & Templin, T.J. (1991). A reflective approach to teaching physical education. Champaign, IL: Human Kinetics.

Hopple, C.J. (1995). Teaching for outcomes in elementary physical education: A guide for curriculum and assessment. Champaign, IL: Human Kinetics.

Kirchner, G. (1989). Physical education for elementary school children (7th ed.). Dubuque, IA: W.C. Brown.

Melograno, V.J. (1996). Designing the physical education curriculum (3rd ed.). Champaign, IL: Human Kinetics.

Melograno, V.J. (1998). Professional and student portofolios for physical education. Champaign, IL: Human Kinetics.

Murray, N., & Wall, J. (1994). Children and movement: Physical education in the elementary school. Madison, WI: Brown & Benchmark.

Murray, N., & Wall, J. (1990). Children and movement. Dubuque, IA: Wm.C. Brown.

NASPE, (1995). Moving Into the Future: National Standards for Physical Education. New York: Mosby.

Rink, J. (1998). Teaching physical education for learning. Boston: WCB/McGraw-Hill.

Thomas, J.R., Thomas, K.T., & Lee, A.M. (1989). Physical education for children. Champaign, IL: Human Kinetics.

MOVEMENT ACTIVITIES:

Allen, L. (1997). Physical activity ideas for action: Elementary level. Champaign, IL: Human Kinetics.

Barbarash, L. (1997). Multicultural Games. Champaign, IL: Human Kinetics.

Belka, D.E. (1994). Teaching children games: Becoming a master teacher. Champaign, IL: Human Kinetics.

Buschner, C.A. (1994). Teaching children movement concepts and skills: Becoming a master teacher. Human Kinetics.

Clements, R.L. (1995). Games and great ideas: A guide for elementary school physical educators and classroom teachers. CT: Greenwood.

Coughenour-Riemer, P., & Price-Bennett, J. (1995). Rhythmic activities and dance. Champaign, IL: Human Kinetics.

Elbourn, J., & Harris, J. (1997). Teaching health-related exercise at key stages 1 and 2. Champaign, IL: Human Kinetics.

Fisher, B., Hopper, C., & Munoz, K.D. (1997). Health-related fitness for grades 1 and 2. Champaign, IL: Human Kinetics.

Fisher, B., Hopper, C., & Munoz, K.D. (1997). Health-related fitness for grades 3 and 4. Champaign, IL: Human Kinetics.

Foster, E.R., Hartinger, K., & Smith, K.A. (1992). Fitness fun. Champaign, IL: Human Kinetics.

Gabbard, C., LeBlance, E. & Lowy, S. (1989). Game, dance, and gymnastic activities for children. Englewood, NJ: Prentice-Hall.

Harris, J.A., Pitman, A.M. & Waller, M. (1988). Dance a while. Minneapolis, MN: Burgess.

Hinson, C. (1995). Fitness for children. Champaign, IL: Human Kinetics.

Lane, C. (1997). <u>Christy Lane's complete guide to party dances.</u> Champaign, IL: Human Kinetics. (videotape)

Lefevre, D. & Strong, T. (1996). <u>Parachute games.</u> Champaign, IL: Human Kinetics.

McCravey-Ratliffe, L., & Ratliffe, T. (1994). <u>Teaching children fitness: Becoming a master teacher.</u> Champaign, IL: Human Kinetics.

McGreevy-Nichols, S. & Scheff, H. (1995). <u>Building dances: A guide to putting movements together.</u> Champaign, IL: Human Kinetics.

Purcell, T.M. (1994). <u>Teaching children dance: Becoming a master teacher.</u> Champaign, IL: Human Kinetics.

Virgilio, S.J. (1997). <u>Fitness for children.</u> Champaign, IL: Human Kinetics.

Ward, P. (1997). <u>Teaching Tumbling.</u> Champaign, IL: Human Kinetics.

Werner, P.H. (1994). <u>Teaching children gymnastics: Becoming a master teacher.</u> Champaign, IL: Human Kinetics.

MOVEMENT ACTIVITIES - COOPERATIVE

Butler, S., & Rohnke, K. (1995). <u>Quicksilver: Adventure games, initiative problems, trust activities, and a guide to effective leadership.</u> Dubuque, IA: Kendall Hunt.

Glover, D.R. & Midura, D.M. (1992). <u>Team building through physical challenges.</u> Champaign, IL: Human Kinetics.

Glover, D.R. & Midura, D.W. (1995). <u>More team building challenges.</u> Champaign, IL: Human Kinetics.

Grineski, S. (1996). <u>Cooperative learning in physical education.</u> Champaign, IL:Human Kinetics.

Rohnke, K. (1989). <u>Cowstails and cobras II: A guide to games, initiatives, ropes courses, and adventure curriculum.</u> Dubuque, IA: Kendall Hunt.

Turner, L. & Turner, S. (1989). <u>P.E. teacher; skill by skill activity bag.</u> West Nyack, NY: Parker Publishing.

REFERENCE LIST 6-8

Allen, L. (1997). <u>Physical activity ideas for action: Secondary Level.</u> Champaign, IL: Human Kinetics.

American Alliance for Health, Physical Education, Recreation and Dance. (1988). <u>Physical best manual.</u> Reston, VA: AAHPERD.

American Alliance for Health, Physical Education, Recreation and Dance. (1987). <u>Basic stuff series.</u> Reston, VA: AAHPERD.

Ashworth, S., & Mosston, D. (1990). <u>The spectrum of teaching styles: From command to discovery.</u> White Plains, NY: Longman.

Bean, J.A. (1990). <u>A middle school curriculum: From rhetoric to reality.</u> Columbus, OH: National Middle School Association.

Blakemore, C., Harrison, J. (1992). <u>Instructional strategies for secondary school physical education</u> (3rd ed.). New York: MacMillan.

Carnes, L.A., Pettigrew, F.E., & Zakrajsek, D.B. (1994). <u>Quality lesson plans for secondary physical education.</u> Champaign, IL: Human Kinetics.

Cestaro, N.G. & Smith, T.K. (1998). <u>Student centered physical education: Strategies for developing middle school fitness and skills.</u> Champaign, IL: Human Kinetics.

Corbin, C.B. & Lindsey, R. (1990). <u>Fitness for life: Physical education components</u> (3rd ed.). Palo Alto, CA: Scott, Foresman.

Darst, P., & Pangrazzi, R. (1991). <u>Dynamic physical education for secondary students: Curriculum and instruction</u> (2nd ed.). New York: Macmillan.

Ermler, K., Mehrhof, J. (1996). <u>Ideas III: Middle school physical activities for a fit generation.</u> Reston, VA: NASPE.

Farrow, A., & Magee, R. (1987). <u>Test questions for physical education activities.</u> Champaign, IL: Human Kinetics.

Fisher, B., Hopper, C., Munoz, K.D. (1997). <u>Health-related fitness for grades 5 and 6.</u> Champaign, IL: Human Kinetics.

Griffin, L.L., Mitchell, S.A., Oslin, J.L. (1997). <u>Teaching sports concepts and skills.</u> Champaign, IL: Human Kinetics.

Gustafson, M., King, C., Wolfe, S. (1991). <u>Great games for young people.</u> Champaign, IL: Human Kinetics.

Hanlon, T. (1998). The sports rule book. Champiagn, IL: Human Kinetics.

Harris, J.A., Pittman, A.M., & Waller, M. (1988). Dance awhile. Minneapolis, MN: Burgess.

Lichtman, B. (1993). Innovative Games. Champaign, IL: Human Kinetics.

Mohnsen, B.S. (1997). Teaching middle school physical education. Champaign, IL: Human Kinetics.

Morris, D. & Stiehl, L. (1989). Changing kids' games. Champaign, IL: Human Kinetics.

National Association for Sport and Physical Education. (1991). Guidelines for secondary school physical education. Reston, VA: AAHPERD.

National Association for Sport and Physical Education. (1991). Guidelines for elementary school physical education. Reston, VA: AAHPERD.

National Association for Sport and Physical Education. (1991). The physically educated person: NASPE outcomes project. Reston, VA: AAHPERD.

Phillips, J. & Wilkerson, J. (1990). Teaching team sports. Champaign, IL: Human Kinetics.

Rohnke, K. (1988). Silver bullets: A guide to initiative problems, adventure games, and trust activities. Hamilton, MA: Project Adventure.

Rohnke, K. (1989). Cowstails and cobras II: A guide to games, initiatives, ropes courses, and adventure curriculum. Dubuque, IL: Kendall/Hunt.

Ryser, O.E. & Brown, J.R. (1991). A manual for tumbling and apparatus stunts (8th ed.). Dubuque, IL: Wm. C. Brown.

Siedentop, D., Mand, C. & Taggart, A. (1986). Physical education: Teaching and curriculum strategies for grades 5-12. Mountain View, CA: Mayfield.

Singer, R.N. (1980). Motor learning and human performance: An application to motor skills and movement behaviors (3rd ed.). New York: MacMillan.

Spindt, G., Monit, W., Holyoak, C., Hennessy, B. & Weinberg, H. (1993). Middle school physical education. Dubuque, IA: Kendall/Hunt.

Vickers, J. (1990). Instructional design for teaching physical education activities. Champaign, IL: Human Kinetics.

NOTES

NOTES

NOTES

NOTES

NOTES

NOTES

NOTES

NOTES

NOTES

NOTES

NOTES